JAPANESE

PHRASEBOOK

Compiled by

LEXUS

www.roughguides.com

Credits

Compiled by Lexus with T. Yahata Hyland and Kumi Liley
Lexus Series Editor: Sally Davies
Rough Guides Reference Director: Andrew Lockett
Rough Guides Series Editor: Mark Ellingham

First edition published in 1998 by Rough Guides Ltd.
Revised in 2001.
This updated edition published in 2006 by
Rough Guides Ltd,
80 Strand, London WC2R 0RL
345 Hudson St, 4th Floor, New York 10014, USA
Email: mail@roughguides.co.uk.

Distributed by the Penguin Group.

Penguin Books Ltd, 80 Strand, London WC2R 0RL
Penguin Putnam, Inc., 375 Hudson Street, NY 10014, USA
Penguin Group (Australia), 250 Camberwell Road,
Camberwell, Victoria 3124, Australia
Penguin Books Canada Ltd, 10 Alcorn Avenue, Toronto,
Ontario, Canada M4V 1E4
Penguin Group (New Zealand), Cnr Rosedale and Airborne Roads,
Albany, Auckland, New Zealand

Typeset in Bembo and Helvetica to an original design by Henry Iles.
Printed in Italy by L.E.G.O. Spa, Lavis (TN)

British Library Cataloguing in Publication Data
A catalogue for this book is available from the British Library.

ISBN 13: 978-1-84353-634-5
ISBN 10: 1-84353-634-X

5 7 9 8 6 4

The publishers and authors have done their best to ensure the
accuracy and currency of all information in The Rough Guide
Japanese Phrasebook however, they can accept no responsibility
for any loss or inconvenience sustained by any reader using the
book.

Online information about Rough Guides can be
found at our website www.roughguides.com

CONTENTS

Introduction

The Rough Guide Japanese dictionary phrasebook is a highly practical introduction to the contemporary language. Laid out in clear A-Z style, it uses key-word referencing to lead you straight to the words and phrases you want – so if you need to book a room, just look up 'room'. The Rough Guide gets straight to the point in every situation, in bars and shops, on trains and buses, and in hotels and banks.

The main part of the Rough Guide is a double dictionary: English-Japanese then Japanese-English. Before that, there's a section called **Basic Phrases** and to get you involved in two-way communication, the Rough Guide includes, in this new edition, a set of **Scenario** dialogues illustrating questions and responses in key situations such as renting a car and asking directions. You can hear these and then download them free from **www.roughguides. com/phrasebooks** for use on your computer or MP3 player.

Forming the heart of the guide, the **English-Japanese** section gives easy-to-use transliterations of the Japanese words wherever pronunciation might be a problem. Throughout this section, cross-references enable you to pinpoint key facts and phrases, while asterisked words indicate where further information can be found in a section at the end of the book called **How the Language Works**. This section sets out the fundamental rules of the language, with plenty of practical examples. You'll also find here other essentials like numbers, dates, telling the time and basic phrases. The **Japanese-English** section is in two parts: a dictionary, arranged phonetically, of all the words and phrases you're likely to hear (starting with a section of slang and colloquialisms); then a compilation, arranged by subject, of various signs, labels, instructions and other basic words you may come across in print or in public places.

Near the back of the book too the Rough Guide offers an extensive **Menu Reader**. Consisting of food and drink sections (each starting with a list of essential terms), it's indispensable whether you're eating out, stopping for a quick drink, or browsing through a local food market.

楽しいご旅行を！
tanoshī goryokō o!
have a good trip!

Basic
Phrases

yes
hai
はい

no
īe
いいえ

OK
ōkē
オーケー

hello
kon·nichi wa
こんにちは

(on phone)
moshi-moshi
もしもし

good morning
ohayō gozaimasu
おはようございます

good evening
komban wa
こんばんは

good night (when leaving)
osaki ni
お先に

(when going to bed)
oyasuminasai
おやすみなさい

goodbye (formal)
sayōnara
さようなら

(informal)
dewa mata
ではまた

(between friends)
jā ne
じゃ あね

see you later!
ja, mata!
じゃ、また！

please (requesting something)
onegai shimasu
お願いします

yes, please
hai, onegai shimasu
はい、お願いします

could you please ...?
... -te kuremasen ka?
…ーてくれませんか？

thank you
arigatō
ありがとう

thank you very much
hontō ni arigatō gozaimasu
ほんとうにありがと
うございます

8

no, thank you
īe kek·kō des*u*
いいえ、けっこうで
す

don't mention it
dō itashimash*i*te
どういたしまして

how do you do?
hajimemash*i*te
はじめまして

how are you?
ogenki des*u* ka?
お元気ですか？

I'm fine, thanks
okagesama de
おかげさまで

nice to meet you
hajimemash*i*te
はじめまして

excuse me (to get past)
shitsurei shimas*u*
失礼します

excuse me! (to get attention)
chot·to sumimasen!
ちょっとすみません！

excuse me/sorry
gomen·nasai
ごめんなさい

sorry?/pardon me?
nante īmash*i*ta ka?
何て言いましたか？

I see/I understand
naruhodo
なるほど

I don't understand
wakarimasen
わかりません

do you speak English?
Eigo o hanasemas*u* ka?
英語を話せますか？

I don't speak Japanese
nihon·go wa hanasemasen
日本語は話せません

could you speak more slowly?
mot·to yuk·kuri hanashite
  kuremasen ka?
もっとゆっくり話し
てくれませんか？

could you repeat that?
mō ichido it·te kuremasen
  ka?
もう一度言ってくれ
ませんか？

Scenarios

1. Accommodation

is there an inexpensive hotel you can recommend?
▶ yasume no hoteru o shōkai sh*i*te kuremas*u* ka?

---

zan·nen des*u* ga, subete yoyaku zumi des*u* ◀
I'm sorry, they all seem to be fully booked

---

can you give me the name of a good middle-range hotel?
▶ chū gurai no hoteru wa arimas*u* ka?

---

sōdes*u* ne, chūshin bu ga ī des*u* ka? ◀
let me have a look; do you want to be in the centre?

---

if possible
▶ dekireba

---

s*u*koshi hazure demo ī des*u* ka? ◀
do you mind being a little way out of town?

---

not too far out
▶ amari tōk*u* nai hō ga ī des*u*

where is it on the map?
▶ chiz*u* no doko des*u* ka?

---

can you write the name and address down?
▶ namae to jyūsho o kaite kudasai

I'm looking for a room in a private house
▶ minsyuk*u* o sagash*i*te imas*u*

I'd like to stay in a ryokan, a Japanese-style hotel
▶ ryokan ni tomaritai des*u*

2. Banks

bank account — ginkō kōza
to change money — ryōgae shimasu
cheque — kogit·te
to deposit — yokin shimasu
pin number — anshō bangō
pound — pondo
to withdraw — hikidashi masu

口座番号
kōza bangō
account number

手数料
tesūryō
commission

当座預金
tōza yokin
current account

貯蓄預金
chochik(u) yokin
savings account

支店コード
shiten kōdo
sort code

can you change this into yen?
▶ yen ni ryōgae shite kudasai

could I have three 10,000 yen notes, two 5,000 yen notes and five 100 yen coins?
▶ ichiman en satsu sanmai, gosen en satsu nimai to hyaku en dama goko kudasai

do you have information in English about opening an account?
▶ kōza ni tsuite Eigo no setsumē wa arimasu ka?

hai, don·na kōza ga ī desu ka? ◀
yes, what sort of account do you want?

I'd like a current account
▶ tōza yokin ga ī desu

pasupōto o misete kudasai ◀
your passport, please

can I use this card to draw some cash?
▶ kono kādo de genkin ga hikidasemasu ka?

kaikē ni it·te kudasai ◀
you have to go to the cashier's desk

I want to transfer this to my account at Nippon Bank
▶ kore o Nip·pon Ginkō no watashi no kōza ni sōkin shite kudasai

shōchi shimashita, demo denwa ryōkin o itadakimasu ◀
OK, but we'll have to charge you for the phonecall

3. Booking a room

shower	shawā
telephone in the room	heya no denwa
payphone in the lobby	kōshūdenwa

do you have any rooms?
▶ heya wa arimasu ka?

▶ nanmē sama desu ka?
for how many people?

for one/for two
▶ hitori desu/futari desu

▶ hai, aki beya ga arimasu
yes, we have rooms free

▶ nanpaku desu ka?
for how many nights?

just for one night
▶ hito ban dake desu

---

how much is it?
▶ ikura desu ka?

---

furo tsuki de ichi man en, furo nashi de hassen en desu ◀
ten thousand yen with bathroom and eight thousand yen without bathroom

---

does that include breakfast?
▶ chōshoku tsuki desu ka?

can I see a room with bathroom?
▶ furo tsuki no heya o misete kuremasu ka?

ok, I'll take it
▶ kore ni shimasu

when do I have to check out?
▶ chek·ku auto wa nanji desu ka?

is there anywhere I can leave luggage?
▶ nimotsu okiba wa arimasu ka?

4. Car hire

automatic	o-tomachik-ku
full tank	mantan
manual	manyuaru
rented car	renta kā

I'd like to rent a car
▶ renta kā o karitaindesu ga

▶ nan nichi kan desu ka?
for how long?

two days
▶ futsuka desu

I'll take the ...
▶ ...ni shimasu

---

is that with unlimited mileage?
▶ sōkō kyori wa musēgen desu ka?

hai ◀
it is

---

menkyo shō o misete kudasai ◀
can I see your driving licence, please?

sorekara pasupōto mo ◀
and your passport

---

is insurance included?
▶ hoken komi desu ka?

---

so desu ga, saisho no ichi man en wa jiko futan gaku desu ◀
yes, but you have to pay the first ten thousand yen

---

hoshōkin wa ichi man en desu ◀
can you leave a deposit of ten thousand yen?

---

and if this office is closed, where do I leave the keys?
▶ kono ofisu ga shimat-te itara dokoni ki o kaeshimashō ka?

---

ano hako ni irete kudasai ◀
you drop them in that box

5. Communications

ADSL modem	ADSL modemu
at	at·to
dial-up modem	daiyaru ap·pu modemu
dot	dot·to
Internet	intānet·to
mobile (phone)	kētai (denwa)
password	pasuwādo
telephone socket adaptor	denwa soket·to adaputā
wireless hotspot	waiyaresu hot·to supot·to

is there an Internet café around here?
▶ kono chikaku ni intānet·to kafe wa arimasu ka?

can I send email from here?
▶ koko kara denshi mēru o okuremasu ka?

where's the at sign on the keyboard?
▶ kono kibōdo dewa dore ga at·to desu ka?

can you switch this to a UK keyboard?
▶ UK kibōdo ni henkan dekimasu ka?

can you help me log on?
▶ rogu in o tetsudat·te kuremasu ka?

I'm not getting a connection, can you help?
▶ setsuzoku dekimasen, mite kuremasu ka?

where can I get a top-up card for my mobile?
▶ doko de kētai denwa no top·pu ap·pu kādo o kaemasu ka?

can you put me through to...?
▶ ...ni tsunaide kudasai

zero	zero	five	go
one	ichi	six	roku
two	ni	seven	nana
three	san	eight	hachi
four	yon	nine	kyū

6. Directions

where?	which direction?
doko?	dochira no hōgaku?

hi, I'm looking for Shinjuku
▶ sumimasen, Shinjuku o sagashite imasu

gomen·nasai, shirimasen ◀
sorry, never heard of it

hi, can you tell me where Shinjuku is?
▶ sumimasen, Shinjuku wa dochira desu ka?

watashi mo shiranaindesu ◀
I'm a stranger here too

hi, Shinjuku, do you know where it is?
▶ sumimasen, Shinjuku wa doko daka wakarimasu ka ?

sono kado ◀
around the corner

futatsume no shingō o hidari ◀
left at the second traffic lights

soshite saisho no migi no michi ◀
then it's the first street on the right

asoko ni over there	...no mae in front of...	mot·to saki further	tōri street
chikaku near	mas·sugu mae straight ahead	...o sugite past the ... sugu ato just after	ushiro back wakare michi turn off
hantai gawa opposite			
hidari ni on the left	migi(gawa) ni on the right	tonari, tsugi next	

7. Emergencies

accident	consul	fire brigade
jiko	ryōjikan	shōbōtai
ambulance	embassy	police
kyūkyūsha	taishikan	kēsatsu

help!
▶ tasukete!

can you help me?
▶ tasukete kudasai

please come with me! it's really very urgent
▶ is·sho ni kite kudasai! kinkyū jitai desu

I've lost (my keys)
▶ (kagi) o nakushimashita

(my car) is not working
▶ (kuruma) ga koshō shimashita

(my purse) has been stolen
▶ (saifu) ga nusumaremashita

I've been mugged
▶ gōtō ni aimashita

---

o namae wa? ◀
what's your name?

pasupōto o misete kudasai ◀
I need to see your passport

I'm sorry, all my papers have been stolen
▶ gomen·nasai, shorui ga zembu nusumaremashita

8. Friends

hi, how're you doing?
▶ kon·nichiwa, o genki desu ka?

hai, anata wa? ◀
OK, and you?

yeah, fine
▶ ee, genki desu

not bad
▶ waruku arimasen

d'you know Mark?
▶ Mark-san o go zonji desu ka?

and this is Hannah
▶ kochira wa Han·nah-san desu

ee, shit·te imasu ◀
yeah, we know each other

where do you know each other from?
▶ doko de o ai ni narimash*i*ta ka?

Kenji-san no tokoro de ai mash*i*ta ◀
we met at Kenji's place

that was some party, eh?
▶ yoi pātī desh*i*ta ne?

saikō ◀
the best

are you guys coming for a beer?
▶ biru o nomini ikimasen ka?

▶ īne, ikimashō
cool, let's go

▶ ie, Yōko-san to aimasu
no, I'm meeting Yōko

see you at Luke's place tonight
▶ Luke-san no tokoro de konya aimashō

jyā ne ◀
see you

download these scenarios as MP3s from:

9. Health

I'm not feeling very well
▶ kibun ga suguremasen

can you get a doctor?
▶ isha o yonde kuremasu ka?

---

doko ga itai desu ka? ◀
where does it hurt?

---

it hurts here
▶ koko ga itai desu

▶ itami wa tsuzuite imasu ka?
is the pain constant?

it's not a constant pain
▶ zut-to itaku wa arimasen

can I make an appointment?
▶ yoyaku wa toremasu ka?

can you give me something for ...?
▶ ...no kusuri o kuremasu ka?

yes, I have insurance
▶ hai, hoken ni hait-te imasu

antibiotics	kōsēbus-shitsu
antiseptic ointment	kanōdome nankō
cystitis	bōkōen
dentist	haisha
diarrhoea	geri
doctor	isha
hospital	byōin
ill	byōki
medicine	kusuri
painkillers	itami dome
pharmacy	yak-kyoku
to prescribe	shohō suru
thrush	kanjida shō

10. Language difficulties

a few words — ikutsu ka no kotoba
interpreter — tsūyaku
to translate — honyaku suru

anata no kurejit·to kādo wa kyohi saremashita ◀
your credit card has been refused

what, I don't understand; do you speak English?
▶ e? wakarimasen, Eigo o hanasemasu ka?

kore wa mukō desu ◀
this isn't valid

could you say that again? | **slowly**
▶ mō ichido it·te kudasai | ▶ yuk·kuri

I understand very little Japanese
▶ Nihongo wa hotondo hanasemasen

I speak Japanese very badly
▶ Nihongo wa amari hanasemasen

kono kādo de harau koto wa dekimasen ◀
you can't use this card to pay

▶ wakarimasu ka? | **sorry, no**
do you understand? | ▶ gomen·nasai, wakarimasen

is there someone who speaks English?
▶ dare ka Eigo o hanaseru hito wa imasu ka?

oh, now I understand
▶ a, ima wakarimashita

is that ok now?
▶ dewa, kore de ī desu ka?

11. Meeting people

hello
▶ kon·nichiwa

kon·nichiwa, watashi wa Kumiko desu ◀
hello, my name's Kumiko

Graham, from England, Thirsk
▶ watashi wa Igirisu no Thirsk kara kita Graham desu

sore wa shirimasen. doko desu ka? ◀
don't know that, where is it?

not far from York, in the North; and you?
▶ hokubu no York no chikaku desu. anata wa?

watashi wa Ōsaka kara kimash/ta. anata wa kochira dewa o hitori
desu ka? ◀
I'm from Ōsaka; here by yourself?

no, I'm with my wife and two kids
▶ ie, tsuma to kodomo futari ga kochira ni imasu

what do you do?   kompyūtā kankē desu ◀
▶ o shigoto wa?   I'm in computers

me too
▶ watashi mo

here's my wife now
▶ kore ga watashi no tsuma desu

hajime mash/te ◀
nice to meet you

12. Post offices

airmail	post card	post office	stamp
kōkūbin	ehagaki	yūbinkyoku	kit·te

what time does the post office close?
▶ yūbinkyoku wa nanji ni shimarimasu ka?

syūjitsu wa goji desu ◀
five o'clock weekdays

is the post office open on Saturdays?
▶ Doyōbi ni yūbinkyoku wa aite imasu ka?

shōgo made ◀
until midday

I'd like to send this registered to England
▶ kore o Igirisu ni kakitome de okuritai no desu ga

wakarimashita, san byaku yen desu ◀
certainly, that will cost 300 yen

and also two stamps for England, please
▶ sorekara Igirisu e no kit·te o ni mai kudasai

do you have some airmail stickers?
▶ kōkūbin no sutek·kā wa arimasu ka?

do you have any mail for me?
▶ watashi e no yūbinbutsu wa arimasu ka?

国内	kokunai	domestic
海外/国際	kaigai/kokusai	international
書簡	shokan	letters
小包	kozutsumi	parcels
局留め郵便	kyokudome yūbin	poste restante

13. Restaurants

bill	kanjō gaki
menu	menyū
table	tēburu

can we have a non-smoking table?
▶ kin'en seki o onegai shimasu?

there are two of us
▶ futari desu

there are four of us
▶ yonin desu

what's this?
▶ korewa nan desu ka?

sakana no is·syu desu ◀
it's a type of fish

kono tochi no mēbutsu desu ◀
it's a local speciality

naka ni dōzo, o mise shimashō ◀
come inside and I'll show you

we would like two of these, one of these, and one of those
▶ kore o futatsu, kore o hitotsu, soshite are o hitotsu kudasai

▶ o nomimono wa?
and to drink?

red wine
▶ aka wain

white wine
▶ shiro wain

a beer and two orange juices
▶ bīru hitotsu to orenji jūsu futatsu

some more bread please
▶ mot·to pan o kudasai

▶ ikaga deshi·ta ka?
how was your meal?

excellent!, very nice!
▶ saikō! totemo oishi/kat·ta desu!

▶ hoka ni wa?
anything else?

just the bill thanks
▶ okanjō onegai shimasu

14. Shopping

nani ka, o sagashi desu ka? ◄
can I help you?

can I just have a look around?   yes, I'm looking for ...
▸ miru dake desu   ▸ hai. ...o kaitaino desu ga

how much is this?
▸ kore wa ikura desu ka?

ni sen en ◄
two thousand yen

OK, I think I'll have to leave it; it's a little too expensive for me
▸ wakarimashita, yamete okimasu, sukoshi taka sugi masu

kore wa dō desu ka? ◄
how about this?

can I pay by credit card?
▸ kurejit-to kādo de haraemasu ka?

it's too big   it's too small
▸ ōki sugi masu   ▸ chīsa sugi masu

it's for my son – he's about this high
▸ musuko no desu – kore gurai no takasa desu

▸ hoka ni nani ka?   that's all thanks
will there be anything else?   ▸ kore de zembu desu

make it five thousand yen and I'll take it
▸ go sen en ni shite kurereba kai masu

fine, I'll take it
▸ ī desu, kaimasu

お支払い	o shiharai	cash desk
閉店	hēten	closed
開店	kaiten	open
バーゲンセール	bāgen sēru	sale
取り替える	torikaeru	to exchange

download these scenarios as MP3s from:

15. Sightseeing

art gallery	bijutsukan	guide	gaido
bus tour	basu tsuā	museum	hakubutsukan
city centre	chūshinbu	open	aite iru
closed	shimat·te iru		

I'm interested in seeing the old town
▶ kyūshigai ga mitai desu

are there guided tours?
▶ gaido tsuki no tsuā wa arimasu ka?

mōshiwake arimasen. manseki desu ◀
I'm sorry, it's fully booked

how much would you charge to drive us around for four hours?
▶ yo jikan no kankō doraibu wa ikura desu ka?

can we book tickets for the concert here?
▶ koko de konsāto no kip·pu o yoyaku dekimasu ka?

▶ hai, o namae wa?	▶ dono kurejit·to kādo?
yes, in what name?	which credit card?

where do we pick up the tickets?
▶ kip·pu wa doko de moraemasu ka?

iriguchi de uketot·te kudasai ◀
just pick them up at the entrance

is it open on Sundays?
▶ Nichiyōbi wa aite imasu ka?

how much is it to get in?
▶ nyūjōryō wa ikura desu ka?

are there reductions for groups of 6?
▶ roku nin no dantai ni waribiki wa arimasu ka?

that was really impressive!
▶ totemo yokat·ta desu!

16. Trains

to change trains	norikaeru
platform	purat·tofōmu
return	ōfuku
single	katamichi
station	eki
stop	eki
ticket	kip·pu

how much is ...?
▶ ...wa ikura desu ka?

a single, second class to ...
▶ katamichi hitori, futsūsha, ... made

two returns, second class to ...
▶ ōfuku futari, futsūsha, ... made

for today	for tomorrow	for next Tuesday
▶ kyō no	▶ ashita no	▶ raisyū no Kayōbi

Shinkansen wa tokubetsu ryōkin desu ◀
there's a supplement for the Bullet Train

zaseki o yoyaku shimasu ka? ◀
do you want to make a seat reservation?

Okayama de norikaete kudasai ◀
you have to change at Okayama

what time is the last train to Kyoto?
▶ Kyoto e no saisyūdensha wa nanji desu ka?

is this seat free?
▶ kono seki wa aite imasu ka?

excuse me, which station are we at?
▶ sumimasen, koko wa doko no eki desu ka?

is this where I change for Okayama?
▶ Okayama e wa koko de norikae desu ka?

English → Japanese

a, an* hitots*u* (no)
ひとつ (の)

about: about 20 ni-jū kurai
20 くらい

it's about 5 o'clock goji goro
5 時ごろ

a film about Japan Nihon ni
tsuite no eiga
日本についての映画

above … no ue ni
…の上に

abroad gaikok de
外国で

absorbent cotton das·shimen
脱脂綿

accelerator akseru
アクセル

accept (present) uketorimas*u*
受け取ります
(credit card etc) ukets*u*kemas*u*
受け付けます

accident jiko
事故

there's been an accident jiko
ga arimash*i*ta
事故がありました

accommodation heya
部屋

account kōza
口座

accurate seikak (na)
正確 (な)

ache itami
痛み

my back aches koshi ga itai
des*u*
腰が痛いです

across: across the road michi
no mukōgawa
道の向う側

adapter adaptā
アダプター

address jūsho
住所

what's your address?
gojūsho wa?
ご住所は ?

address book jūshorok
住所録

admission charge
nyūjōryō
入場料

adult otona
大人

advance: in advance mae-
mot·te
前もって

aeroplane hikōki
飛行機

after … no ato de
…の後で

after you dōzo osaki ni
どうぞお先に

after lunch chūshok*u*-go ni
昼食後に

after all kek·kyok*u*
結局

afternoon gogo
午後
in the afternoon gogo ni
午後に
this afternoon kyō no gogo ni
今日の午後に
aftershave afutā-shēbu
アフターシェイブ
aftersun cream afutāsan-rōshon
アフターサンローション
afterwards ato de
後で
again mata
また
against (opposed to) ... to hantai (no)
…と反対（の）
(position) ... ni tatekakete
…に立てかけて
age toshi
年
agent dairinin
代理人
ago mae
前
a week ago is·shūkan-mae
一週間前
an hour ago ichijikan-mae
一時間前
agree: I agree dōkan desu
同感です
agreement kyōtei
協定

AIDS eizu
エイズ
air kūki
空気
by air (travel) hikōki de
飛行機で
(send) kōkūbin de
航空便で
air-conditioning eya-kon
エアコン
airmail: by airmail kōkūbin de
航空便で
airmail envelope kōkūbin-yō fūtō
航空便用ふうとう
airplane hikōki
飛行機
airport kūkō
空港
to the airport, please kūkō made, onegai shimasu
空港までお願いします
airport bus rimujin-basu
リムジンバス
aisle seat tsūrogawa no seki
通路側の席
alarm clock mezamashi-dokei
目覚まし時計
alcohol arukōru
アルコール
alcoholic drink osake
お酒

all: all the ... ... wa min·na
…はみんな

all of it sore zembu
それぜんぶ

all of them zembu
ぜんぶ

that's all, thanks sore dake
des*u*, dōmo arigatō
それだけです、どう
もありがとう

allergic: I'm allergic to ...
watashi wa ... arerugī des*u*
私は…アレルギーで
す

allowed: is it allowed? ī des*u*
ka?
いいですか？

all right kek·kō des*u*
けっこうです

(I agree) dōkan des*u*
同感です

I'm all right daijōb*u* des*u*
大丈夫です

are you all right? daijōb*u*
des*u* ka?
大丈夫ですか？

almost hotondo
ほとんど

alone hitori
ひとり

already mō
もう

also ... mo
…も

although ... keredomo

けれども

although it's expensive takai
keredomo
高いけれども

altogether zembu de
ぜんぶで

always its*u*mo
いつも

am*: I am watashi wa ... des*u*
私は…です

am: at 7am gozen shichiji ni
午前７時に

at 1am gozen ichiji ni
午後１時に

amazing (surprising) odoroku-
beki
驚くべき

(very good) subarashī
すばらしい

ambulance kyūkyūsha
救急車

call an ambulance!
kyūkyūsha o yonde
kudasai!
救急車を呼んでくだ
さい！

America Amerika
アメリカ

American (adj) Amerika (no)
アメリカ（の）

I'm American watashi wa
Amerika-jin des*u*
私はアメリカ人です

among ... no naka de
…のなかで

amount ryō

量

(of money) gak

額

amp: a 13-amp fuse
jūsan-ampeya no hyūz

13アンペアのヒューズ

and* soshite

そして

(with nouns) to

と

(at beginning of sentence)

sorekara

それから

angry okot·ta

怒った

animal dōbutsu

動物

ankle ashikubi

足首

anniversary (wedding)

kek·kon-kinen-bi

結婚記念日

**annoy: this man's annoying
me** kono hito wa watashi o
komarasete imasu

このひとは私を困らせています

annoying iraira suru

いらいらする

another (different) betsu no

別の

(one more) mō hitotsu

もうひとつ

can we have another room?
betsu no heya wa arimasu
ka?

別の部屋はありますか？

another beer, please bīru o
mō hitotsu onegai shimasu

ビールをもうひとつお願いします

antibiotics kōsei-bus·shitsu

抗生物質

antihistamine kō-hisutamin-
zai

坑ヒスタミン剤

antique: is it an antique? sore
wa kot·tōhin desu ka?

それは骨董品ですか？

antique shop kot·tōhin-ten

骨董品店

antiseptic shōdoku-zai

消毒剤

any: do you have any ...? … o
mot·te imasu ka?

…を持っていますか？

**have you got any bread/
cherries?** pan/sakuranbo wa
arimasu ka?

パン／さくらんぼはありますか？

sorry, I don't have any
sumimasen, mot·te imasen

すみません、持っていません

anybody dare ka
だれか
does anybody speak English? dare ka Eigo ga hanasemasu ka?
だれか英語が話せますか？
there wasn't anybody there soko niwa dare mo imasen deshita
そこにはだれもいませんでした
anything nani ka
何か

dialogue

anything else? hoka ni nani ka?
nothing else, thanks hoka niwa nai desu, arigatō
would you like anything to drink? nani ka nomimasu ka?
I don't want anything, thanks nani mo hoshiku arimasen, arigatō

apart from … igai dewa
…以外では
apartment apāt(o)
アパート
apartment block manshon
マンション
appetizer zensai
前菜
apple rin·go
りんご
appointment yoyaku
予約

dialogue

good morning, how can I help you? ohayō gozaimasu, ikaga itashimashō?
I'd like to make an appointment yoyaku o shitai no desu ga
what time would you like? nanji ga yoroshī desu ka?
three o'clock sanji ga ī desu
I'm afraid that's not possible, is four o'clock all right? mōshiwake arimasen ga sanji wa ip·pai desu, yoji dewa ikaga desu ka?
yes, that will be fine hai, ī desu
the name was? onamae o itadakemasu ka?

apricot anzu
あんず
April Shigatsu
四月

are* des*u*
です

you are (sing) anata wa … des*u*
あなたは…です

they are (men/women) karera/kanojotachi wa … des*u*
彼ら／彼女たちは…です

area chīki
地域

area code shigai-kyok*u*ban
市外局番

arm ude
うで

arrange tehai shimas*u*
手配します

will you arrange it for us? sore o tehai shite kuremas*u* ka?
それを手配してくれますか？

arrival tōchak*u*
到着

arrive ts*u*kimas*u*
着きます

when do we arrive? itsu ts*u*kimas*u* ka?
いつ着きますか？

has my fax arrived yet? watashi no fak·k*u*s wa todokimash*i*ta ka?
私のファックスは届きましたか？

we arrived today kyō ts*u*kimash*i*ta

art bijuts*u*
美術

art gallery bijuts*u*-kan
美術館

artist geijuts*u*-ka
芸術家

as: as big as … … to onaji ōkisa no
…と同じ大きさの

as soon as possible dekiru dake hayak*u*
できるだけ早く

ashtray haizara
灰皿

Asia Ajia
アジア

Asian (adj) Ajia (no)
アジア（の）

(noun) Ajia-jin
アジア人

ask tanomimas*u*
頼みます

I didn't ask for this kore wa tanonde imasen
これは頼んでいません

could you ask him to …? kare ni … yō tanonde kuremasen ka?
彼に…よう頼んでくれませんか？

asleep: she's asleep kanojo wa nemut·te imas*u*
彼女は眠っています

aspirin asupirin
アスピリン

asthma zensoku
ぜんそく

astonishing odoroku hodo (no)
驚くほど（の）

at: at the hotel hoteru de
ホテルで

at the station eki de
駅で

at six o'clock rokuji ni
6時に

at Yukiko's Yukiko-san no tokoro de
ゆきこさんのところで

ATM genkin-jidō-shiharaiki
現金自動支払機

attractive miryoku-teki (na)
魅力的（な）

August Hachigatsu
八月

aunt (one's own) oba
おば

(someone else's) oba-san
おばさん

Australia Ōsutoraria
オーストラリア

Australian (adj) Ōsutoraria (no)
オーストラリア（の）

I'm Australian watashi wa Ōsutoraria-jin desu
私はオーストラリア人です

automatic (adj) jidō (no)
自動（の）

(noun: car) ōtomachik·ku
オートマティック

autumn aki
秋

in the autumn aki ni
秋に

avalanche nadare
なだれ

avenue ōdōri
大通り

average (not good) heikin-teki (na)
平均的（な）

on average heikin shite
平均して

awake: is he awake? kare wa okite imasu ka?
彼は起きていますか？

away: go away! at·chi e it·te!
あっちへいって！

is it far away? tōi desu ka?
遠いですか？

awful hidoi
ひどい

B

baby akachan
赤ちゃん

baby food bebī-fūdo
ベビーフード

baby's bottle honyūbin
ほ乳びん

baby-sitter bebī-shit·tā
ベビーシッター

back (of body) senaka
背中

(back part) ura
裏

at the back ushiro ni
後ろに

can I have my money back?
okane o kaeshite
kuremasen ka?
お金を返してくれま
せんか？

to come back modot·te
kimasu
戻ってきます

to go back modot·te
ikimasu
戻っていきます

backache koshi no itami
腰の痛み

bacon bēkon
ベーコン

bad warui
悪い

a bad headache hidoi zutsū
ひどい頭痛

not bad māmā desu
まあまあです

badly hidoku
ひどく

badminton badominton
バドミントン

bag kaban
かばん

(paper bag) fukuro
袋

(carrier bag) binīru-bukuro
ビニール袋

(handbag) handobag·gu
ハンドバッグ

baggage nimotsu
荷物

baggage checkroom
tenimotsu-azukari-jo
手荷物預り所

baggage claim
tenimotsu-uketori-jo
手荷物受取所

baker's pan-ya
パン屋

balcony beranda
ベランダ

a room with a balcony
beranda-tsuki no heya
ベランダ付きの部屋

ball bōru
ボール

ballpoint pen bōru-pen
ボールペン

bamboo take
竹

bamboo shoots takenoko
たけのこ

banana banana
バナナ

band (musical) bando
バンド

bandage hōtai
包帯

Bandaid® bando-eido
バンドエイド

bank (money) ginkō
銀行

bank account ginkō-kōza
銀行口座

banker's draft kawase-tegata
為替手形

bar bā
バー

a bar of chocolate
chokorēto-bā
チョコレートバー

barber's toko-ya
床屋

baseball yakyū
野球

basket kago
かご

(in shop) basuket-to
バスケット

basketball basuket-to-borū
バスケットボール

bath ofuro
お風呂

can I have a bath? ofuro ni
hait-te mo ī desu ka?
お風呂にはいっても
いいですか？

bathroom ofuro-ba
お風呂場

with a private bathroom
basu-tsuki no heya
バス付きの部屋

bath towel basu-taoru
バスタオル

bathtub yokusō
浴槽

battery (for radio etc)
denchi
電池

(for car) bat·terī
バッテリー

bay wan
湾

be* desu
です

beach hamabe
浜辺

on the beach hamabe de
浜辺で

bean curd tōfu
豆腐

beans mame
豆

soya beans daizu
大豆

beard hige
ひげ

beautiful (object, painting)
subarashī
すばらしい

(person, view) kirei (na)
きれいな

(building) utsukushī
美しい

because nazenara
なぜなら

because of ... ... no tame ni
…のために

bed (Western-style) bed·do
ベッド

(Japanese-style) nedoko
寝床

I'm going to bed now
sorosoro nemas*u*
そろそろ寝ます

bed and breakfast
chōshok*u*-ts*u*ki yado
朝食付き宿

bedding (Japanese) futon
ふとん

bedroom shinshits*u*
寝室

beef gyūnik*u*
牛肉

beer bīru
ビール

two beers, please bīru
futats*u*, onegai shimas*u*
ビールふたつ、お願
いします

before ... mae ni
…前に

begin hajimarimas*u*
始まります

when does it begin? itsu
hajimarimas*u* ka?
いつ始まりますか？

beginner shoshinsha
初心者

beginning: at the beginning
hajime ni
始めに

behind ... no ushiro ni
…の後ろに

behind me watashi no
ushiro ni
私の後ろに

below ... no shita ni
…の下に

belt beruto
ベルト

bend (in road) kāb*u*
カーブ

berth (on ship) shindai
寝台

beside ... no soba ni
…のそばに

best saikō (no)
最高（の）

better mot·to ī
もっと良い

are you feeling better?
kibun wa yok*u* narimash*i*ta
ka?
気分はよくなりまし
たか？

between ... no aida ni
…の間に

beyond ... no mukō ni
…の向こうに

bicycle jitensha
自転車

big ōkī
大きい

too big ōkīsugimas*u*

大きすぎます

it's not big enough

chīsasugimas*u*

小さすぎます

bikini bikini

ビキニ

bill seikyūsho

請求書

(in restaurant, bar etc) okanjō

お勘定

(US: banknote) shihei

紙幣

could I have the bill, please?

okanjō o onegai shimas*u*

お勘定をお願いします

bin gomibako

ごみ箱

bird tori

鳥

birthday tanjōbi

誕生日

happy birthday! otanjōbi omedetō gozaimas*u*!

お誕生日おめでとうございます

biscuit bis*u*ket·to

ビスケット

bit: a little bit s*u*koshi

すこし

a big bit ōkī bubun

大きい部分

a bit of ... ... o s*u*koshi

…をすこし

a bit expensive chot·to takai des*u*

ちょっと高いです

bite (by insect) mushi-sasare

虫さされ

(by dog) inu no kamikizu

犬の噛み傷

bitter (taste etc) nigai

にがい

black kuroi

黒い

blanket mōf*u*

毛布

blind me no fujiyū na hito (no)

目の不自由な人（の）

blinds buraindo

ブラインド

blocked (road, pipe) fusagat·ta

ふさがった

(sink) tsumat·ta

つまった

blond (adj) kimpatsu (no)

金髪（の）

blood ketsu·eki

血液

high blood pressure

kōketsu·atsu

高血圧

blouse buraus*u*

ブラウス

blow-dry burō-dorai

ブロードライ

I'd like a cut and blow-dry

kat·to to burō-dorai o
onegai shimasu

カットとブロードラ
イをお願いします

blue aoi

青い

boarding pass tōjōken

搭乗券

boat bōto

ボート

(for passengers) fune

船

body karada

からだ

boiled egg yude-tamago

ゆでたまご

boiled rice gohan

ごはん

bone hone

ほね

bonnet (of car) bon·net·to

ボンネット

book (noun) hon

本

(verb) yoyaku shimasu

予約します

can I book a seat? seki o
yoyaku dekimasu ka?

席を予約できます
か？

dialogue

I'd like to book a table for
two tēburu o futari-yō ni

yoyaku shitai no desu ga
**what time would you like it
booked for?** nanji ni
otorishimashō ka?
half past seven shichiji-
han ni onegai shimasu
that's fine o-uke-
itashimasu
and your name?
dochirasama desu ka?

bookshop, bookstore hon-ya

本屋

boot (footwear) būtsu

ブーツ

(of car) toranku

トランク

border (of country) kok·kyō

国境

bored: I'm bored taikutsu
desu

退屈です

boring taikutsu (na)

退屈な

born: I was born in ... (place)
... de umaremashita

…で生まれました

(year) ... ni umaremashita

に生まれました

borrow karimasu

借ります

may I borrow ...? ... o
okarishite mo ī desu ka?

…をお借りしてもい
いですか？

both ryōhō
両方

bother: sorry to bother you
otesū o okakeshite
sumimasen
お手数をおかけして
すみません

bottle bin
びん

a bottle of sake sake ip·pon
酒一本

bottle-opener sen·nuki
栓抜き

bottom (of person) oshiri
お尻

at the bottom of the ... ... no
soko ni
…の底に

(hill, mountain) ... no fumoto
ni
…のふもとに

(road, street) ... no tsukiatari
ni
…のつきあたりに

bowl (porcelain) chawan
茶碗

(wooden) owan
お椀

box hako
箱

(wooden) kibako
木箱

box office kip·p-uriba
切符売り場

boy otoko no ko
男の子

boyfriend bōi-frendo
ボーイフレンド

bra brajā
ブラジャー

bracelet buresuret·to
ブレスレット

brake (noun) burēki
ブレーキ

brandy burandē
ブランデー

bread pan
パン

white bread shiro-pan
白パン

brown bread kuro-pan
黒パン

wholemeal bread zenryūko
no pan
全粒粉のパン

break (verb) kowashimasu
壊します

I've broken the ... ... o
kowashite shimai-
mashita
…を壊してしまい
ました

I think I've broken my wrist
dōmo tekubi o ot·ta yō
desu
どうも手首を折った
ようです

break down koshō shimasu
故障します

I've broken down kuruma ga

enko shimash*i*ta

車がエンコしました

breakdown koshō

故障

breakdown service rek·kā-sha

レッカー車

breakfast chōshok*u*

朝食

break-in: I've had a break-in

dorobō ni hairaremash*i*ta

どろぼうにはいられ
ました

breast chibusa

乳房

bridge (over river) hashi

橋

brief mijikai

短い

briefcase bur*ī*f*u*-kēs*u*

ブリーフケース

bright (light etc) akarui

あかるい

(colour) azayaka (na)

あざやか（な）

brilliant subarashī

すばらしい

bring mot·te kimas*u*

持ってきます

I'll bring it back later atode

kaesh*i* ni kimas*u*

後で返しにきます

Britain Eikok*u*

英国

British (adj) Eikok*u* (no)

英国（の）

brochure panfret·to

パンフレット

broken kowareta

壊れた

(leg etc) hone ga oreta

骨が折れた

brooch burōchi

ブローチ

brother kyōdai

兄弟

(elder: one's own) ani

兄

(someone else's) onī-san

お兄さん

(younger: one's own) otōto

弟

(someone else's) otōto-san

弟さん

brother-in-law giri no kyōdai

義理の兄弟

(elder: one's own) giri no ani

義理の兄

(someone else's) giri no
onī-san

義理のお兄さん

(younger: one's own) giri no
otōto

義理の弟

(someone else's) giri no
otōto-san

義理の弟さん

brown cha-iro (no)

茶色

bruise dabok*u*-shō

打撲傷

brush (for hair) burashi
ブラシ
(artist's) efude
絵筆
(for cleaning) hōki
ほうき
Buddha hotoke-sama
仏様
Buddhism Buk·kyō
仏教
Buddhist (adj) Buk·kyō (no)
仏教（の）
(noun) Buk·kyōto
仏教徒
buffet car shokudōsha
食堂車
buggy (for child) uba-guruma
乳母車
building biru
ビル
bullet train shinkansen
新幹線
bunk shindai
寝台
bureau de change ryōgae-jo
両替所
burglary oshikomi-gōtō
押し込み強盗
burn (noun) yakedo
やけど
(verb) yakedo shimasu
やけどします
burnt: this is burnt (food) kore
wa kogete imasu
これは焦げています

bus basu
バス
what number bus is it to ...?
…-iki no basu wa namban
desu ka?
…―行きのバスは
何番ですか？
when is the next bus to ...?
tsugi no …-iki no basu wa
nanji desu ka?
次の…―行きのバス
は何時ですか？
what time is the last bus?
saishū basu wa nanji desu
ka?
最終バスは何時です
か？

dialogue

does this bus go to ...?
kono basu wa …-iki
desu ka?
no, you need a number ...
īe, … ban no basu desu

business shigoto
仕事
(company) kaisha
会社
business card meishi
名刺
business hotel
bijinesu-hoteru
ビジネスホテル

businessman bijines*u*-man
ビジネスマン

business trip shut·chō
出張

businesswoman kyaria-ūman
キャリアウーマン

bus station bas*u*-tāminaru
バスターミナル

bus stop bas*u*-tei
バス停

bust bas*u*to
バスト

busy (restaurant etc) konde iru
込んでいる

I'm busy tomorrow ash*i*ta wa
isogash*ī* des*u*
あしたは忙しいです

but demo
でも

butcher's nik*u*-ya
肉屋

butter batā
バター

button botan
ボタン

buy kaimas*u*
買います

where can I buy ...? doko de
... ga kaemas*u* ka?
どこで…が買えま
すか？

by: by car kuruma de
車で

by bus bas*u* de
バスで

written by ... ... ga kaita
…が書いた

by the window mado no soba
窓のそば

by the sea umi no soba
海のそば

by Thursday Mok*u*·yōbi
made ni
木曜日までに

bye dewa mata
ではまた

(between friends) jā ne
じゃあね

C

cabin (on ship) senshits*u*
船室

(in mountains) yamagoya
山小屋

cable car kēburu-kā
ケーブルカー

café kis·saten
喫茶店

cake kēki
ケーキ

cake shop kēki-ya
ケーキ屋

calendar karendā
カレンダー

lunar calendar kyūreki
旧暦

call (verb: to phone) denwa
shimas*u*

電話します

what's it called? kore wa nan to īmasu ka?

これはなんと言
いますか？

he/she is called ... kare/kanojo wa ... to īmasu

彼／彼女は…と言
います

please call the doctor isha o yonde kudasai

医者を呼んで
ください

please give me a call at 7.30am tomorrow ashita no asa shichi-ji han ni denwa o kudasai

あしたの朝7時半に
電話をください

please ask him to call me kare ni denwa o kureru yō tsutaete kudasai

彼に電話をくれるよ
う伝えてください

call back: I'll call back later ato de mata ukagaimasu

後でまたうかがい
ます

(phone back) ato de mata denwa shimasu

後でまた電話します

call round: I'll call round tomorrow ashita ukagaimasu

あしたうかがいます

calligraphy shodō

書道

camcorder bideo-kamera

ビデオカメラ

camera kamera

カメラ

camera shop kamera-ya

カメラ屋

campsite kyamp-jō

キャンプ場

can kanzume

缶詰め

a can of beer kan-bīru

缶ビール

can*: can you ...? ...-koto ga dekimasu ka?

…―ことができます
か？

can I have ...? ... o morat-te mo ī desu ka?

…をもらってもいい
ですか？

I can't ... ...-koto ga dekimasen

…―ことができませ
ん

Canada Kanada

カナダ

Canadian (adj) Kanada (no)

カナダ（の）

I'm Canadian watashi wa Kanada-jin desu

私はカナダ人です

canal un·ga

運河

cancel torikeshimasu
取り消します

candies kyandī
キャンディー

candle rōsoku
ロウソク

canoe kanū
カヌー

canoeing kanūingu
カヌーイング

can-opener kankiri
缶切り

cap (hat) bōshi
ぼうし

(of bottle) futa
ふた

car kuruma
車

by car kuruma de
車で

card (birthday etc) kādo
カード

New Year's card nen-gajō
年賀状

here's my (business) card
watashi no meishi desu
私の名刺です

cardphone kādo-denwa
カード電話

careful chūibukai
注意深い

be careful! ki o tsukete!
気をつけて！

carp koi
こい

car park chūshajō
駐車場

carpet jūtan
じゅうたん

carp streamer koi-nobori
こいのぼり

car rental rentakā
レンタカー

carriage (of train) kyakusha
客車

carrier bag binīru-bukuro
ビニール袋

carrot ninjin
にんじん

carry mochimasu
持ちます

carry-cot keitai-yō
bebī-bed-do
携帯用ベビーベッド

carton pak-ku
パック

cartoon (film) animēshon
アニメーション

cash (noun) genkin
現金

(verb) genkin ni kaemasu
現金に換えます

will you cash this for me?
genkin ni kaete kuremasen
ka?
現金に換えてくれま
せんか？

cash desk kaikei
会計

cash dispenser

genkin-jidō-shiharaiki
現金自動支払機

cassette kaset·to
カセット

cassette recorder
kaset·to-rekōdā
カセットレコーダー

castle shiro
城

casualty department
kyūkyūbyōtō
救急病棟

cat neko
ねこ

catch tsukamaemasu
捕まえます

**where do we catch the bus
to ...?** ...-iki no basu wa
doko kara dete imasu ka?
…―行きのバスはど
こから出ています
か？

Catholic (adj) Katorik·ku (no)
カトリック（の）

cauliflower karifurawā
カリフラワー

cave hora-ana
洞穴

CD shī-dī
シーディー

ceiling tenjō
天井

cemetery bochi
墓地

centigrade ses·shi
摂氏

centimetre senchi-mētoru
センチメートル

central chūshin (no)
中心（の）

centre chūshin
中心

**how do we get to the city
centre?** hankagai niwa dō
ikimasu ka?
繁華街にはどう行き
ますか？

cereal kōnfurēku
コーンフレーク

ceremony shikiten
式典

opening ceremony
kaikaishiki
開会式

tea ceremony chakai
茶会

certainly tashika ni
たしかに

certainly not! (that's wrong)
zet·tai chigaimasu!
絶対違います！

(refusal) dame desu!
だめです！

certificate shōmeisho
証明書

chair isu
いす

change (verb: replace)
torikaemasu
取りかえます

49

(trains etc) norikaemas*u*

乗り換えます

(money) kuzushimas*u*

くずします

(noun: money) kozeni

小銭

can I change this for ...,
please? kore o ... to
torikaete kudasai

これを…と取りかえ
てください

where do I change trains?
doko de norikaereba ī des*u*
ka?

どこで乗り換えれば
いいですか？

I don't have any change
kozeni ga arimasen

小銭がありません

can you give me change for a
1,000-yen note?
sen-en-sats*u* o kuzushite
kuremasen ka?

千円札をくずして
くれませんか？

dialogue

do we have to change
(trains)? norikae-nak*u*te
wa narimasen ka?
yes, change at Tokyo/no,
it's a direct train hai,
Tokyo-eki de norikae
des*u*/īe, chok*u*tsū des*u*

changed: to get changed
kigaemas*u*

着替えます

character (written) kanji

漢字

charge (noun) ryōkin

料金

(verb) seikyū shimas*u*

請求します

charge card kurejit·to-kādo

クレジットカード

cheap yasui

安い

do you have anything
cheaper? mō s*u*koshi yasui
no wa arimas*u* ka?

もう少し安いの
はありますか？

check (US: noun) kogit·te

小切手

(bill) seikyūsho

請求書

(in restaurant, bar etc) okanjō

お勘定

could I have the check,
please? okanjō o onegai
shimas*u*

お勘定をお願します

check (verb) shirabemas*u*

調べます

could you check the ...? ... o
shirabete kuremasen ka?

…を調べてくれ
ませんか？

check-in chek·k*u*-in

check in chek·k*u*-in shimas*u*
チェックインします

where do we have to check in?
doko de chek·k*u*-in
shinak*u*te wa narimasen ka?
どこでチェックイン
しなくてはなりませ
んか？

cheek (on face) hō
ほお

cheerio! bai-bai!
バイバイ！

cheers! (toast) kampai!
乾杯！

cheese chīz*u*
チーズ

chemist's yak·kyok*u*
薬局

cheque kogit·te
小切手

cherry sakuranbo
さくらんぼ

cherry blossom sakura
桜

cherry tree sakura no ki
桜の木

chess (Western) ches*u*
チェス
(Japanese) shōgi
将棋

chest mune
胸

chestnut kuri
くり

chewing gum chūin·gam
チューインガム

chicken (meat) torinik*u*
鶏肉

chickenpox mizubōsō
水ぼうそう

child kodomo
子供

children kodomo-tachi
子供たち

child minder komori
子守

children's pool kodomo-yō
pūru
子供用プール

children's portion
okosama-yō
お子様用

chin ago
あご

china setomono
瀬戸もの

China Chūgok*u*
中国

Chinese (adj) Chūgok*u* (no)
中国（の）

chips (French fries) f*u*rench-frai
フレンチフライ
(US) poteto-chip·p*u*
ポテトチップ

chocolate chokorēto
チョコレート

milk chocolate
miruk*u*-chokorēto
ミルクチョコレート

plain chocolate
burak·ku-chokorēto
ブラックチョコレート

a hot chocolate kokoa
ココア

choose erabimasu
選びます

chopstick rest hashioki
はしおき

chopsticks hashi
はし

Christmas Kurismasu
クリスマス

merry Christmas!
Merī-Kurismasu!
メリークリスマス

Christmas Eve
Kurismasu-Ibu
クリスマスイブ

church kyōkai
教会

cider rin·goshu
りんご酒

cigar hamaki
葉巻

cigarette tabako
タバコ

cigarette lighter raitā
ライター

cinema eiga
映画

circle en
円
(in theatre) barukonī-seki
バルコニー席

city toshi
都市

city centre hankagai
繁華街

clean (adj) kirei (na)
きれい (な)
(verb) kirei ni shimasu
きれいにします

can you clean these for me?
kore o kirei ni shite
kuremasen ka?
これをきれいにして
くれませんか ?

cleaning solution (for contact
lenses) kontakuto-renzu-yō
kurīnā
コンタクトレンズ用
クリーナー

cleansing lotion
kurenjing-rōshon
クレンジングロー
ション

clear tōmei (na)
透明 (な)
(obvious) akiraka (na)
明らか (な)

clever kashikoi
かしこい

client irainin
依頼人

cliff gake
崖

climbing tozan
登山

clinic shinryōjo
診療所

cloakroom kurōku
クローク

clock tokei
時計

close (verb) shimarimasu
閉まります

dialogue

what time do you close?
nanji ni shimarimasu ka?
we close at 8pm on
weekdays, and 6pm on
Saturdays heijitsu wa
hachiji, Doyōbi wa rokji
ni shimarimasu
do you close for lunch?
hiruyasumi wa arimasu
ka?
yes, between 12 and 1pm
hai, jūniji kara ichiji desu

closed (door) shimat·ta
閉まった
(shop) heiten (no)
閉店 (の)

cloth (fabric) nunoji
布地
(for cleaning etc) zōkin
ぞうきん

clothes (Western) yōfuku
洋服
(Japanese) kimono

着物

cloudy kumori (no)
くもり (の)

clutch (in car) kurat·chi
クラッチ

coach (bus) chōkyori-basu
長距離バス
(on train) kyaksha
客車

coach station basu-tāminaru
バスターミナル

coach trip basu-ryokō
バス旅行

coast kaigan
海岸
on the coast engan ni
沿岸に

coat (long coat) kōto
コート
(jacket) jaket·to
ジャケット

coathanger han·gā
ハンガー

code (for phoning)
shigai-kyokban
市外局番
what's the (dialling) code for
Osaka? Ōsaka no shigai-
kyokban wa namban desu
ka?
大阪の市外局番は
何番ですか？

coffee kōhī
コーヒー
two coffees, please kōhī

futatsu, onegai shimasu
コーヒーふたつ、
お願いします

coin kōka
硬貨

Coke® kōla
コーラ

cold tsumetai
冷たい
(weather, person) samui
寒い
I'm cold samui desu
寒いです
I have a cold kaze o
hikimashita
風邪を引きました

collar eri
えり

collect atsumemasu
集めます
I've come to collect ... ... o
tori ni kimashita
…を取りに来ました

collect call korekuto-kōru
コレクトコール

college daigaku
大学

colour iro
色
do you have this in other
colours? hoka no iro wa
arimasu ka?
ほかの色はあります
か？

colour film karā-firumu

カラーフィルム

comb kushi
くし

come kimasu
来ます

dialogue

where do you come from?
doko kara
iras·shaimashita ka?
I come from Edinburgh
Ejinbara kara kimashita

come back modot·te kimasu
戻ってきます
I'll come back tomorrow
mata ashita kimasu
またあした来ます

come in hairimasu
入ります

comfortable yut·tari shita
ゆったりした

comic book man·ga
漫画

compact disc
kompakuto-disuku
コンパクトディスク

company (business) kaisha
会社

compare kurabemasu
比べます

compartment (on train)
koshitsu
個室

compass kompas*u*
コンパス

complain kujō o īmas*u*
苦情を言います

complaint kujō
苦情

I have a complaint kujō ga
arimas*u*
苦情があります

completely kanzen ni
完全に

computer kompyūtā
コンピューター

concert konsāto
コンサート

conditioner (for hair) rins*u*
リンス

condom kondōm*u*
コンドーム

conference kaigi
会議

conference room kaigijō
会議場

confirm kak*u*nin shimas*u*
確認します

congratulations! omedetō!
おめでとう！

connecting flight
setsuzok*u*bin
接続便

connection (in travelling)
setsuzok*u*
接続

constipation bempi
便秘

consulate ryōjikan
領事館

contact (verb) renrak*u*
shimas*u*
連絡します

contact lenses
kontak*u*to-renzu
コンタクトレンズ

contract keiyak*u*
契約

convenient (time) tsugō no ī
都合のいい
(location, object) benri (na)
便利（な）

that's not convenient sore wa
tsugō ga yok*u* arimasen
それは都合がよくあ
りません

cook (verb) ryōri shimas*u*
料理します

not cooked han·nama (na)
半なま（な）

cooker renji
レンジ

cookie bis*u*ket·to
ビスケット

cool suzushī
涼しい

cork koruk*u*
コルク

corkscrew koruk*u*-nuki
コルク抜き

corner: on the corner
machikado ni
街角に

in the corner sumi ni

隅に

cornflakes kōnfurēku

コーンフレーク

correct (right) tadashī

正しい

corridor rōka

廊下

cosmetics keshōhin

化粧品

cost (noun) hiyō

費用

(verb) hiyō ga kakarimasu

費用がかかります

how much does it cost?

ikura desu ka?

いくらですか？

cot bebī-bed·do

ベビーベッド

cotton momen

木綿

cotton wool das·shimen

脱脂綿

couchette shindai

寝台

cough (noun) seki

せき

cough medicine sekidome

せき止め

could: could you ...? ...-te

kuremasen ka?

……ーてくれません

か？

could I have ...? ... o

kuremasen ka?

…をくれませんか？

I couldn't ... ... koto wa

dekimasen deshita

…ことはできません

でした

country (nation) kuni

国

(countryside) inaka

いなか

countryside inaka

いなか

couple: a couple of ...

... futatsu

…ふたつ

courier gaido

ガイド

course kōsu

コース

of course mochiron

もちろん

of course not mochiron

chigaimasu

もちろん違います

cousin itoko

いとこ

crab kani

かに

cracker (biscuit) kurak·kā

クラッカー

craft shop min·geihin-ten

民芸品店

crash (noun) shōtotsu-jiko

衝突事故

I've had a crash

shōtotsu-jiko ni aimashita

衝突事故にあい
ました
crazy muchū (na)
夢中（な）
cream kurīm*u*
クリーム
creche tak*u*ji-sho
託児所
credit card kurejit·to-kādo
クレジットカード
do you take credit cards?
kurejit·to-kādo wa
ts*u*kemas*u* ka?
クレジットカードは
使えますか？

dialogue

can I pay by credit card?
kurejit·to-kādo de
haraemas*u* ka?
which card do you want to
use? doko no kādo des*u*
ka?
Mastercard/Visa
mas*u*tā/biza des*u*
yes, sir hai, oshiharai
itadakemas*u*
what's the number?
ban·gō o itadakemas*u* ka?
and the expiry date?
yūkōkigen wa its*u* des*u*
ka?

crisps poteto-chip·p*u*

ポテトチップ
crockery tōjiki
陶磁器
crossing (by sea) ōdan
横断
crossroads jūjiro
十字路
crowd hitogomi
ひと込み
crowded konda
込んだ
crown (dental) kuraun
クラウン
cruise kōkai
航海
crutches mats*u*bazue
松葉杖
cry (verb) nakimas*u*
泣きます
cucumber kyūri
きゅうり
cup kap·p*u*
カップ
a cup of ..., please ... o
hitots*u* kudasai
…をひとつください
cupboard oshīre
押し入れ
(with shelves) todana
戸棚
curly kārī-hea (no)
カーリーヘア
（の）
curtains kāten
カーテン

cushion kus·shon
クッション
　floor cushion zabuton
　ざぶとん
custom shūkan
習慣
customer kyaku
客
Customs zeikan
税関
cut (noun) kirikizu
切り傷
　(verb) kirimasu
　切ります
　I've cut myself kit·te
　shimaimashita
　切ってしまいました
cutlery naifu-fōku-rui
ナイフ・フォーク類
cycling saikuringu
サイクリング
cyclist saikurisuto
サイクリスト

D

daily mainichi (no)
毎日
damage (verb) kowashimasu
壊します
　damaged kowareta
　壊れた
　I'm sorry, I've damaged this
　sumimasen, kore o

kowashite shimaimashita
すみません、これを
壊してしまいまし
た
damn! chikushō!
ちくしょう！
damp shimet·ta
しめった
dance (noun) dansu
ダンス
　(verb) odorimasu
　おどります
　would you like to dance?
　odorimasen ka?
　おどりませんか？
dangerous abunai
危ない
Danish (adj) Dem·māku (no)
デンマーク（の）
dark (adj: colour) koi
濃い
　(hair) kuroi
　黒い
　it's getting dark kuraku
　nat·te kimashita
　暗くなってきました
date*: **what's the date today?**
kyō wa nan·nichi desu ka?
きょうは何日です
か？
　let's make a date for next
　Monday raishū no
　Getsuyōbi ni shimashō
　来週の月曜日に
　しましょう

daughter (one's own) musume

娘

(someone else's) ojō-san

お嬢さん

daughter-in-law (one's own) giri no musume

義理の娘

(someone else's) giri no musume-san

義理の娘さん

dawn yoake

夜明け

at dawn yoake ni

夜明けに

day hi

日

the day after sono tsugi no hi

その次の日

the day after tomorrow

as·sat·te

あさって

the day before sono mae no hi

その前の日

the day before yesterday

ototoi

おととい

every day mainichi

毎日

all day ichinichi-jū

一日中

in two days' time

futsuka-inai ni

二日以内に

have a nice day! gokigen·yō!

ごきげんよう！

day trip higaeri-ryokō

日帰り旅行

dead shinda

死んだ

deaf mimi ga kikoenai

耳がきこえない

deal (business) torihiki

取り引き

it's a deal sore de te o uchimashō

それで手を打ちま
しょう

death shi

死

decaffeinated coffee kafein nuki no kōhī

カフェイン抜き
のコーヒー

December Jūnigatsu

十二月

decide kimemasu

決めます

we haven't decided yet mada kimete imasen

まだ決めていません

decision ket·tei

決定

deck (on ship) dek·ki

デッキ

deckchair dek·ki-chea

デッキチェア

deep fukai

深い

definitely mat·tak*u* sono tōri des*u*

まったくそのとおりです

definitely not mat·tak*u* chigaimas*u*

まったく違います

degree do

度

(qualification) gakui

学位

delay (noun) okure

遅れ

deliberately waza to

わざと

delicatessen sōzai-ya

惣菜屋

delicious totemo oishī

とてもおいしい

deliver haitats*u* shimas*u*

配達します

delivery haitats*u*

配達

Denmark Den·māk*u*

デンマーク

dental floss dentaru-f*u*ros*u*

デンタルフロス

dentist haisha

歯医者

dialogue

it's this one here koko no kore des*u*
this one? kore des*u* ka?

no that one īe, sore des*u*
here? koko des*u* ka?
yes hai

dentures ireba

入れ歯

deodorant deodoranto

デオドラント

department bumon

部門

department store depāto

デパート

departure shup·pats*u*

出発

departure lounge shup·pats*u*-raunji

出発ラウンジ

depend: it depends bāi ni yorimas*u*

場合によります

it depends on ... ... ni yorimas*u*

…によります

deposit (for bike/boat hire) hoshōkin

保証金

(as part payment) atamakin

頭金

description sets*u*mei

説明

design dezain

デザイン

dessert dezāto

デザート

destination mok*u*tekichi

目的地

develop genzō shimas*u*
現像します

dialogue

could you develop these films? kono firum*u* o genzō shite kuremasen ka?
yes, certainly hai, genzō des*u* ne
when will they be ready? itsu dekiagarimas*u* ka?
tomorrow afternoon ashita no gogo des*u*
how much is the four-hour service? yojikan no sābis*u* wa ikura des*u* ka?

diabetic (noun) tōnyōbyō-kanja
糖尿病患者
diabetic foods tōnyōbyō-kanja-yō shok*u*hin
糖尿病患者用食品
dial (verb) daiyaru shimas*u*
ダイヤルします
dialling code shigai-kyok*u*ban
市外局番
diamond daiyamondo
ダイアモンド
diaper omuts*u*

おむつ
diarrhoea geri
下痢
do you have any medicine for diarrhoea? geridome wa arimas*u* ka?
下痢止めはあります か？
diary (business etc) techō
手帳
(for personal experiences) nik·ki
日記
dictionary jisho
辞書
didn't* ...-masen desh*i*ta
…―ませんでした
see not
die shinimas*u*
死にます
diesel dīzeru-sha
ディーセル車
diet daiet·to
ダイエット
I'm on a diet daiet·to-chū des*u*
ダイエット中です
I have to follow a special diet shok*u*ji-seigen ga arimas*u*
食事制限があります
difference chigai
違い
what's the difference? chigai wa nan des*u* ka?
違いは何ですか？

different chigau
違う
this one is different kore wa chigaimasu
これは違います
a different table chigau tēburu
違うテーブル

difficult muzukashī
むずかしい

dining room shokudō
食堂

dinner (evening meal) yūshoku
夕食
to have dinner shokuji o shimasu
食事をします

direct (adj) chokusetsu (no)
直接（の）
is there a direct train? chokutsū no densha wa arimasu ka?
直通の電車はありますか？

direction hōkō
方向
which direction is it? dotchi no hōkō desu ka?
どっちの方向ですか？
is it in this direction? kono hōkō desu ka?
この方向ですか？

director (section chief) kachō
課長

(of department) buchō
部長
(of company) shachō
社長

directory enquiries denwa-ban·gō-an·nai
電話番号案内

dirt yogore
汚れ

dirty kitanai
汚い

disabled: disabled person shintai-shōgai-sha
身体障害者
is there access for the disabled? shintai-shōgai-sha mo riyō dekimasu ka?
身体障害者も利用できますか？

disappear nakunarimasu
なくなります
it's disappeared nakunarimashita
なくなりました

disappointed gak·kari sh(i)ta
がっかりした

disappointing kitai hazure (no)
期待はずれ（の）

disaster saigai
災害
this is a disaster kore wa hidoi desu
これはひどいです

disco disuko
ディスコ

discount waribiki

割引

is there a discount? waribiki
ni narimasu ka?

割引になりますか？

disease byōki

病気

disgusting iya (na)

いや（な）

dish (meal) ryōri

料理

(plate) sara

皿

disk (for computer) disuku

ディスク

disposable diapers/nappies
kami-omutsu

紙おむつ

distance kyori

距離

in the distance tōku ni

遠くに

district chihō

地方

disturb jama shimasu

じゃまします

do not disturb okosanaide
kudasai

起こさないで
ください

diversion (detour)
mawari-michi

回り道

divorced rikon shita

離婚した

dizzy: I feel dizzy memai ga
shimasu

めまいがします

do (verb) shimasu

します

what shall we do? nani o
shimashō ka?

何をしましょうか？

how do you do it? dōyat·te
surundesu ka?

どうやってするん
ですか？

will you do it for me? sōshite
kuremasen ka?

そうしてくれません
か？

dialogue

how do you do?
hajimemashite, dōzo
yoroshiku
nice to meet you
o-aidekite ureshīdes
what do you do? (work)
oshigoto wa nan desu
ka?
I'm a teacher, and you?
watashi wa kyōshi desu
ga anata wa?
I'm a student watashi wa
gakusei desu
**what are you doing
tonight?** komban wa nani
o shite imasu ka?

we're going out for a drink, do you want to join us? watashitachi wa nomi ni ikimasu ga, is·sho ni kimasen ka?

do you want tea? ocha wa ikaga desu ka?
I do, but she doesn't watashi wa itadakimasu ga, kanojo niwa kek·kō desu

doctor isha
医者
we need a doctor isha ga hitsuyō desu
医者が必要です
please call a doctor isha o yonde kudasai
医者を呼んで
ください

dialogue

where does it hurt? doko ga itai desu ka?
right here koko desu
does that hurt now? kore wa itai desu ka?
yes hai
take this to the chemist kore o mot·te kusuri-ya ni ikinasai

document shorui
書類
dog inu
犬
doll nin·gyō
人形
domestic flight kokunaisen
国内線
don't!* dame!
だめ！
don't do that! yoshinasai!
よしなさい！
see not
door doa
ドア
(of house: Japanese-style) to
戸
sliding door (wooden lattice and paper) shōji
障子
(patterned) fusuma
ふすま
doorman doaman
ドアマン
doorway genkan
玄関
double nibai (no)
二倍
double bed daburu–bed·do
ダブルベッド
double room daburu
ダブル
double whisky daburu
ダブル
doughnut dōnat·tsu

ドーナッツ

down: down here kono shita
desu

この下です

put it down over there soko
ni oite kudasai

そこに置いて
ください

it's down there on the right
soko o it·te migi desu

そこを行って右です

it's further down the road
mot·to saki desu

もっと先です

downmarket (restaurant etc)
yasup·poi

安っぽい

downstairs shita

下

dozen ichi-dāsu (no)

1ダース

half a dozen han-dās (no)

半ダース

draught beer nama-bīru

生ビール

draughty: it's draughty
sukima-kaze ga hairimasu

すきま風がはいり
ます

drawer hikidashi

引出し

drawing e

絵

dreadful hidoi

ひどい

dream (noun) yume

夢

dress (noun) doresu

ドレス

dressed: to get dressed fuku
o kimasu

服を着ます

dressing gown gaun

ガウン

drink (noun) nomimono

飲物

(alcoholic) osake

お酒

(non-alcoholic) seiryō-inryō

清涼飲料

(verb) nomimasu

飲みます

a cold drink tsumetai
nomimono

冷たい飲物

can I get you a drink?
nomimono wa ikaga desu
ka?

飲物はいかがです
か？

**what would you like (to
drink)?** nani o nomimasu
ka?

何を飲みますか？

no thanks, I don't drink
arigatō, demo arukōru wa
nomimasen

ありがとう、でもア
ルコールは飲み
ません

I'll just have a drink of water
mizu o kudasai
水をください

drinking water inryōsui
飲料水

is this drinking water? kore
wa inryōsui desu ka?
これは飲料水です
か？

drive (verb) unten shimasu
運転します

we drove here kuruma de
kimashita
車で来ました

I'll drive you home okut·te
ikimasu
送って行きます

driver untenshu
運転手

driving licence
unten-menkyo-shō
運転免許証

drop: just a drop, please (of
drink) hon no sukoshi dake
kudasai
ほんの少しだけ
ください

drug (medicine) kusuri
薬

drugs (narcotics) mayaku
麻薬

drunk (adj) yop·parat·ta
酔っぱらった

dry (adj) kawaita
乾いた

(wine) karakuchi (no)
辛口（の）

dry-cleaner's kurīning-ya
クリーニング屋

due: he was due to arrive
yesterday kare wa kinō
tōchaku suru hazu deshita
彼はきのう到着する
はずでした

when is the train due?
densha wa itsu kuru hazu
desu ka?
電車はいつ来るはず
ですか？

dull (pain) zuki-zuki
ずきずき

(weather) kumori (no)
くもり（の）

(uninteresting) tsumaranai
つまらない

dummy (baby's) oshaburi
おしゃぶり

during ... no aida ni
…の間に

dust hokori
ほこり

dustbin gomibako
ごみ箱

dusty hokorip·poi
ほこりっぽい

Dutch (adj) Oranda (no)
オランダ

duty-free (goods)
menzei(hin)
免税（品）

English → Japanese

duty-free shop
menzeihin-ten
免税品店

duvet kakebuton
かけぶとん

E

each (every) sorezore (no)
それぞれ（の）
  how much are they each?
  hitotsu ikura desu ka?
  ひとついくらですか？

ear mimi
耳

earache: I have earache mimi
ga itai desu
耳が痛いです

early hayai
早い
  early in the morning asa
  hayaku
  朝早く
  I called by earlier sakihodo
  mo ukagaimashita
  先程もうかがいました

earrings iyaringu
イヤリング

earthquake jishin
地震

east higashi
東
  in the east higashi ni
  東に

Easter Fuk·katsu-sai
復活祭

Eastern (oriental) tōyō (no)
東洋（の）

easy yasashī
やさしい

eat tabemasu
食べます
  we've already eaten
  watashitachi wa mō
  tabemashita
  私たちはもう食べ
  ました

eau de toilette
ō-do-toware
オードトワレ

economy class ekonomī-
kurasu
エコノミークラス

eel unagi
うなぎ

egg tamago
たまご

either: either ... or ... … ka …
ka
…か…か
  either of them dochiraka
  どちらか

elbow hiji
ひじ

electric denki (no)
電気（の）

electrical appliances
denki-kigu
電気器具

electrician denki-ya
電気屋

electricity denki
電気

elevator erebētā
エレベーター

else: something else nani ka
hoka no mono
何かほかのもの

somewhere else doko ka
hoka no tokoro
どこかほかのところ

dialogue

would you like anything
else? hoka ni nani ka
irimasu ka?
no, nothing else, thanks īe,
hoka niwa nani mo
irimasen, arigatō

e-mail ī-mēru
イーメール

embassy taishikan
大使館

emergency kinkyū
緊急

this is an emergency! kinkyū
desu!
緊急です

emergency exit hijōguchi
非常口

Emperor of Japan Ten·nō-
Heika
天皇陛下

Empress of Japan Kōgō-
Heika
皇后陛下

empty kara (no)
から（の）

end (noun) owari
終わり

at the end of the street sono
michi no tsukiatari ni
その道の突き当たり
に

when does it end? itsu owari
masu ka?
いつ終わりますか？

engaged (toilet) shiyō-chū
使用中
(phone) hanashi-chū
話し中
(to be married) kon·yaku shita
婚約した

engine (car) enjin
エンジン

England Igirisu
イギリス

English (adj) Igirisu (no)
イギリス（の）
(language) Eigo
英語

I'm English watashi wa
Igirisu-jin desu
私はイギリス人です

do you speak English? Eigo
ga hanasemasu ka?
英語が話せますか？

enjoy: to enjoy oneself
tanoshimimas*u*

楽しみます

dialogue

how did you like the film?
eiga wa dō desh*i*ta ka?
I enjoyed it very much, did
you enjoy it? totemo
tanoshikat·ta des*u*, anata
wa dō desh*i*ta ka?

enlargement (of photo)
hiki-nobashi

引き伸ばし

enormous totemo ōkī

とても大きい

enough jūbun

十分

there's not enough tarimasen

たりません

it's not big enough
ch*i*sasugimas*u*

小さすぎます

that's enough sore de jūbun
des*u*

それで十分です

entrance iriguchi

入り口

(of house) genkan

玄関

envelope fūtō

ふうとう

epileptic tenkan-kanja

てんかん患者

equipment setsu*bi*

設備

(for climbing etc) sōbi

装備

error machigai

まちがい

especially tok*u* ni

とくに

essential hits*u*yō (na)

必要（な）

it is essential that ... ...-koto
wa hits*u*yō des*u*

…—ことは必要です

Europe Yōrop·pa

ヨーロッパ

European (adj) Yōrop·pa (no)

ヨーロッパ（の）

even: even the ... ... demo

…でも

even if ... moshi ... demo

もし…でも

evening yūgata

夕方

this evening komban

今晩

in the evening yoru ni

夜に

evening meal yūshok*u*

夕食

eventually tsui ni

ついに

ever: I hardly ever ... hotondo
...-masen

ほとんど…—ません

dialogue

have you ever been to Hiroshima? Hiroshima ni it·ta koto ga arimas*u* ka?
yes, I was there two years ago hai, ni-nen mae ni ikimash*i*ta

every subete no
すべての
every day mainichi
毎日
everyone mina-san
皆さん
everything subete
すべて
everywhere doko demo
どこでも
exactly! sono tōri des*u*!
そのとおりです！
exam shiken
試験
example rei
例
for example tatoeba
たとえば
excellent subarashī
すばらしい
(food) totemo oishī
とてもおいしい
(hotel) ichiryū (no)
一流（の）
excellent! subarashī!
すばらしい！

except … igai wa
…以外は
excess baggage chōka-tenimots*u*
超過手荷物
exchange rate ryōgae-rēto
両替レート
exciting omoshiroi
おもしろい
excuse me (to get past) shitsurei shimas*u*
失礼します・
(to say sorry) gomen·nasai
ごめんなさい
(to get attention) chot·to sumimasen!
ちょっとすみません
executive kanrishok*u*
管理職
exhaust (pipe) haikikan
排気管
exhibition tenrankai
展覧会
exit deguchi
出口
where's the nearest exit? ichiban chikai deguchi wa doko des*u* ka?
いちばん近い出口は どこですか？
expensive takai
高い
experienced keiken no aru
経験のある
explain sets*u*mei shimas*u*

説明します
can you explain that?
setsumei shite kuremasen
ka?
説明してくれません
か？

express (mail) sokutatsu
速達

(train) tok·kyū
特急

extension (telephone) naisen
内線

extension ..., please naisen
no ..., onegai shimasu
内線の…、お願いし
ます

extension lead encho-kōdo
延長コード

**extra: can we have an extra
one?** mō hitotsu
moraemasen ka?
もうひとつもらえま
せんか？

do you charge extra for that?
sore wa betsu-ryōkin desu
ka?
それは別料金です
か？

extraordinary mezurashī
めずらしい

extremely totemo
とても

eye me
目

will you keep an eye on my

suitcase for me? chot·to
sūtsukēs o mite ite
kuremasen ka?
ちょっとスーツケー
スを見ていてくれま
せんか？

eyeglasses (US: spectacles)
megane
めがね

eyeliner ai-rainā
アイライナー

eye make-up remover
ai-mēku-otoshi
アイメーク落し

eye shadow ai-shadō
アイシャドウ

F

face kao
かお

face mask (for colds) masuku
マスク

factory kōjō
工場

Fahrenheit kashi
華氏

faint (verb) ki o
ushinaimasu
気を失います

she's fainted kanojo wa ki o
ushinaimashita
彼女は気を失いまし
た

I feel faint fura-fura shimasu
ふらふらします
fair (funfair) yūenchi
遊園地
(trade fair) mihon-ichi
見本市
(impartial) kōhei (na)
公平（な）
(amount) kanari (no)
かなり（の）
fairly (quite) kanari
かなり
fake (adj) nise (no)
にせ（の）
fall (US: season) aki
秋
in the fall aki ni
秋に
fall (verb) korobimasu
ころびます
she's had a fall kanojo wa
korobimashita
彼女はころびました
false (not true) machigat·ta
まちがった
family kazoku
家族
famous yūmei (na)
有名（な）
fan (electrical) sempūki
扇風機
(handheld) sensu
せんす
(sports) fan
ファン

fantastic subarashī
すばらしい
far tōi
遠い

dialogue

is it far from here? koko
kara tōi desu ka?
no, not very far īe, amari
tōku nai desu
well, how far? dono kurai
desu ka?
it's about 20 kilometres ni-
juk·kiro kurai desu

fare ryōkin
料金
fare box (on buses)
ryōkinbako
料金箱
farm nōjō
農場
fashionable oshare (na)
おしゃれ（な）
fast hayai
速い
fat (person) futot·ta
太った
(on meat) aburami
あぶらみ
father (one's own) chichi
父
(someone else's) otō-san
お父さん

father-in-law (one's own) giri no chichi
義理の父
(someone else's) giri no otō–san
義理のお父さん

faucet jaguchi
じゃ口

fault: sorry, it was my fault gomen·nasai, watashi no sei deshita
ごめんなさい、私の せいでした

it's not my fault watashi no sei dewa arimasen
私のせいではあり ません

faulty chōshi ga okashī
調子がおかしい

favourite oki ni iri (no)
お気に入り（の）

fax (noun) fak·ksu
ファックス
(verb) fak·ksu o okurimasu
ファックスを送り ます

February Nigatsu
二月

feel kanjimasu
感じます

I feel hot atsui desu
暑いです

I feel unwell kibun ga yoku nai desu
気分がよくないです

I feel like going for a walk sampo ni ikitai desu
散歩にいきたいです

how are you feeling? ikaga desu ka?
いかがですか？

I'm feeling better zut·to ī desu
ずっといいです

fence (noun) hei
塀

fencing fensingu
フェンシング

Japanese fencing kendō
剣道

ferry ferī
フェリー

festival omatsuri
お祭り

fetch (person) tsurete kimasu
連れてきます
(object) tot·te kimasu
取ってきます

I'll fetch him kare o yonde kimashō
彼を呼んでききま しょう

will you come and fetch me later? atode mukae ni kite kuremasen ka?
後でむかえに来て くれませんか？

feverish netsup·poi
熱っぽい

few: a few sukoshi no
少しの
a few days ni-san nichi
二三日
fiancé(e) kon·yakusha
婚約者
field hatake
畑
fight (noun) kenka
けんか
fill in kinyū shimasu
記入します
do I have to fill this in? kinyū shinakute wa narimasen ka?
記入しなくてはなり
ませんか？
fill up ip·pai ni shimasu
いっぱいにします
fill it up, please ip·pai ni shite kudasai
いっぱいにして
ください
filling (in cake, sandwich) nakami
なかみ
(in tooth) ha no tsumemono
歯の詰めもの
film (movie) eiga
映画
(for camera) firumu
フィルム

dialogue

do you have this kind of film? kon·na firumu wa

arimasu ka?

yes, how many exposures? hai, nan·mai dori desu ka?

36 san-jū-roku-mai desu

film processing genzō
現像
final (adj) saigo (no)
最後（の）
find (verb) mitsukemasu
見つけます
I can't find it mitsukarimasen
見つかりません
I've found it mitsukemashita
見つけました
find out shirabemasu
調べます
could you find out for me? shirabete kuremasen ka?
調べてくれません
か？
fine (weather) hareta
晴れた
(punishment) bak·kin
罰金

dialogue

how are you? ogenki desu ka?
I'm fine, thanks okagesama de

is that OK? sore de ī desu ka?

that's fine, thanks ē,
kek·kō des*u*

finger yubi
指

finish (verb) owarimas*u*
終わります

I haven't finished yet mada
owat·te imasen
まだ終わっていませ
ん

when does it finish? its*u*
owarimas*u* ka?
いつ終わりますか？

fire (in hearth) hi
火

(blaze) kaji
火事

fire! kaji da!
火事だ！

can we light a fire here?
koko de hi o taite mo ī
des*u* ka?
ここで火をたいても
いいですか？

it's on fire kaji des*u*
火事です

fire alarm kasai-hōchiki
火災報知機

fire brigade shōbōtai
消防隊

fire escape hijōguchi
非常口

fire extinguisher shōkaki
消火器

fireworks hanabi
花火

first saisho (no)
最初（の）

I was first watashi ga saki
desh*i*ta
私が先でした

at first saisho ni
最初に

the first time hajimete
はじめて

first on the left hidarigawa
no saisho
左がわの最初

first aid ōkyū-te-ate
応急手当

first-aid kit kyūkyūbako
救急箱

first class (train) gurīnsha
グリーン車

(plane) fās*u*to-kuras*u*
ファーストクラス

first-class ticket (train)
gurīnsha jōshaken
グリーン車乗車券

(plane) fās*u*to-kuras*u*
chiket·to
ファーストクラスチ
ケット

first floor ni-kai
二階

(US) ik·kai
一階

first name namae
名前

fish (noun) sakana
さかな

fishmonger's sakana-ya
魚屋

fit (attack) hos·sa
発作

fit: it doesn't fit me sore wa
watashi ni aimasen
それは私に合い
ません

fitting room shichaku-shitsu
試着室

fix (verb: arrange) tehai shimasu
手配します

　can you fix this? (repair)
naosemasu ka?
なおせますか？

fizzy tansan (no)
炭酸（の）

fizzy orange tansan-iri orenji
jūsu
炭酸入りオレンジ
ジュース

flag hata
はた

flannel taoru
タオル

flash (for camera) furashu
フラッシュ

flat (noun: apartment) apāto
アパート

　(adj) taira (na)
たいら（な）

　I've got a flat tyre taiya ga
panku shimashita

タイヤがパンクし
ました

flavour fūmi
風味

flea nomi
のみ

flight hikō
飛行

flight number bin·mei
便名

flood kōzui
洪水

floor (of room) yuka
床

　(storey) kai
階

　on the floor yuka ni
床に

florist's hana-ya
花屋

flower hana
花

flower arranging ikebana
生け花

flu infuruenza
インフルエンザ

**fluent: he speaks fluent
Japanese** kare wa ryūchō
na Nihon-go o
hanashimasu
彼は流暢な日本語を
話します

fly (noun) hae
ハエ

　(verb) tobimasu

飛びます
can we fly there? hikōki de
ikemasu ka?
飛行機で行けます
か？
fog kiri
霧
foggy: it's foggy kiri ga dete
imasu
霧が出ています
food (in general) tabemono
食べ物
(in shop) shokuryōhin
食料品
(in restaurant) ryōri
料理
food poisoning
shokuchūdoku
食中毒
food shop/store
shokuryōhin-ten
食料品店
foot (of person) ashi
足
on foot aruite
歩いて
football (game) sak·kā
サッカー
(ball) sak·kā-bōru
サッカーボール
footwarmer kotatsu
こたつ
**for: do you have something for
...?** (headache/diarrhoea etc) …
ni kik kusuri wa arimasu

ka?
…に効く薬はありま
すか？

dialogues

who's the tempura for?
tempura wa dochira desu
ka?
that's for me watashi desu
and this one? kore wa
dochira desu ka?
that's for her kanojo desu

**where do I get the bus for
Shinjuku?** Shinjuku-iki
no basu wa doko de
noremasu ka?
**the bus for Shinjuku leaves
from Tokyo station**
Shinjuku-iki no basu wa
Tōkyō eki kara dete
imasu

**how long have you been
here?** koko niwa mō
dono kurai ni narimasu
ka?
**I've been here for two
days, how about you?**
futsuka desu ga, anata
wa?
I've been here for a week
is·shūkan ni narimasu

forehead odeko
おでこ

foreign gaikoku (no)
外国

foreigner gaijin
外人

forest mori
森

forget wasuremasu
忘れます

I forget, I've forgotten
wasurete shimaimashita
忘れてしまいました

fork fōk
フォーク

(in road) bunkiten
分岐点

form (document) yōshi
用紙

formal seishiki (na)
正式（な）

(dress) aratamat·ta
あらたまった

fortnight nishūkan
二週間

fortunately un·yoku
運よく

forward: could you forward my mail? tegami o tensō shite kuremasen ka?
手紙を転送して
くれませんか？

forwarding address tensō saki
転送先

foundation (make-up)

fandēshon
ファンデーション

fountain (ornamental) funsui
噴水

(for drinking) kyūsuiki
給水器

foyer robī
ロビー

fracture (noun) kos·setsu
骨折

France Furansu
フランス

free (no charge) tada, muryō
ただ、無料

is it free (of charge)? muryō desu ka?
無料ですか？

freeway kōsokudōro
高速道路

freezer reitōko
冷凍庫

French (adj) Furansu (no)
フランス（の）

(language) Furansu-go
フランス語

French fries furenchi-furai
フレンチフライ

frequent tabitabi (no)
たびたび（の）

how frequent is the bus to Kobe? Kōbe-iki no basu wa nambon kurai dete imasu ka?
神戸行きのバスは何
本くらいでています
か？

fresh (food) shinsen (na)
新鮮（な）
Friday Kin·yōbi
金曜日
fridge reizōko
冷蔵庫
fried itameta
いためた
fried egg medamayaki
めだまやき
fried rice chāhan
チャーハン
friend tomodachi
友達
friendly shinsetsu (na)
親切（な）
from kara
から
**when does the next train
from Hakata arrive?** tsugi no
Hakata hatsu no res·sha wa
itsu tsukimasu ka?
次の博多発の列車は
いつ着きますか？
from Monday to Friday
Getsuyōbi kara Kin·yōbi
月曜日から金曜日
from next Thursday tsugi no
Mok·yōbi kara
次の木曜日から

dialogue

where are you from? doko
kara kimashita ka?

I'm from Manchester
Manchesutā kara desu

front mae
前
in front mae ni
前に
in front of the hotel hoteru
no mae ni
ホテルの前に
at the front mae de
前で
frost shimo
霜
frozen reitō shita
冷凍した
fruit kudamono
くだもの
fruit juice frūtsu-jūsu
フルーツジュース
full ip·pai
いっぱい
it's full of ... ... de ip·pai
desu
…でいっぱいです
I'm full onaka ga ip·pai desu
おなかがいっぱい
です
full board san-shoku-tsuki
三食付き
fun: it was fun
omoshirokat·ta desu
おもしろかったです
funeral osōshiki
お葬式

funny (strange) okashī
おかしい
(amusing) omoshiroi
おもしろい
furniture kagu
家具
further mot·to tōku
もっと遠く
it's further down the road
sono michi no mot·to saki
desu
その道のもっと先
です

dialogue

how much further is it to
Kinkakuji? Kinkakuji ewa
dono kurai arimasu ka?
about 5 kilometres
go-kiro kurai desu

fuse (noun) hyūzu
ヒューズ
future shōrai
将来
in future kore kara
これから

G

gallon garon
ガロン
game (cards etc) gēmu

ゲーム
(match) shiai
試合
garage (for fuel) gasorin-
sutando
ガソリンスタンド
(for repairs) shūrikōjō
修理工場
(for parking) shako
車庫
garden niwa
庭
garlic nin·niku
ニンニク
gas gasu
ガス
(US) gasorin
ガソリン
gas permeable lenses
sanso-tōka-sei kontakuto-
renzu
酸素透過性コンタク
トレンズ
gas station (US) gasorin-
sutando
ガソリンスタンド
gate mon
門
(at airport) gēto
ゲート
gay homo (no)
ホモ
gay bar gei-bā
ゲイバー
gears (in car) gia

ギア

general (adj) ip·pan-teki (na)

一般的（な）

gents' toilet dansei-yō toire

男性用トイレ

genuine (antique etc)
hon·mono (no)

本物（の）

German (adj) Doits*u* (no)

ドイツ（の）

Germany Doits*u*

ドイツ

get (fetch) te ni iremas*u*

手に入れます

**could you get me another
one, please?** mō hitots*u*
moraemas*u* ka?

もうひとつもらえ
ますか？

how do I get to ...? ... ewa
dō ikeba ī des*u* ka?

…へはどう行けば
いいですか？

**do you know where I can get
them?** sore wa dokode te ni
hairimas*u* ka?

それはどこで手に入
りますか？

dialogue

can I get you a drink?
nomimono wa ikaga
des*u* ka?

no, I'll get this one, what

would you like? īe, kore
wa watashi mochi des*u*,
nani ga ī des*u* ka?

a beer, please bīru kudasai

get back (return) modorimas*u*

戻ります

get in (arrive) tōchak*u* shimas*u*

到着します

get off orimas*u*

降ります

where do I get off? doko de
orireba ī des*u* ka?

どこで降りればいい
ですか？

get on (to train etc) norimas*u*

乗ります

get out (of car etc) orimas*u*

降ります

(take out) toridashimas*u*

取り出します

get up (in the morning) okimas*u*

起きます

gift okurimono

贈り物

gift shop gif*u*to-shop·p*u*

ギフトショップ

gin jin

ジン

a gin and tonic, please jin-
tonik·k*u* o onegai shimas*u*

ジントニックをお願
いします

girl on·na no ko

女の子

81

girlfriend gāru-furendo
ガールフレンド

give agemasu
あげます

can you give me some change? kore o kuzushite kuremasen ka?
これをくずしてくれませんか？

I gave it to him sore wa kare ni watashimashita
それは彼にわたしました

will you give this to ...? kore o … ni watashite kuremasen ka?
これを…にわたしてくれませんか？

give back kaeshimasu
返します

glad ureshī
うれしい

glass (material) garasu
ガラス

(for drinking) kop·pu
コップ

a glass of wine wain o ip·pai
ワインを一杯

glasses (spectacles) megane
めがね

gloves tebukuro
手袋

glue (noun) set·chaku-zai
接着剤

go ikimasu
行きます

we'd like to go to Tokyo Disneyland Tōkyō-Dizunīrando ni it·te mitai desu
東京ディズニーランドに行ってみたいです

where are you going? doko e ikundesu ka?
どこへ行くんですか？

where does this bus go? kono basu wa doko e ikimasu ka?
このバスはどこへ行きますか？

let's go! ikimashō!
行きましょう！

hamburger to go hambāgā o teiku-auto de
ハンバーガーをテイクアウトで

she's gone (left) kanojo wa it·te shimaimashita
彼女は行ってしまいました

where has he gone? kare wa doko e ikimashita ka?
彼はどこへ行きましたか？

I went there last week senshū soko e ikimashita
先週そこへ行き

ました
go away dekakemas*u*

出かけます
go away! at·chi e it·te!

あっちへいって！
go back (return) kaerimas*u*

帰ります
go down (the stairs etc) shita e ikimas*u*

下へ行きます
go in naka e hairimas*u*

なかへ入ります
go out (in the evening) gaishuts*u* shimas*u*

外出します
do you want to go out tonight? komban dekaketai des*u* ka?

今晩出かけたいです
か？
go through tōrinukemas*u*

通り抜けます
go up (the stairs etc) ue e ikimas*u*

上へ行きます
God kami-sama

神様
goggles gōguru

ゴーグル
gold kin

金
goldfish kin·gyo

金魚
golf goruf*u*

ゴルフ
golf course goruf*u*-jō

ゴルフ場
good ī

いい
good! yokat·ta!

よかった！
it's no good sore wa dame des*u*

それはだめです
goodbye (formal) sayōnara

さようなら
(informal) dewa mata

ではまた
(between friends) jā ne

じゃあね
good evening komban wa

こんばんは
Good Friday Sei-Kin·yōbi

聖金曜日
good morning ohayō gozaimas*u*

おはようございま
す
good night (when leaving) osaki ni

お先に
(when going to bed) oyasuminasai

おやすみなさい
got: we've got to leave mō ikanakereba narimasen

もう行かなければな
りません
have you got any ...? ... o mot·te imas*u* ka?

を持っていますか？

government seifu
政府

gradually dandan
だんだん

gram(me) guramu
グラム

granddaughter (one's own)
magomusme
孫娘
(someone else's) omago-san
お孫さん

grandfather (one's own) sofu
祖父
(someone else's) oji-san
おじいさん

grandmother (one's own)
sobo
祖母
(someone else's) obā-san
おばあさん

grandson (one's own)
magomusuko
孫息子
(someone else's) omago-san
お孫さん

grapefruit gurēpu-frūtsu
グレープフルーツ

grapes budō
ぶどう

grass kusa
草

grateful ureshī
うれしい

gravy gurēbī-sōsu
グレービーソース

great (excellent) subarashī
すばらしい

that's great! sore wa sugoi!
それはすごい！

a great success daiseikō
大成功

Great Britain Eikoku
英国

greedy yokubari (na)
よくばり（な）
(for food) kuishimbō (no)
くいしんぼうの

green midori (no)
みどり（の）

green card (car insurance)
jidōsha-hoken
自動車保険

greengrocer's yao-ya
八百屋

grey hai-iro (no)
灰色（の）

grilled guriru de yaita
グリルで焼いた

grocer's shokuryōhin-ten
食料品店

ground jimen
地面

on the ground jimen ni
地面に

ground floor ik·kai
一階

group gurūpu
グループ

guarantee (noun) hoshō
保証

is it guaranteed? hoshō-
tsuki desu ka?
保証付きですか？

guest okyaku-sama
お客さま

guesthouse minshuku
民宿

guide (person) gaido
ガイド

guidebook gaido-buk·ku
ガイドブック

guided tour gaido-tsuki tuā
ガイド付きツアー

gum (in mouth) haguki
歯ぐき

gun (rifle) jū
銃

(pistol) pisutoru
ピストル

gym jimu
ジム

H

hair kami
髪

hairbrush burashi
ブラシ

haircut (man's) sampatsu
散髪

(woman's) heya-kat·to
ヘアカット

hairdresser's (men's) toko-ya
床屋

(women's) biyōin
美容院

hairdryer doraiyā
ドライヤー

hair gel jeru
ジェル

hairgrips heya-pin
ヘヤピン

hair spray heya-supurē
ヘヤスプレー

half hambun
半分

half an hour han-jikan
半時間

half a litre han-rit·toru
半リットル

about half that sono
hambun kurai
その半分くらい

half board
asayū-nishoku-tsuki
朝夕二食付き

half-bottle hāfu-botoru
ハーフボトル

half fare hangaku
半額

half-price hangaku
(no)
半額（の）

ham hamu
ハム

hamburger hambāgā
ハンバーガー

hand te
手

handbag handobag·gu
ハンドバッグ

handbrake handoburēki
ハンドブレーキ

handkerchief hankachi
ハンカチ

handle (on door) tot·te
取っ手
(on suitcase) mochite
持ち手

hand luggage tenimotsu
手荷物

hang-gliding hanguraidingu
ハンググライディング

hangover futsukayoi
ふつか酔い

I've got a hangover
futsukayoi desu
ふつか酔いです

happen okorimasu
起ります

what's happening? dō nat·te
imasu ka?
どうなっていますか？

(what's on?) nani o yat·te
imasu ka?
何をやっています
か？

(what's wrong?) dō shitandesu
ka?
どうしたんですか？

what has happened? nani ga
at·tandesu ka?
何があったんです
か？

happy ureshī
うれしい

I'm not happy about this sore
niwa nat·toku dekimasen
それには納得でき
ません

harbour minato
港

hard katai
かたい
(difficult) muzukashī
むずかしい

hard-boiled egg
katayude-tamago
かたゆでたまご

hard lenses hādo-kontakuto
ハードコンタクト

hardly: I hardly ever ...
hotondo …-masen
ほとんど…ません

I hardly ever go met·ta ni
ikimasen
めったに行きません

I hardly know him kare no
koto wa hotondo
shirimasen
彼のことはほとんど
知りません

hardware shop kanamono-ya
金物屋

hat bōshi
ぼうし

hate (verb) kirai desu
きらいです

have mochimasu

持ちます
can I have a ...? ... o
morat·te mo ī desu ka?
…をもらってもいい
ですか？
can we have some ...? ... o
ikutsuka moraemasu ka?
…をいくつかもらえ
ますか？
do you have ...? ... o mot·te
imasu ka?
…を持っています
か？
what'll you have (to drink)?
nani ni shimasu ka?
何にしますか？
I have to ... ...-nakute wa
narimasen
…ーなくてはなり
ません
I have to leave now mō
ikanakute wa narimasen
もう行かなくてはな
りません
do I have to ...? ...-nakute
wa narimasen ka?
…ーなくてはなり
ませんか？
hayfever kafun-shō
花粉症
he* kare
彼
head atama
あたま
headache zutsū

頭痛
headlights hed·do·raito
ヘッドライト
headphones hed·do·hon
ヘッドホン
healthy (person) kenkō (na)
健康（な）
(food) karada ni ī
からだにいい
hear kikoemasu
きこえます

dialogue

> **can you hear me?**
> kikoemasu ka?
> **I can't hear you, could you
> repeat that?** kikoemasen,
> mō ichido it·te
> kuremasen ka?

hearing aid hochōki
補聴器
heart shinzō
心臓
heart attack shinzōmahi
心臓麻痺
heat atsusa
暑さ
heater (in room) dambō
暖房
(in car) hītā
ヒーター
heating dambō
暖房

heavy omoi
おもい

heel (of foot) kakato
かかと

(of shoe) hīru
ヒール

could you heel these? hīru o
naoshite kuremasen ka?
ヒールをなおして
くれませんか？

height (of person) shincho
身長

(of object) takasa
高さ

helicopter herikoptā
ヘリコプター

hello kon·nichi wa
こんにちは

(on phone) moshi-moshi
もしもし

helmet (for motorcycle)
herumet·to
ヘルメット

help (noun) kyōryoku
協力

(verb) tetsudaimasu
手伝います

help! tasukete!
たすけて！

can you help me? tetsudat·te
kuremasen ka?
手伝ってくれません
か？

**thank you very much for your
help** tetsudat·te kurete

dōmo arigatō
手伝ってくれてどう
もありがとう

helpful yaku ni tatsu
役に立つ

hepatitis kan-en
肝炎

her* kanojo (o)
彼女（を）

to her kanojo ni
彼女に

with her kanojo to
彼女と

for her kanojo no tame
ni
彼女のために

that's her kanojo desu
彼女です

I haven't seen her kanojo
niwa at·te imasen
彼女には会って
いません

her ... kanojo no ...
彼女の…

it's her car sore wa kanojo
no kuruma desu
それは彼女の車です

herbal tea hābu-tī
ハーブティー

herbs (for cooking) hābu
ハーブ

(medicinal) yakusō
薬草

here koko
ここ

here is/are ... ... wa koko des*u*

…はここです

here you are (offering) hai, dōzo

はい、どうぞ

hers* kanojo no

彼女の

that's hers sore wa kanojo no des*u*

それは彼女のです

hey! chot·to!

ちょっと！

hi! (hello) dōmo!

どうも！

high takai

高い

highchair bebī-chea

ベビーチェア

highway kōsok*u*dōro

高速道路

hill oka

丘

him* kare (o)

彼（を）

to him kare ni

彼に

with him kare to

彼と

for him kare no tame ni

彼のために

that's him kare des*u*

彼です

I haven't seen him kare niwa at·te imasen

彼には会って
いません

hip oshiri

おしり

hire karimas*u*

借ります

for hire rentaru (no)

レンタル（の）

where can I hire a bike? doko de jitensha ga kariraremas*u* ka?

どこで自転車が借り
られますか？

his* kare no

彼の

it's his car sore wa kare no kuruma des*u*

それは彼の車です

that's his sore wa kare no des*u*

それは彼のです

hitch-hike hit·chi-haik*u*

ヒッチハイク

hobby shumi

趣味

hold (verb) mochimas*u*

持ちます

hole ana

あな

holiday yasumi

休み

on holiday yasumi de

休みで

Holland Oranda

オランダ

home uchi
うち
at home (in my house) uchi de
うちで
(in my country) watashi no
kuni de
私の国で
we go home tomorrow
watashitachi wa ashita
kikoku shimasu
私たちはあした帰国
します
honey hachimitsu
はちみつ
honeymoon shinkon-ryokō
新婚旅行
hood (US: of car) bon·net·to
ボンネット
hope kibō
希望
I hope so sō da to ī desu ne
そうだといいですね
I hope not sō de nai to ī
desu ne
そうでないといい
ですね
hopefully dekireba
できれば
horrible osoroshī
おそろしい
horse uma
馬
horse riding jōba
乗馬
hospital byōin

病院
hospitality omotenashi
おもてなし
thank you for your hospitality
omotenashi dōmo arigatō
gozaimashita
おもてなしどうもあ
りがとうございまし
た
hot atsui
暑い
(spicy) karai
からい
I'm hot atsui desu
暑いです
it's hot today kyō wa atsui
desu
きょうは暑いです
hotel hoteru
ホテル
(Japanese-style) ryokan
旅館
hotel room hoteru no heya
ホテルの部屋
hot spring onsen
温泉
hour jikan
時間
house ie
家
hovercraft hobā-kurafuto
ホバークラフト
how dō
どう
how many? ikutsu?

いくつ？
how do you do? hajimemash*i*te
はじめまして

dialogues

how are you? ogenki des*u* ka?

fine, thanks, and you? e, okagesama de, sochira wa dō des*u* ka?

how much is it? ik*u*ra des*u* ka?

520 yen go-hyak*u*-ni-jū-en des*u*

I'll take it ja, sore o k*u*dasai

---

humid mushi-atsui
蒸し暑い

hungry onaka ga suita
おなかがすいた

are you hungry? onaka ga sukimash*i*ta ka?
おなかがすきました
か？

hurry (verb) isogimas*u*
急ぎます

I'm in a hurry isoide imas*u*
急いでいます

there's no hurry isog*u* koto wa arimasen
急ぐことはあり

ません

hurry up! isoide kudasai!
急いでください！

hurt (verb) itamimas*u*
痛みます

it really hurts totemo itamimas*u*
とても痛みます

husband (one's own) shujin
主人

(someone else's) goshujin
御主人

my husband uchi no shujin
うちの主人

hydrofoil suichū-yok*u*sen
水中翼船

I

I watashi
私

ice kōri
氷

with ice kōri-iri
氷入り

no ice, thanks kōri wa ī des*u*
氷はいいです

ice cream ais*u*-kurīm*u*
アイスクリーム

ice-cream cone ais*u*-kurīm*u* no kōn
アイスクリームの
コーン

ice lolly aisu-kyandī
アイスキャンディー

idea kan·gae
考え

idiot hakuchi
白痴

if moshi
もし

ill byōki (no)
病気（の）

I feel ill kibun ga warui desu
気分が悪いです

illness byōki
病気

imitation (leather etc) mozōhin
模造品

immediately sugu
すぐ

important taisetsu (na)
大切（な）

it's very important totemo
taisetsu desu
とても大切です

it's not important dō demo ī
koto desu
どうでもいいこと
です

impossible fukanō (na)
不可能（な）

impressive inshō-teki (na)
印象的（な）

improve: I want to improve my
Japanese Nihon-go ga
umaku naritai desu
日本語がうまくなり

たいです

in: it's in the centre sore wa
hankagai ni arimasu
それは繁華街にあり
ます

in my car watashi no
kuruma no naka
私の車のなか

in Sapporo Sapporo ni
札幌に

in May Gogatsu ni
五月に

in English Eigo de
英語で

in Japanese Nihon-go de
日本語で

in two days from now ima
kara futsuka de
いまから二日で

in five minutes go-fun de
五分で

is he in? kare wa imasu ka?
彼はいますか？

incense okō
お香

inch inchi
インチ

include fukumimasu
含みます

does that include meals?
shokuji wa komi desu ka?
食事は込みですか？

is that included? sore mo
ryōkin ni fukumarete imasu
ka?

それも料金に含
まれていますか？

inconvenient fuben (na)
不便（な）

incredible shinjirarenai
信じられない

Indian (adj) Indo (no)
インド（の）

indicator winkā
ウィンカー

indigestion shōkafuryō
消化不良

indoor pool okunai-pūru
屋内プール

indoors okunai
屋内

inexpensive tegoro (na)
手ごろ（な）

infection kansenshō
感染症

infectious densensei (no)
伝染性（の）

inflammation enshō
炎症

informal kudaketa
くだけた

information jōhō
情報

do you have any information
about ...? ... ni tsuite no
jōhō ga arimasu ka?
…についての情報が
ありますか？

information desk an·naisho
案内所

injection chūsha
注射

injured kega o shita
けがをした

she's been injured kanojo
wa kega o shimashita
彼女はけがをし
ました

inn (Japanese-style) ryokan
旅館

inner tube (for tyre) chūbu
チューブ

insect mushi
虫

insect bite mushi-sasare
虫さされ

do you have anything for
insect bites? mushi-sasare
no kusuri wa arimasu ka?
虫さされの薬はあり
ますか？

insect repellent
mushiyoke
虫よけ

inside: inside the hotel hoteru
no naka
ホテルのなか

let's sit inside naka ni
suwarimashō
なかに座りましょう

insist īharimasu
言いはります

I insist dōka zehi
どうかぜひ

if you insist dō shitemo to

iunara

どうしてもと
いうなら

instant coffee insutanto-kōhī

インスタント
コーヒー

**instead: give me that one
instead** kawari ni sotchi o
kudasai

かわりにそっちを
ください

instead of ... ... no kawari
ni

…のかわりに

insulin inshurin

インシュリン

insurance hoken

保険

intelligent atama ga ī

あたまがいい

interested: I'm interested in ...
... ni kyōmi ga arimasu

…に興味があります

interesting omoshiroi

おもしろい

that's very interesting sore
wa totemo omoshiroi desu

それはとてもおもし
ろいです

international kokusai-teki
(na)

国際的（な）

Internet intānetto

インターネット

interpreter tsūyaku

intersection kōsaten

交差点

interval (at theatre) kyūkei-
jikan

休憩時間

into ... ni

…に

I'm not into ... ... wa suki
dewa arimasen

…は好きではあり
ません

introduce shōkai shimasu

紹介します

may I introduce ...? (formal)
... o goshōkai itashimasu

…をご紹介いたし
ます

(informal) ... o shōkai
shimasu

…を紹介します

invitation shōtai

招待

invite shōtai shimasu

招待します

invoice seikyūsho

請求書

Ireland Airurando

アイルランド

Irish Airurando (no)

アイルランド
（の）

I'm Irish watashi wa
Airurando-jin desu

私はアイルランド人

です

iron (for ironing) airon
アイロン

　can you iron these for me?
kore ni airon o kakete
kuremasen ka?
これにアイロンをか
けてくれませんか？

is* ... desu
…です

island shima
島

it sore
それ

　it is ... sore wa ... desu
それは…です

is it ...? ... desu ka?
…ですか？

where is it? doko desu ka?
どこですか？

it's him kare desu
彼です

it was ... ... deshita
…でした

Italian (adj) Itaria (no)
イタリア（の）

Italy Itaria
イタリア

itch: it itches kayui desu
かゆいです

ivory zōge
ぞうげ

J

jacket jaket·to
ジャケット

jam (preserve) jamu
ジャム

jammed: it's jammed
tsumat·te imasu
つまっています

January Ichigatsu
一月

Japan Nihon
日本

Japanese (adj) Nihon
(no)
日本（の）

(noun) Nihon-jin
日本人

(language) Nihon-go
日本語

　the Japanese Nihon-jin
日本人

Japanese food washoku
和食

Japanese-style wafū
和風

Japan Sea Nihon-kai
日本海

jar (noun) bin
びん

jaw ago
あご

jazz jazu
ジャズ

jeans jīnzu
ジーンズ

jellyfish kurage
くらげ

jersey sētā
セーター

jetty sambashi
さんばし

jeweller's hōseki-ten
宝石店

jewellery hōseki
宝石

Jewish Yudaya (no)
ユダヤ（の）

job shigoto
仕事

jogging jogingu
ジョギング

joke jōdan
冗談

joss stick osenkō
お線香

journey ryokō
旅行

have a good journey! sore
dewa tanoshī ryokō o!
それでは楽しい旅行
を！

judo jūdō
柔道

jug mizusashi
水さし

a jug of water mizusashi
ip·pai no mizu
水さし一杯の水

juice fres·shu-jūsu
フレッシュジュース

July Shichigatsu
七月

jump (verb) jampu shimasu
ジャンプします

junction (in road) kōsaten
交差点
(on motorway) intāchenji
インターチェンジ

June Rokgatsu
六月

just (only) … dake
…だけ

just two futatsu dake
ふたつだけ

just for me watashi ni dake
私にだけ

just here chōdo koko de
ちょうどここで

not just now ima wa dame
desu
いまはだめです

we've just arrived ima tsuita
tokoro desu
いま着いたところ
です

K

keep (verb) tot·te okimasu
取っておきます

keep the change otsuri wa
kek·kō desu

おつりはけっこうです
can I keep it? morat·te mo ī
des*u* ka?
もらってもいいです
か？

please keep it dōzo omochi
kudasai
どうぞお持ち
ください

ketchup kechap·p*u*
ケチャップ

kettle yakan
やかん

key kagi
かぎ

the key for room 201, please
ni-maru-ichi-gō no kagi o
onegai shimas*u*
201号のかぎをお願
いします

keyring kīhorudā
キーホルダー

kidneys jinzō
腎臓

kilo kiro
キロ

kilometre kiromētoru
キロメートル

**how many kilometres is it to
...?** … made nan-kiro
arimas*u* ka?
…まで何キロあり
ますか？

kind (generous) shinsetsu
親切

that's very kind sore wa
goshinsets*u* ni
それはご親切に

dialogue

which kind do you want?
dochira ga ī des*u* ka?
I want this/that kind kono/
sono shurui ga hoshī des*u*

kiosk kios*u*k*u*
キオスク

kiss (noun) kis*u*
キス

(verb) kis*u* shimas*u*
キスします

kitchen daidokoro
台所

kite tako
たこ

kite-flying tako-age
たこあげ

Kleenex® tis·shu-pēpā
ティッシュペーパー

knee hiza
ひざ

knickers shōts*u*
ショーツ

knife naif*u*
ナイフ

knock (verb) nok·k*u* shimas*u*
ノックします

knock over (object) hik·kuri
kaeshimasu

ひっくり返します
(pedestrian) hanemasu
はねます

he's been knocked over kare
wa kuruma ni
haneraremashita
彼は車にはねられ
ました

know shit·te imasu
知っています

I don't know shirimasen
知りません

I didn't know that sore wa
shirimasen deshita
それは知りません
でした

do you know where I can
find ...? doko de ... ga te ni
hairimasu ka?
どこで…が手に入り
ますか？

Korean (adj) Kankoku (no)
韓国（の）

L

label raberu
ラベル

lacquerware shik·ki
漆器

ladies' room, ladies' toilets
keshōshitsu
化粧室

ladies' wear fujinfuku-uriba
婦人服売り場

lady josei
女性

lager ragā-bīru
ラガービール

lake mizūmi
湖

lamb (meat) kohitsuji
仔羊

lamp sutando
スタンド

lane (motorway) shasen
車線

(small road) roji
路地

language kotoba
言葉

(foreign language) gaikoku-go
外国語

language course
gogaku-kōsu
語学コース

large ōkī
大きい

last (final) saigo (no)
最後（の）

last week senshū
先週

last Friday senshū no
Kin·yōbi
先週の金曜日

last night yūbe
ゆうべ

what time is the last train to
Yokohama? Yokohama-iki

no saishū-densha wa nanji desu ka?

横浜行きの最終電車は何時ですか？

late osoi

遅い

sorry I'm late okurete sumimasen

遅れてすみません

the train was late densha ga okuremashita

電車が遅れました

we must go – we'll be late ikanaito chikoku shite shimaimasu

行かないと遅刻してしまいます

it's getting late zuibun osoku narimashita

ずいぶん遅くなりました

later ato de

あとで

I'll come back later ato de modot·te kimasu

あとで戻ってきます

see you later sore jā mata

それじゃあまた

later on ato de

あとで

latest (most recent) saishin (no)

最新（の）

by Wednesday at the latest osoku-tomo Suiyōbi made ni

遅くとも水曜日までに

laugh (verb) waraimasu

笑います

launderette, laundromat koin-randorī

コインランドリー

laundry (clothes) sentaku-mono

せんたくもの

(place) sentaku-ya

せんたく屋

lavatory toire

トイレ

law hōritsu

法律

lawn shibafu

しばふ

lawyer ben·goshi

弁護士

laxative gezai

下剤

lazy namake-mono

なまけもの

lead (electrical) kōdo

コード

lead (verb) tsūjite imasu

通じています

where does this road lead? kono michi wa doko ni tsūjite imas ka?

この道はどこに通じていますか？

leaf hap·pa

葉っぱ

leaflet chirashi
ちらし

leak (noun) more
もれ

the roof leaks amamori ga shimasu
雨もりがします

learn naraimasu
習います

least: not in the least zenzen
ぜんぜん

at least sukunaku-tomo
すくなくとも

leather kawa
革

leave (verb: depart) shup·patsu shimasu
出発します

(put somewhere) okimasu
置きます

(forget) okiwasuremasu
置き忘れます

I am leaving tomorrow ashita shup·patsu shimasu
あした出発します

he left yesterday kare wa kinō tachimashita
彼はきのう立ちました

when does the bus for Kanazawa leave? Kanazawa-iki no basu wa itsu shup·patsu shimasu ka?
金沢行きのバスはいつ出発しますか？

may I leave this here? koko ni oite mo ī desu ka?
ここに置いてもいいですか？

I left my coat in the bar bā ni kōto o okiwasuremashita
バーにコートを置き忘れました

left hidari
左

on the left hidari ni
左に

to the left hidari e
左へ

turn left hidari e magat·te kudasai
左へ曲がってください

there's none left mō arimasen
もうありません

left-handed hidari-kiki (no)
左きき

left luggage (office) tenimotsu-azukari-jo
手荷物預り所

leg ashi
足

lemon remon
レモン

lemonade remonēdo
レモネード

lend kashimasu
貸します

will you lend me your ...?

... o kashite kuremasen ka?

…を貸してくれ
ませんか？

lens (of camera) renzu

レンズ

lesbian rezubian

レズビアン

less mot·to sukunaku

もっとすくなく

less than ... ika

…以下

less expensive sore hodo takaku nai

それほど高くない

lesson jugyō

授業

let: will you let me know?
shirasete kuremasen ka?

知らせてくれません
か？

I'll let you know oshirase shimasu

お知らせします

let's go for something to eat
nani ka tabe ni ikimashō

何か食べに行き
ましょう

let off oroshimasu

降ろします

will you let me off at ...? ... de oroshite kuremasen ka?

…で降ろしてくれ
ませんか？

letter tegami

手紙

do you have any letters for me? watashi-ate no tegami wa arimasu ka?

私宛ての手紙はあり
ますか？

letterbox posuto

ポスト

lettuce retasu

レタス

library toshokan

図書館

licence menkyo

免許

lid futa

ふた

lie (verb: tell untruth) uso o tsukimasu

うそをつきます

lie down yoko ni narimasu

横になります

lifebelt kyūmeitai

救命帯

lifeguard raifu-gādo

ライフガード

life jacket kyūmei-dōi

救命胴衣

lift (elevator) erebētā

エレベーター

could you give me a lift?
nosete kuremasen ka?

乗せてくれません
か？

would you like a lift? nosete

agemashō ka?

乗せてあげましょう
か？

light (noun) hikari

ひかり

(electric) denki

電気

(adj: not heavy) karui

かるい

do you have a light? (for
cigarette) hi o mot·te imasu
ka?

火を持っています
か？

light green usu-midori (no)

うすみどり（の）

light bulb denkyū

電球

I need a new light bulb
atarashī denkyū ga hitsuyō
desu

新しい電球が必要
です

lighter (cigarette) raitā

ライター

lightning inabikari

いなびかり

like (verb) suki desu

好きです

I like it suki desu

好きです

I like going for walks sampo
ni ikuno ga suki desu

散歩にいくのが好き
です

I like you anata ga suki
desu

あなたが好きです

I don't like it suki ja
arimasen

好きじゃありません

do you like ...? ... ga suki
desu ka?

…が好きですか？

I'd like a beer bīru ga hoshī
desu

ビールが欲しいです

I'd like to go swimming oyogi
ni ikitai desu

泳ぎにいきたいです

would you like a drink?
nomimono wa ikaga desu
ka?

飲み物はいかがです
か？

would you like to go for a
walk? sampo ni ikitaku
arimasen ka?

散歩にいきたくあり
ませんか？

what's it like? dō yū kanji
desu ka?

どういう感じです
か？

I want one like this kon·na
no ga hoshī desu

こんなのが欲しい
です

lime raimu

ライム

Ll

102

line sen
線

could you give me an outside
line? gaisen ni tsunaide
kudasai
外線につないで
ください

lips kuchibiru
くちびる

lipstick kuchibeni
口紅

liqueur rikyūru
リキュール

listen kikimasu
聞きます

litre rit·toru
リットル

little sukoshi
すこし

just a little, thanks arigatō,
hon no sukoshi
ありがとう、ほんの
すこし

a little milk miruku o hon
no sukoshi
ミルクをほんの
すこし

a little bit more mō sukoshi
もうすこし

live (verb) sunde imasu
住んでいます

we live together is·sho ni
sunde imasu
一緒に住んでいます

dialogue

where do you live? doko
ni sunde imasu ka?
I live in London Rondon
ni sunde imasu

lively iki-iki shita
いきいきした

liver (in body) kanzō
肝臓
(food) rebā
レバー

lobby (in hotel) robī
ロビー

lobster ise-ebi
いせえび

local jimoto no
地元の

lock (noun) kagi
かぎ

it's locked kagi ga kakat·te
imasu
かぎがかかって
います

lock in tojikomemasu
閉じ込めます

lock out
shimedashimasu
締め出します

I've locked myself out of my
room kagi o naka ni
wasuremashita
かぎを中に忘れ
ました

locker (for luggage etc) rok·kā
ロッカー

lollipop kyandī
キャンディー

London Rondon
ロンドン

long nagai
長い

how long will it take to fix it?
naosu no ni dono kurai
kakarimasu ka?
なおすのにどのくら
いかかりますか？

how long does it take? dono
kurai kakarimasu ka?
どのくらいかかり
ますか？

a long time nagai aida
長い間

long-distance call
chōkyori-denwa
長距離電話

look: I'm just looking, thanks
miteru dake desu, arigatō
見てるだけです、
ありがとう

you don't look well guai ga
yoku nasasō desu ne
具合いがよくなさそ
うですね

look out! ki o tsuete!
気をつけて！

can I have a look? chot·to
misete kuremasen ka?
ちょっと見せてくれ

ませんか？

look after sewa o shimasu
世話をします

look at mimasu
見ます

look for sagashimasu
さがします

I'm looking for ... ... o
sagashite imasu
…をさがしています

look forward to tanoshimi ni
shimasu
楽しみにします

I'm looking forward to it
tanoshimi ni shite imasu
楽しみにしています

loose (handle etc) yurui
ゆるい

lorry torak·ku
トラック

lose nakushimasu
なくします

I've lost my way michi ni
mayot·te shimaimashita
道に迷ってしまい
ました

I'm lost, I want to get to ...
... e ikitai no desu ga,
mayot·te shimaimashita
…へ行きたいのです
が、迷ってしまい
ました

I've lost my bag bag·gu o
nakshimashita
バッグをなくし

ました
lost property (office)
ishitsubutsu-toriatsukai-jo
遺失物取扱所
lot: a lot, lots takusan
たくさん
not a lot an-mari ōku naku
あんまり多くなく
a lot of people takusan no hito
たくさんのひと
a lot bigger zut·to ōkī
ずっとおおきい
I like it a lot totemo suki desu
とても好きです
lotion rōshon
ローション
loud sawagashī
騒がしい
lounge raunji
ラウンジ
love (noun) ai
愛
(verb) daisuki desu
大好きです
I love Japan Nihon ga daisuki desu
日本が大好きです
lovely steki (na)
すてき (な)
low (prices) yasui
安い
(bridge) hikui
低い

luck un
運
good luck! umaku ikimasu yōni!
うまくいきます
ように！
luggage nimotsu
荷物
luggage trolley nimotsu-yō kāto
荷物用カート
lunch chūshoku
昼食
boxed lunch obentō
おべんとう
lungs hai
肺
luxurious zeitaku (na)
ぜいたく (な)

M

machine kikai
機械
magazine zas·shi
雑誌
maid (in hotel) kyakushitsu-gakari
客室係
(in Japanese inn, restaurant) nakai-san
仲居さん
maiden name kyūsei
旧姓

mail (noun) yūbin
郵便
(verb) yūsō shimasu
郵送します
is there any mail for me?
nani ka yūbin ga kite imasu
ka?
何か郵便がきて
いますか？
mailbox posuto
ポスト
main omo (na)
主（な）
main course mein-kōsu
メインコース
main post office yūbinkyoku
no honkyok
郵便局の本局
main road ōdōri
大通り
mains switch dengen
電源
make (brand name) shurui
種類
(verb) tsukurimasu
つくります
I make it 500 yen tat·ta
go-hyaku-en desu
たった五百円です
what is it made of? nani de
dekite imasu ka?
何で出来ています
か？
make-up keshō
化粧

Malaysia Marēshia
マレーシア
Malaysian (adj) Marēshia
(no)
マレーシア（の）
man otoko no hito
男の人
manager (in restaurant, hotel)
shihainin
支配人
(in shop) tenchō
店長
(in business) keieisha
経営者
can I see the manager?
shihainin ni awasete
kuremasen ka?
支配人に会わせて
くれませんか？
managing director shachō
社長
manual (car with manual gears)
manyuaru (no)
マニュアル（の）
many takusan (no)
たくさん（の）
not many amari ōk nai
あまり多くない
map chizu
地図
network map rosenzu
路線図
March San·gatsu
三月
margarine māgarin

マーガリン

market ichiba
市場

(in business) shijō
市場

marmalade māmarēdo
マーマレード

married: I'm married kek·kon
shite imasu
結婚しています

are you married? kek·kon
shite imasu ka?
結婚していますか？

martial arts budō
武道

mascara masukara
マスカラ

massage (noun) mas·sāji
マッサージ

mat (Japanese) tatami
たたみ

match (football etc) shiai
試合

matches mat·chi
マッチ

material (fabric) kiji
生地

matter: it doesn't matter nan
demo ī desu
なんでもいいです

what's the matter? dō
shimashita ka?
どうしましたか？

mattress futon
ふとん

May Gogatsu
五月

may: may I have another one?
mō hitotsu morat·te mo ī
· desu ka?
もうひとつもらって
もいいですか？

may I come in? hait·te mo ī
desu ka?
入ってもいいです
か？

may I see it? mite mo ī desu
ka?
見てもいいですか？

may I sit here? koko ni
suwat·te mo ī desu ka?
ここに座ってもいい
ですか？

maybe tabun
たぶん

mayonnaise mayonēzu
マヨネーズ

me* watashi (o)
私（を）

that's for me sore wa
watashi no desu
それは私のです

send it to me okut·te
kudasai
送ってください

me too watashi mo
私も

meal gohan, shokuji
ごはん、食事

dialogue

did you enjoy your meal?
oshokuji no hō wa ikaga
deshita ka?

it was excellent, thank you
arigatō gozaimasu,
totemo oishikat·ta desu

mean: what do you mean? dō
iu koto desu ka?
どういうことですか？

dialogue

what does this word
mean? kono kotoba wa
dō iu imi desu ka?
it means ... in English Eigo
de ... to iu imi desu

measles hashika
はしか
German measles fūshin
風疹
meat niku
肉
mechanic shūrikō
修理工
medicine kusuri
薬
medium (adj) chū kurai (no)
中くらい（の）
(clothes) emu-saizu
エムサイズ

medium-dry chū kurai no
karasa (no)
中くらいの辛さ
（の）
medium-rare midiamu-rea
(no)
ミディアム・レア
（の）
medium-sized chū kurai (no)
中くらい（の）
meet aimasu
会います
nice to meet you
hajimemashite
はじめまして
where shall I meet you? doko
de aimashō ka?
どこで会いましょう
か？
meeting shūkai
集会
(business) kaigi
会議
meeting place
machi-awase-basho
待ち合わせ場所
men dansei
男性
mend naoshimasu
なおします
could you mend this for me?
kore o naoshite kuremasen
ka?
これをなおして
くれませんか？

men's room dansei-yō toire

男性用トイレ

menswear shinshifuku-uriba

紳士服売り場

mention: don't mention it dō
itashimash*i*te

どういたしまして

menu menyū

メニュー

may I see the menu, please?
menyū o onegai shimas*u*

メニューをお願いし
ます

see menu reader page 266

message dengon

伝言

**are there any messages for
me?** dengon ga nani ka
arimasen desh*i*ta ka?

伝言が何かありませ
んでしたか？

**I want to leave a message
for ...** ...-san ni dengon o
onegai shimas*u*

…—さんに伝言をお
願いします

metal kinzok*u*

金属

metre mētoru

メートル

microwave (oven) denshi-
renji

電子レンジ

midday shōgo

正午

at midday shōgo ni

正午に

middle: in the middle
man·naka ni

真ん中に

in the middle of the night
mayonaka ni

真夜中に

the middle one man·naka
no

真ん中の

midnight mayonaka

真夜中

at midnight mayonaka ni

真夜中に

might: I might go iku kamo
shiremasen

行くかもしれません

I might not go ikanai kamo
shiremasen

行かないかもしれ
ません

**I might want to stay another
day** mō ip·pak*u* suru kamo
shiremasen

もう一泊する
かもしれません

migraine henzutsū

偏頭痛

mild (taste) usuaji (no)

うすあじ（の）

(weather) atatakai

あたたかい

mile mairu

マイル

milk miruk*u*
ミルク

milkshake miruk*u*-sēki
ミルクセーキ

millimetre mirimētoru
ミリメートル

mind: never mind ki ni
sh*i*naide kudasai
気にしないで
ください

I've changed my mind ki ga
kawarimash*i*ta
気が変わりました

dialogue

do you mind if I open the
window? mado o akete
mo ī desho ka?
no, I don't mind ē, dōzo

mine*: it's mine watashi no
des*u*
私のです

mineral water mineraru-uōtā
ミネラルウォーター

mints minto
ミント

minute fun
分

in a minute sug ni
すぐに

just a minute chot·to mat·te
kudasai
ちょっと待って

くださいい

mirror kagami
かがみ

Miss ... ...-san
…ーさん

miss: I missed the bus bas*u* ni
noriokuremash*i*ta
バスに乗り遅れ
ました

missing: one of my ... is
missing ... ga hitots*u*
miatarimasen
…がひとつ見あたり
ません

there's a suitcase missing
sūts*u*ēs*u* ga miatarimasen
スーツケースが見あ
たりません

mist kiri
霧

mistake (noun) machigai
まちがい

I think there's a mistake
dōmo machigai ga aru yō
nan des*u* ga
どうもまちがいがあ
るようなんですが

sorry, I've made a mistake
sumimasen,
machigaemash*i*ta
すみません、まちが
えました

mix-up: sorry, there's been a
mix-up sumimasen, techigai
desh*i*ta

110

すみません、手違い
でした
mobile phone keitaidenwa
携帯電話
modern modan (na)
モダン（な）
moisturizer nyūeki
乳液
moment: I won't be a moment
sugu modorimasu
すぐ戻ります
monastery sōin
僧院
Monday Getsuyōbi
月曜日
money okane
お金
month (this, last, next etc) getsu
月
(one, two, three etc) kagetsu
ヶ月
monument kinenhi
記念碑
moon tsuki
月
moped tansha
単車
more* mot·to
もっと
**can I have some more water,
please?** omizu o mō
sukoshi moraemasu ka?
お水をもうすこし
もらえますか？
more expensive/interesting

mot·to takai/omoshiroi
もっと高い／おも
しろい
more than 50 go-jū ijō
５０以上
more than that sore ijō
それ以上
a lot more mot·to takusan
もっとたくさん

dialogue

> **would you like some
> more?** mō sukoshi ikaga
> desu ka?
> **no, no more for me,
> thanks** īe, mō kek·ko
> desu
> **how about you?** sochira
> wa dō desu ka?
> **I don't want any more,
> thanks** mō kek·ko desu

morning asa
朝
this morning kesa
けさ
in the morning asa ni
朝に
mosquito ka
蚊
mosquito repellent
kayoke-supurē
蚊よけスプレー
most: I like this one most of all

kore ga ichiban suki desu
これがいちばん好き
です

most of the time taitei
たいてい

most tourists taitei no ryokōkyaku
たいていの旅行客

mostly taitei
たいてい

mother (one's own) haha
母

(someone else's) okā-san
お母さん

mother-in-law (one's own) giri no haha
義理の母

(someone else's) giri no okā-san
義理のお母さん

motorbike ōtobai
オートバイ

motorboat mōtābōto
モーターボート

motorway kōsokudōro
高速道路

mountain yama
山

up in the mountains yama ni
山に

mountaineering tozan
登山

mouse nezumi
ねずみ

moustache kuchihige

くちひげ

mouth kuchi
口

move (verb) ugokashimasu
動かします

he's moved to another room kare wa hik·koshimashita
彼は引っ越しました

could you move your car?
kuruma o ugokashite kuremasen ka?
車を動かしてくれま
せんか？

could you move up a little?
sukoshi tsumete kuremasen ka?
すこしつめてくれま
せんか？

movie eiga
映画

movie theater (US) eigakan
映画館

Mr ...-san
…―さん

Mrs ...-san
…―さん

Ms ...-san
…―さん

much takusan (no)
たくさん（の）

much better zut·to ī desu
ずっといいです

much worse nao warui desu
なお悪いです

much hotter zut·to atsui
ずっと暑い

not much sukoshi
すこし

not very much amari
あまり

I don't want very much amari
hoshiku nai desu
あまり欲しくない
です

mud doro
どろ

mug (for drinking) magukap·pu
マグカップ

I've been mugged gōtō ni
osowaremashita
強盗におそわれ
ました

mum mama
ママ

mumps otafuku-kaze
おたふくかぜ

museum hakubutsuan
博物館

mushrooms kinoko
きのこ

music on·gaku
音楽

musician on·gak-ka
音楽家

Muslim (adj) Isuramukyo (no)
イスラム教

mussels mūrugai
ムール貝

must: I must ... ...-nakereba

narimasen
…―なければなりま
せん

I mustn't drink alcohol
watashi wa arukōru o
nonde wa ikenain desu
私はアルコールを飲
んではいけないん
です

mustard masutādo
マスタード

(Japanese) karashi
からし

my* watashi no
私の

myself: I'll do it myself jibun
de shimasu
自分でします

by myself jibun de
自分で

N

nail (finger) tsume
つめ

(metal) kugi
くぎ

nailbrush tsume-burashi
つめブラシ

nail varnish manikyua
マニキュア

name namae
名前

my name's John watashi no

namae wa John des*u*

私の名前はジョン
です

what's your name? shitsurei
des*u* ga, onamae wa?

失礼ですがお名前
は？

**what is the name of this
street?** kono tōri no namae
wa nan des*u* ka?

この通りの名前は何
ですか？

napkin nap*u*kin

ナプキン

nappy omuts*u*

おむつ

narrow (street) semai

せまい

nasty (person) iya (na)

いや（な）

(weather, accident etc) hidoi

ひどい

national kok*u*rits*u* (no)

国立（の）

nationality kok*u*seki

国籍

natural shizen (na)

自然（な）

nausea hakike

吐き気

navy (blue) kon-iro (no)

紺色（の）

near … no soba

…のそば

is it near the city centre?

hankagai kara chikai des*u*
ka?

繁華街から近いです
か？

do you go near the Osaka-jo?

Ōsaka-jo no chikak*u* e
ikimas*u* ka?

大阪城の近くへ行き
ますか？

where is the nearest ...?

ichiban chikai … wa doko
des*u* ka?

いちばん近い…はど
こですか？

nearby chikai

近い

nearly hotondo

ほとんど

necessary hits*u*yō (na)

必要（な）

neck kubi

くび

necklace nek·kures*u*

ネックレス

necktie nek*u*tai

ネクタイ

need: I need ... … ga hitsuyō
des*u*

…が必要です

do I need to pay? okane wa
haraun deshō ka?

お金は払うん
でしょうか？

needle hari

針

negative (film) nega
ネガ

neither: neither (one) of them
dochira demo nai
どちらでもない

neither ... nor ... ... demo ...
demo nai
…でも…でもない

nephew (one's own) oi
甥

(someone else's) oigo-san
甥御さん

net (in sport) net·to
ネット

net price seika
正価

never* kes·shite …-masen
けっして…―ません

I never go there soko e wa
kes·shite ikimasen
そこへはけっして
行きません

(never been/done) … koto ga
arimasen
…ことがありません

dialogue

have you ever been to
Tokyo? Tōkyō ni it·ta
koto wa arimasu ka?

no, I've never been there
īe, ichido mo it·ta koto
ga arimasen

new atarashī
新しい

news (radio, TV etc) nyūs
ニュース

newsagent's shimbun-ya
新聞屋

newspaper shimbun
新聞

New Year oshōgatsu
お正月

Happy New Year!
akemashite omedetō
gozaimasu!
明けましておめでと
うございます！

New Year's Day gantan
元旦

New Year's Eve ōmisoka
大晦日

New Zealand Nyū-Jīrando
ニュージーランド

New Zealander: I'm a New
Zealander watashi wa Nyū-
Jīrando-jin desu
私はニュージーラン
ド人です

next tsugi (no)
次（の）

the next turning/street on the
left tsugi no hidari no
magarikado/michi
次の左の曲り角／道

at the next stop tsugi no
teiryū-jo de
次の停留所で

next week raishū
来週
next to ... no tonari
…のとなり
nice (food) oishī
おいしい
(looks, view etc) kirei (na)
きれい（な）
(person) shinsetsu (na)
親切（な）
niece (one's own) mei
姪
(someone else's) meigo-san
姪御さん
night yoru
夜
at night yoru ni
夜に
good night oyasuminasai
おやすみなさい

dialogue

do you have a single room
for one night? ip·paku
desu ga shinguru wa aite
imasu ka?
yes, madam hai,
gozaimasu
how much is it per night?
ip·paku ikura desu ka?
5,000 yen ip·paku go-
sen-en ni narimasu
thank you, I'll take it ja,
onegai shimasu

nightclub naitokurabu
ナイトクラブ
nightdress naitodoresu
ナイトドレス
night porter yakan no
furonto-gakari
夜間のフロント係
no* (answer) īe
いいえ
no ... ... ga arimasen
…がありません
I've no change kozeni ga
arimasen
小銭がありません
there's no ... left ... ga mō
arimasen
…がもうありません
no way! tondemo nai!
とんでもない！
oh no! (upset) masaka!
まさか！
nobody* dare mo ...-masen
だれも…ーません
there's nobody there soko
niwa dare mo imasen
そこにはだれもい
ません
noise sō-on
騒音
noisy urusai
うるさい
non-alcoholic arukōru-nuki
(no)
アルコール抜き
（の）

none* (people) dare mo
…-masen
だれも…ーません
(things) dore mo …-masen
どれも…ーません

nonsmoking compartment
kin·en-koshitsu
禁煙個室

noodles menrui
めん類

noon shōgo
正午

at noon shōgo ni
正午に

no-one* dare mo …-masen
だれも…ーません

nor: nor do I watashi mo sō
desu
私もそうです

normal futsū (no)
ふつう（の）

north kita
北

in the north kita ni
北に

to the north kita e
北へ

north of Kanazawa
Kanazawa no kita
金沢の北

northeast hokutō
北東

Northern Ireland Kita-
Airurando
北アイルランド

North Korea Kita-Chōsen
北朝鮮

northwest hokusei
北西

Norway Noruē
ノルウェー

Norwegian (adj) Noruē (no)
ノルウェー（の）

nose hana
鼻

not* …-masen
…ーません

no, I'm not hungry īe, onaka
ga suite imasen
いいえ、おなかが
すいていません

I don't want any, thank you
arigatō, demo watashi wa
kek·kō desu
ありがとう、でも私
はけっこうです

it's not necessary hitsuyō
nai desu
必要ないです

I didn't know that sore wa
shirimasen deshita
それは知りません
でした

not that one sore ja
arimasen
それじゃありません

not that one, this one sore ja
nakute, kore desu
それじゃなくてこれ
です

note (banknote) shihei
紙幣
notebook techō
手帳
nothing nani mo …-masen
何も…ーません
nothing for me, thanks nani
mo irimasen
何もいりません
novel shōsetsu
小説
November Jūichigatsu
十一月
now ima
いま
number ban·gō
番号
(figure) sūji
数字
I've got the wrong number
ban·go o
machigaemashita
番号をまちがえ
ました
what is your phone number?
denwaban·go wa nan-ban
desu ka?
電話番号は何番です
か？
number plate nambā-purēto
ナンバープレート
nurse (man) kan·goshi
看護士
(woman) kan·gofu
看護婦

nuts nat·tsu
ナッツ

O

Occidental seiyō (no)
西洋（の）
occupied (phone) hanashi-chū
話し中
(toilet) shiyō-chū
使用中
October Jūgatsu
十月
o'clock ji
時
odd (strange) kawat·ta
変わった
of* … no
…の
off (lights) kiete iru
消えている
it's just off ... sore wa …
kara sugu desu
それは…からすぐです
we're off tomorrow ashita
tachimasu
あした立ちます
office (place of work) jimusho
事務所
officer (said to policeman)
omawari-san
おまわりさん
often yoku
よく

not often met·ta ni

めったに

how often are the buses?
bas*u* wa nan-bon kurai
arimas*u* ka?

バスは何本くらいあ
りますか？

oil (for car) oiru

オイル

(for cooking) abura

あぶら

(for salad) sarada-oiru

サラダオイル

ointment nankō

軟膏

OK ōkē

オーケー

are you OK? daijōb*u* des*u*
ka?

大丈夫ですか？

is that OK with you? sore de
ī des*u* ka?

それでいいですか？

is it OK to ...? … shite mo ī
des*u* ka?

…してもいいです
か？

that's OK, thanks sore de
kamaimasen, arigatō

それでかまいませ
ん、ありがとう

I'm OK (nothing for me) watashi
wa kek·ko des*u*

私はけっこうです

(I feel OK) daijōb*u* des*u*

is this train OK for ...? kono
densha wa … e ikimas*u* ka?

この電車は…へ行き
ますか？

old (person) toshi o tot·ta

年をとった

(thing) furui

古い

dialogue

> **how old are you?** oikuts*u*
> des*u* ka?
> **I'm 25** ni-jū-go des*u*
> **and you?** anata wa?

old-fashioned mukashi-fū
(no)

昔風（の）

old town (old part of town)
kyūshigai

旧市街

in the old town kyūshigai ni

旧市街に

omelette omurets*u*

オムレツ

on … no ue

…の上

on the street tōri de

通りで

is it on this road? sore wa
kono michizoi des*u* ka?

それはこの道沿い
ですか？

on the plane hikōki de
飛行機で

on Saturday Doyōbi ni
土曜日に

on television terebi de
テレビで

I haven't got it on me ima
mot·te imasen
いま持っていません

this one's on me (drink) kore
wa watashi mochi desu
これは私持ちです

the light wasn't on denki ga
tsuite imasen deshita
電気がついてい
ませんでした

what's on tonight? komban
wa nani o yat·te imasu ka?
今晩は何をやって
いますか？

once (on one occasion) ik·kai
一回

(formerly) mae ni
前に

(as soon as) it·tan ...-tara
いったん…―たら

at once (immediately) sugu
すぐ

one* hitotsu
ひとつ

the white one shiroi no
しろいの

one-way ticket katamichi-
kip·pu
片道切符

a one-way ticket to ...
... made katamichi-kip·pu
o ichi-mai
…までの片道切符を
一枚

onion tamanegi
たまねぎ

only ... dake
…だけ

only one hitotsu dake
ひとつだけ

it's only 6 o'clock mada
rokuji desu
まだ6時です

I've only just got here mada
tsuita bakari desu
まだ着いたばかり
です

on/off switch suit·chi
スイッチ

open (adj) hiraita
開いた

(verb: door) akemasu
開けます

(of shop) eigyō-chū
営業中

when do you open? koko wa
itsu akimasu ka?
ここはいつ開きます
か？

I can't get it open akimasen
開きません

in the open air kogai de
戸外で

opening times eigyōjikan

営業時間

open ticket ōpun-chiket·to
オープンチケット

opera opera
オペラ

operation (medical) shujutsu
手術

operator (telephone) operētā
オペレーター

opposite: the opposite
direction hantaihōkō
反対方向

the bar opposite mukai no
bā
向かいのバー

opposite my hotel hoteru no
mukaigawa ni
ホテルの向かい側に

optician megane-ya
めがね屋

or mata wa
または

orange (fruit) orenji
オレンジ

(colour) orenji-iro (no)
オレンジ色（の）

orange juice orenji-jūsu
オレンジジュース

orchestra ōkesutora
オーケストラ

order (noun) chūmon
注文

(verb) chūmon shimasu
注文します

can we order now? (in

restaurant) chūmon shite mo
ī desu ka?
注文してもいいです
か？

I've already ordered mō
chūmon shimashita
もう注文しました

I didn't order this kore wa
chūmon shimasen deshita
これは注文しません
でした

out of order kowarete imasu
こわれています

ordinary futsū (no)
ふつう（の）

other hoka no
ほか（の）

the other one mō katahō no
もう片方の

the other day sūjitsu mae
数日前

I'm waiting for the others hoka
no hitotachi o mat·te imasu
ほかのひとたちを
待っています

do you have any others?
hoka nimo arimasu ka?
ほかにもありますか？

otherwise samonaito
さもないと

Oriental tōyō (no)
東洋（の）

our(s)* watashitachi no
私たちの

out: he's out kare wa

gaishutsu-chū desu
彼は外出中です

three kilometres out of town
machi kara san-kiro
町から3キロ

outdoor pool okugai-pūru
屋外プール

outside … no soto ni
…の外に

can we sit outside? soto ni
suwaremasu ka?
外に座れますか？

oven ōbun
オーブン

over: over here koko ni
ここに

over there asoko ni
あそこに

over 500 go-hyaku ijō
500以上

it's over owarimashita
終わりました

overcharge: you've overcharged
me kore wa torisugi desu
これは取りすぎです

overcoat ōbā
オーバー

overland mail sarubin
サル便

overnight (travel) ip-paku (no)
一泊（の）

overtake oikoshimasu
追い越します

owe: how much do I owe you?
ikura haraeba ī desu ka?

いくら払えばいい
ですか？

own: my own …
watashi-jishin no …
私自身の…

are you on your own? ohitori
desu ka?
おひとりですか？

I'm on my own hitori desu
ひとりです

owner mochinushi
持ち主

oyster kaki
かき

P

Pacific Ocean Taiheiyō
太平洋

pack (verb) nimotsu o
tsumemasu
荷物をつめます

a pack of … … hito-pak·ku
ひとパック

package (parcel) kozutsumi
小包

package holiday pak·ku-
ryokō
パック旅行

packed lunch obentō
お弁当

packet: a packet of cigarettes
tabako hito-hako
たばこ1箱

paddy field tambo
たんぼ

page (of book) pēji
ページ

  could you page Mr ...? ...-san
o yobidashite kuremasen ka?
……—さんを呼び出
しでくれませんか？

pagoda tō
塔

pain itami
痛み

  I have a pain here koko ga
itai desu
ここが痛いです

painful itai
痛い

painkillers itamidome
痛み止め

painting e
絵

pair: a pair of ... hito-kumi
no ...
一組の…

palace kyūden
宮殿

pale (colour) usu-...
うす—…

  pale blue usu-aoi
うすあおい

pan furaipan
フライパン

panties (women's underwear)
shōtsu
ショーツ

pants (underwear: men's) pantsu
パンツ

  (women's) shōtsu
ショーツ

  (US: trousers) zubon
ズボン

pantyhose pantī-sutok·kingu
パンティーストッキ
ング

paper kami
紙

  (Japanese) washi
和紙

  (newspaper) shimbun
新聞

  a piece of paper kami
ichi-mai
紙一枚

paper folding origami
折り紙

paper handkerchiefs tis·shu–
pēpā
ティッシュペーパー

parcel kozutsumi
小包

pardon (me)? (didn't
understand/hear) nante
īmashita ka?
なんて言いました
か？

parents (one's own) ryōshin
両親

  (someone else's) goryōshin
御両親

park (noun) kōen

公園
(verb) chūshajō
駐車場
can I park here? koko ni
chūsha shite mo ī desu ka?
ここに駐車しても
いいですか？
parking lot chūshajō
駐車場
part (noun) bubun
部分
partner (boyfriend, girlfriend etc)
pātonā
パートナー
(in business) kyōdō-keiei-sha
共同経営者
party (group) dantai
団体
(celebration) pātī
パーティー
passenger jōkyaku
乗客
passport pasupōto
パスポート
past*: in the past mae ni
まえに
just past the information
office an-naijo o koete sugu
案内所を越えてすぐ
path komichi
小道
pattern moyō
もよう
pavement hodō
歩道

on the pavement hodō de
歩道で
pavilion tenjikan
展示館
pay (verb) shiharaimasu
支払います
can I pay, please? okanjō o
onegai shimasu
お勘定をお願い
します
it's already paid for mō
harat·te arimasu
もう払ってあります

dialogue

who's paying? dare ga
haraimasu ka?
I'll pay watashi ga
haraimasu
no, you paid last time, I'll
pay īe, konomae harat·te
moraimashita, watashi ga
haraimasu

payment shiharai
支払い
payphone kōshūdenwa
公衆電話
peaceful shizuka (na)
しずか（な）
peach momo
もも
peanuts pīnat·tsu
ピーナッツ

pear nashi
なし

pearl shinju
真珠

peculiar (strange) kawat·ta
変わった

pedestrian crossing ōdanhodō
横断歩道

pedestrian zone hokōsha-
ten·goku
歩行者天国

peg (for washing) sentaku-
basami
せんたくばさみ
(for tent) pegu
ペグ

pen pen
ペン

pencil empitsu
えんぴつ

penfriend pemparu
ペンパル

penicillin penishirin
ペニシリン

penknife poket·to-naifu
ポケットナイフ

pensioner
nenkin-seikatsu·sha
年金生活者

people hito
ひと

the other people in the hotel
hoteru no hoka no
tomarikyaku
ホテルのほかの泊り

客

too many people hito ga
ōsugi
ひとが多すぎ

pepper (spice) koshō
こしょう

per: per night hito-ban ni
tsui
一晩につき

how much per day?
ichinichi ikura desu ka?
一日いくらですか？

per cent pāsento
パーセント

perfect kampeki (na)
完璧（な）

perfume kōsui
香水

perhaps tabun
たぶん

perhaps not tabun chigau
deshō
たぶん違うでしょう

period (of time) kikan
期間
(menstruation) seiri
生理

permit (noun) kyoka
許可

person hito
ひと

personal stereo uōkuman
ウォークマン

petrol gasorin
ガソリン

petrol can sekiyukan
石油缶

petrol station gasorin-sutando
ガソリンスタンド

pharmacy yak·kyok*u*, k*u*suri-ya
薬局、薬屋

Philippines Firipin
フィリピン

phone (noun) denwa
電話

(verb) denwa shimas*u*
電話します

phone book denwachō
電話帳

phone box kōshūdenwa
公衆電話

phonecard terefōn-kādo
テレホンカード

phone number denwaban·gō
電話番号

photo shashin
写真

excuse me, could you take a photo of us? chot·to sumimasen, shashin tot·te kuremasen ka?
ちょっとすみません、写真とってくれませんか？

phrasebook kaiwa-hyōgen-shū
会話表現集

piano piano
ピアノ

pickpocket suri
スリ

pick up: will you be there to pick me up? soko made mukae ni kite kuremasen ka?
そこまでむかえに来てくれませんか？

picnic (noun) piknik·k*u*
ピクニック

picture (painting) e
絵

(photo) shashin
写真

piece hitotsu
ひとつ

a piece of ... hito-kire no ...
ひときれの…

pill piru
ピル

I'm on the pill piru o nonde imas*u*
ピルを飲んでいます

pillow makura
まくら

pillow case makura-kabā
まくらカバー

pin (noun) pin
ピン

pinball pachinko
パチンコ

pine matsu
松

pineapple painap·puru
パイナップル

pink pink*u*-iro (no)
ピンク色（の）

pipe (for smoking) paip*u*
パイプ

(for water) suidōkan
水道管

pity: it's a pity
zan·nen des*u*
残念です

pizza piza
ピザ

place (noun) tokoro
ところ

at your place anata no
tokoro de
あなたのところで

at his place kare no tokoro
de
彼のところで

plain (not patterned) muji (no)
無地（の）

plane hikōki
飛行機

by plane hikōki de
飛行機で

plant shok*u*butsu
植物

plasters bansōkō
ばんそうこう

plastic purastik·k*u*
プラスティック

(credit cards) kurejit·to-kādo
クレジットカード

plastic bag binīru-bukuro
ビニール袋

plate sara
さら

platform purat·to-hōm*u*
プラットホーム

which platform is it for Nara?
Nara-iki wa dono purat·to-
hōm*u* des*u* ka?
奈良行きはどのプ
ラットホームです
か？

play (verb: sports, game) shimas*u*
します

(musical instrument) hikimas*u*
ひきます

(music) kakemas*u*
かけます

(noun: in theatre) shibai
芝居

playground asobiba
あそび場

pleasant kimochi no ī
気持ちのいい

please (requesting) onegai
shimas*u*
お願いします

(go ahead) dōzo
どうぞ

yes, please hai, onegai
shimas*u*
はい、お願いします

could you please ...? ... -te
kuremasen ka?
…ーてくれません
か？

please don't dōka yamete

kudasai
どうかやめてくだ
さい

pleased: pleased to meet you
hajime*mashite*
はじめまして

pleasure: my pleasure dō
itashima*shite*
どういたしまして

plenty: plenty of ... tak*u*san no
...
たくさんの…

there's plenty of time jikan
wa jūbun arima*su*
時間は十分あります

that's plenty, thanks mō
kek·kō de*su*, dōmo
もうけっこうです、
どうも

plug (electrical, for car) purag*u*
プラグ

(in sink) sen
せん

plum (Western) sumomo
すもも

(Japanese) ume
うめ

plumber suidō-ya
水道屋

pm gogo
午後

poached egg otoshi-tamago
おとしたまご

pocket poket·to
ポケット

point: two point five ni-ten-
go
2.5

there's no point muda de*su*
むだです

poisonous yūdok*u* (na)
有毒 (な)

police keisatsu
警察

call the police! keisatsu o
yonde kudasai!
警察を呼んでくだ
さい

policeman keikan
警官

police station keisatsu-sho
警察署

policewoman fukei
婦警

polish (noun) tsuyadashi
つや出し

polite teinei (na)
ていねい (な)

polluted yogoreta
よごれた

pool (for swimming) pūru
プール

poor (not rich) bimbō (na)
びんぼう (な)

(quality) somatsu (na)
そまつ (な)

pop music pop·ps*u*
ポップス

pop singer kashu
歌手

popular ninki no aru
人気のある

pork butaniku
豚肉

port (for boats) minato
みなと

(drink) pōto-wain
ポートワイン

porter (in hotel) bōi
ボーイ

portrait shōzōga
肖像画

posh (restaurant) shareta
しゃれた

(people) jōhin (na)
上品（な）

possible kanō (na)
可能（な）

is it possible to ...?
... -koto ga dekimasu ka?
…ことができます
か？

as ... as possible dekirudake ...
できるだけ…

post (noun: mail) yūbin
郵便

(verb) yūsō shimasu
郵送します

could you post this for me?
kore o tōkan shite
kuremasen ka?
これを投函してくれ
ませんか？

postcard ehagaki

絵はがき

postcode yūbimban-gō
郵便番号

poster posutā
ポスター

poste restante
kyoku-dome-yūbin
局止め郵便

post office yūbinkyoku
郵便局

potato chips (US: crisps)
poteto-chip-pu
ポテトチップ

pottery (objects) tōki
陶器

pound (money) pondo
ポンド

(weight) paundo
パウンド

power cut teiden
停電

power point konsento
コンセント

practise: I want to practise my
Japanese Nihon-go o
renshū shitai desu
日本語を練習したい
です

prawns ebi
えび

prefer: I prefer ... ... no hō ga
suki desu
…のほうが好きです

pregnant ninshin-chū (no)
妊娠中（の）

129

prescription (for medicine) shohōsen
処方せん

present (gift) purezento
プレゼント

president (of country) daitōryō
大統領

(of company) shachō
社長

pretty kirei (na)
きれい（な）

it's pretty expensive kanari takai desu
かなり高いです

price nedan
値段

priest obō-san
お坊さん

(Shinto) kan·nushi-san
神主さん

prime minister sōridaijin
総理大臣

printed matter insatsubutsu
印刷物

prison keimusho
刑務所

private shi-teki (na)
私的（な）

private bathroom sen·yō no basu-toire
専用のバス・トイレ

probably osoraku
おそらく

problem mondai
問題

no problem! daijōbu!
大丈夫！

product seihin
製品

program(me) (TV, radio) ban·gumi
番組

(theatre, computer) puroguramu
プログラム

promise: I promise yakusoku shimasu
約束します

pronounce: how is this pronounced? kore wa dō hatsu·on shimasu ka?
これはどう発音しますか？

properly (repaired, locked etc) chanto
ちゃんと

protection factor fakutā
ファクター

Protestant purotesutanto
プロテスタント

public baths sentō
銭湯

public holiday saijitsu
祭日

public toilets kōshūbenjo
公衆便所

pull hikimasu
引きます

puncture (noun) panku
パンク

puppet nin·gyō

人形
puppet show nin·gyō-geki
人形劇
puppet theatre (Japanese traditional) bunraku
文楽
purple murasaki (no)
むらさき（の）
purse (for money) saifu
さいふ
(US: handbag) handobag·gu
ハンドバッグ
push oshimasu
押します
pushchair kuruma-isu
車いす
put okimasu
置きます
where can I put ...? ... o doko ni okimashō ka?
…をどこに置きましょうか？
could you put us up for the night? komban tomete itadakemasen deshō ka?
今晩泊めていただけませんでしょうか？
pyjamas pajama
パジャマ

Q

quality hinshitsu
品質

quarantine ken·eki
検疫
quarter (amount) yom-bun no ichi
四分の一
(time) jū-go-fun
15分
quayside: on the quayside hatoba de
波止場で
question shitsumon
質問
queue (noun) gyōretsu
行列
quick hayai
速い
that was quick hayakat·ta desu
速かったです
what's the quickest way there? soko ni iku niwa nani ga ichiban hayai desu ka?
そこに行くには何がいちばん速いですか？
fancy a quick drink? ip·pai yat·te ikimasen ka?
一杯やっていきませんか？
quickly hayaku
速く
quiet (place, hotel) shizuka (na)
しずか（な）
quiet! shizuka ni!
しずかに！

Qu

131

quite (fairly) kanari
かなり
(very) totemo
とても
that's quite right mat·tak*u*
sono tōri des*u*
まったくそのとおり
です
quite a lot kanari takusan
かなりたくさん

R

race (for horses) keiba
競馬
(for cars, runners) rēs*u*
レース
racket (tennis, squash) raket·to
ラケット
radiator (of car) rajiētā
ラジエーター
(in room) dambōki
暖房器
radio rajio
ラジオ
on the radio rajio de
ラジオで
rail: by rail tets*u*dō de
鉄道で
rail pass teikiken
定期券
railway tets*u*dō
鉄道
rain (noun) ame

雨
in the rain ame no naka de
雨の中で
it's raining ame ga fut·te
imas*u*
雨が降っています
rainy season tsuyu
梅雨
raincoat reinkōto
レインコート
rape (noun) fujobōkō
婦女暴行
rare (uncommon) mezurashī
めずらしい
(steak) reya
レア
rash (on skin) fukidemono
ふきでもの
raspberry raz*u*berī
ラズベリー
rat nezumi
ねずみ
rate (for changing money)
ryōgae-rēto
両替レート
rather: it's rather good
nakanaka ī des*u*
なかなかいいです
I'd rather ... ... hō ga ī des*u*
…ほうがいいです
raw nama (no)
なま（の）
raw fish sashimi
さしみ
razor kamisori

かみそり
(electric) denki-kamisori
電気かみそり

read yomimasu
読みます

ready yōi ga dekita
用意ができた

are you ready? mō ī desu ka?
もういいですか？

I'm not ready yet mada yōi ga dekite imasen
まだ用意ができていません

dialogue

when will it be ready? itsu dekimasu ka?

it should be ready in a couple of days ni-san-nichi-chū ni dekimasu

real hom·mono (no)
本物（の）

really hontō ni
ほんとう（の）

I'm really sorry hontō ni sumimasen
ほんとうにすみません

that's really great sore wa hontō ni sugoi desu
それはほんとうにすごいです

really? (doubt) hontō?

ほんとう？
(polite interest) hontō desu ka?
ほんとうですか？

rear lights tēru-rampu
テールランプ

reasonable (prices etc) tegoro (na)
手ごろ（な）

receipt reshīto
レシート

recently saikin
最近

reception (in hotel) furonto
フロント

(for guests) kan·geikai
歓迎会

at reception uketsuke de
受付で

reception desk uketsuke
受付

receptionist uketsuke-gakari
受付係

(in hotel) furonto-gakari
フロント係

recognize ki ga tsukimasu
気がつきます

recommend: could you recommend ...? osusume no ... o oshiete kuremasen ka?
おすすめの…をおしえてくれませんか？

record (music) rekōdo
レコード

red akai
赤い

red wine aka-wain
赤ワイン

refund (noun) harai-modoshi
払い戻し

can I have a refund? okane o
haraimodoshite kure-masen
ka?
お金を払い戻して
くれませんか？

region chihō
地方

registered: by registered mail
kakitome-yūbin de
書留郵便

registration number
tōrokuban·gō
登録番号

religion shūkyō
宗教

remember: I don't remember
oboete imasen
おぼえていません

I remember oboete imasu
おぼえています

do you remember? oboete
imasu ka?
おぼえていますか？

rent (noun: for apartment) yachin
家賃

(verb: car etc) karimasu
借ります

to rent rentaru (no)
レンタル

rental (for car, boat etc) ryōkin
料金

rented car renta-kā
レンタカー

repair (verb) shūri shimasu
修理します

can you repair it? shūri
dekimasu ka?
修理できますか？

repeat kurikaeshimasu
繰り返します

could you repeat that? mō
ichido it·te kuremasen ka?
もう一度言ってくれ
ませんか？

representative (noun: of
company) daihyō
代表

reservation yoyaku
予約

I'd like to make a reservation
yoyaku o shitai no desu ga
予約をしたいのです
が

dialogue

I have a reservation
yoyaku o shite arimasu
yes sir, what name please?
kashikomarimashita,
dochira-sama desu ka?

reserve (verb) yoyaku
shimasu
予約します

dialogue

can I reserve a table for tonight? tēburu o komban yoyaku dekimasu ka?

yes madam, for how many people? hai, uketamawarimasu, nam·mei-sama desu ka?

for two futari desu

and for what time? ojikan wa?

for eight o'clock hachiji ni onegai shimasu

and could I have your name please? onamae o itadakemasu ka?

rest: I need a rest hitoyasumi sasete kudasai
ひと休みさせて
ください
the rest of the group hoka no hitotachi
ほかのひとたち
restaurant restoran
レストラン
restaurant car shokudōsha
食堂車
rest room toire
トイレ
retired: I'm retired watashi wa teinen-taishoku shimashita

私は定年退職し
ました
return: a return to ... ... made no ōfuku-kip·pu o ichi-mai
…までの往復切符
を一枚
return ticket ōfuku-kip·pu
往復切符
reverse charge call korekuto-kōru
コレクトコール
reverse gear bak·ku–giya
バックギア
revolting fuyukai (na)
ふゆかい（な）
rib abarabone
あばらぼね
rice (uncooked) kome
こめ
(boiled) gohan
ごはん
(fried) chāhan
チャーハン
rich (person) kanemochi (no)
金持ち（の）
(food) kot·teri shita
こってりした
ridiculous bakageta
ばかげた
right (correct) tadashī
正しい
(not left) migi (no)
右（の）
you were right anata no iu

tōri deshita
あなたの言うとおり
でした

that's right sō desu
そうです

this can't be right kon·na
hazu wa nai desu
こんなはずはない
です

right here chōdo koko de
ちょうどこ こで

is this the right road for ...?
…e iku niwa kono michi
de ī desu ka?
…へ行くにはこの道
でいいですか？

on the right migi ni
右に

to the right migi e
右へ

turn right migi e magat·te
kudasai
右へ曲がってくだ
さい

right-hand drive migi-
handoru (no)
右ハンドル

ring (on finger) yubiwa
ゆびわ

I'll ring you atode denwa
shimasu
あとで電話します

ring back orikaeshi denwa
shimasu
折り返し電話します

ripe (fruit) jukushita
熟した

rip-off: it's a rip-off! hōgai na
nedan desu!
法外な値段です！

rip-off prices hōgai na
nedan
法外な値段

risky kiken (na)
危険な

river kawa
川

road michi
道

is this the road for ...? kore
wa … e iku michi desu ka?
これは…へ行く道
ですか？

down the road konosaki
このさき

road map dōrochizu
道路地図

roadsign dōro-hyōshiki
道路標識

rob: I've been robbed gōtō ni
osowaremashita
強盗におそわれ
ました

rock iwa
岩

(music) rok·ku
ロック

on the rocks (whisky)
on-za-rok·ku de
オンザロック

roll (bread) rōrupan
ロールパン

roof (of house) yane
やね

(of car) rūfu
ルーフ

room heya
部屋

in my room watashi no heya de
私の部屋で

room service rūmu-sābisu
ルームサービス

rope rōpu
ロープ

rosé (wine) roze
ロゼ

roughly (approximately) daitai
だいたい

round: it's my round watashi no ban desu
私の番です

round-trip ticket ōfuku-kip·pu
往復切符

a round-trip ticket to ...
... made no ōfuku-kip·pu o ichi-mai
…までの往復切符を一枚

route ikikata
行き方

what's the best route? dore ga ichiban ī ikikata desu ka?

どれがいちばんいい
行き方ですか？

rubber (material) gomu
ゴム

(eraser) keshigomu
消しゴム

rubber band wagomu
輪ゴム

rubbish (waste) gomi
ごみ

(poor quality goods) garakuta
がらくた

rubbish! (nonsense) bakabakashī!
ばかばかしい！

rucksack ryuk·ku-sak·ku
リュックサック

rude shitsurei (na)
失礼（な）

ruins iseki
遺跡

rum ramu-shu
ラム酒

rum and Coke® ramu-shu no kōra-wari
ラム酒のコーラ割り

run (verb: person) hashirimasu
走ります

I've run out of money okane ga soko o tsukimashita
お金が底をつきました

rush hour ras·shu-awā
ラッシュアワー

S

sad kanashī
かなしい

saddle (for bike) sadoru
サドル

safe (adj) anzen (na)
安全（な）

safety pin anzen-pin
安全ピン

sailboard (noun) sāfubōdo
サーフボード

sailboarding uindosāfingu
ウィンドサーフィング

sailing sēringu
セーリング

sake bottle tok·kuri
とっくり

sake cup sakazuki
さかずき

salad sarada
サラダ

salad dressing dores·shingu
ドレッシング

sale: for sale uridashi-chū
売り出し中

salesman sērusuman
セールスマン

salmon sake
さけ

salt shio
しお

same: the same onaji
同じ

the same as this kore to onaji no
これと同じの

the same again, please onaji no o mō hitotsu kudasai
同じのをもうひとつください

it's all the same to me dot·chi demo onaji desu
どっちでも同じです

sand suna
すな

sandals sandaru
サンダル

(wooden) geta
げた

sandwich sandoit·chi
サンドイッチ

sanitary napkins/towels seiri-yō napukin
生理用ナプキン

sash obi
帯

Saturday Doyōbi
土曜日

sauce sōsu
ソース

saucepan katatenabe
片手なべ

saucer ukezara
受け皿

sauna sauna
サウナ

sausage sōsēji

ソーセージ

say (verb) īmas*u*
言います

how do you say ... in Japanese? Nihon-go de ... o nan te īmas*u* ka?
日本語で…を何て
言いますか？

what did he say? k*a*re wa nan te īmash*i*ta ka?
彼は何て言いました
か？

she said ... kanojo wa ... to īmash*i*ta
彼女は…と言い
ました

could you say that again? mō ichido it·te kuremasen ka?
もういちど言って
くれませんか？

scarf s*u*kāf*u*
スカーフ

scenery keshiki
けしき

schedule yotei
予定

(US: timetable) jikok*u*hyō
時刻表

scheduled flight teikibin
定期便

school gak·kō
学校

scissors: a pair of scissors
hasami

はさみ

scooter s*u*kūtā
スクーター

scotch S*u*kot·chi-uis*u*kī
スコッチウィスキー

Scotch tape® serotēp*u*
セロテープ

Scotland S*u*kot·torando
スコットランド

Scottish (adj) S*u*kot·torando (no)
スコットランド
（の）

I'm Scottish watashi wa S*u*kot·torando-jin des*u*
私はスコットランド
人です

scrambled eggs iri-tamago
いりたまご

screen (Japanese) byōb*u*
びょうぶ

scroll (hanging) kakejik*u*
かけじく

(rolled) makimono
まきもの

sea umi
海

by the sea umibe de
海辺で

seafood shīfūdo
シーフード

seafront kaigan-zoi
海岸沿い

on the seafront kaigan-zoi ni
海岸沿いに

seal: personal seal hanko
はんこ

search (verb) sagashimasu
さがします

seasick: I feel seasick fune ni
yoimashita
船に酔いました

I get seasick funayoi suru
tachi desu
船酔いするたちです

seaside: by the seaside
kaigan de
海岸で

seat seki
席

is this seat taken? kono seki
wa fusagat·te imasu ka?
この席はふさがっ
ていますか？

seat belt shīto-beruto
シートベルト

seaweed kaisō
海草

secluded hempi (na)
へんぴ（な）

second (adj) ni-bam·me (no)
二番目（の）

(of time) byō
秒

just a second! chot·to
mat·te kudasai!
ちょっと待ってくだ
さい

second class (train etc)
futsūseki

普通席

second-hand chūko (no)
中古（の）

second floor san-kai
三階

(US) ni-kai
二階

secretary hisho
秘書

see mimasu
見ます

can I see? mite mo ī desu
ka?
見てもいいですか？

have you seen ...? ... o
mimashita ka?
…を見ましたか？

I saw him this morning kesa
kare ni aimashita
けさ彼に会いました

see you! ja, mata!
じゃ、また！

I see (I understand)
naruhodo
なるほど

self-service serufu-sābisu
セルフサービス

sell urimasu
売ります

do you sell ...? ... wa
arimasu ka?
…はありますか？

Sellotape® serotēpu
セロテープ

send okurimasu

送ります
I want to send this to England
kore o Igirisu ni okuritai
no desu ga
これをイギリスに
送りたいのですが

separate betsubetsu (no)
べつべつ（の）

separated: I'm separated
watashi wa bek·kyo-chū
desu
私は別居中です

separately (pay, travel)
betsubetsu ni
べつべつに

September Kugatsu
九月

serious (problem) jūdai (na)
重大（な）
(illness) omoi
おもい
(person) majime (na)
まじめ（な）

service charge (in restaurant)
sābisu-ryo
サービス料

service station
gasorin-sutando
ガソリンスタンド

serviette napukin
ナプキン

set menu teishoku
定食

several ikutsuka (no)
いくつか（の）

sew nuimasu
ぬいます

could you sew this back on?
kore o nuitsukete
kuremasen ka?
これをぬいつけて
くれませんか？

sex sek·kusu
セックス

sexy sekushī (na)
セクシー（な）

shade: in the shade hikage
ni
ひかげに

shallow (water) asai
浅い

shame: what a shame! (it's a
pity) zan·nen!
残念！

shampoo (noun) shampū
シャンプー

shampoo and set shampū to
set·to
シャンプーとセット

share (verb: room) aibeya ni
narimasu
相部屋になります
(table) aiseki shimasu
相席します

sharp (knife) yoku kireru
よく切れる
(pain) surudoi
するどい

shaver denki-kamisori
電気かみそり

shaving foam shēbing*u*-fōm*u*
シェービングフォー
ム

shaving point
denki-kamisori-yō
konsento
電気かみそり用
コンセント

she* kanojo
彼女

is she here? kanojo wa
imas*u* ka?
彼女はいますか？

sheet (for bed) shīts*u*
シーツ

shelf tana
たな

shellfish kai
貝

sherry sherī
シェリー

Shinto (adj) Shintō (no)
神道（の）

Shintoism Shintō
神道

ship fune
船

by ship fune de
船で

shirt shats*u*
シャツ

shit! k*u*so!
くそ！

shock (noun) shok·k*u*
ショック

**I got an electric shock from
the ...** … de kanden
shimash*i*ta
…で感電しました

shocking hidoi
ひどい

shoe kuts*u*
くつ

a pair of shoes kuts*u* is·sok*u*
くつ一足

shoelaces kuts*u*·himo
くつひも

shoe polish kuts*u*zumi
くつずみ

shoe repairer kuts*u*naoshi
くつなおし

shop mise
店

shopping: I'm going shopping
kaimono ni ikimas*u*
買物にいきます

shopping centre
shop·ping*u*-sentā
ショッピングセン
ター

shop window shōuindō
ショーウィンドー

shore (of sea) umibe
海辺

(of lake) kishibe
岸辺

short (person) se no hikui
背の低い

(time, journey) mijikai
みじかい

shortcut chikamichi
近道

shorts pants*u*
パンツ

should: what should I do? do shitara ī desho?
どうしたらいい でしょう？

you should ... ... -ta hō ga ī des*u*
…―たほうがいい です

you shouldn't ... ... -nai hō ga ī des*u*
…―ないほうがいい です

he should be back soon kare wa sug*u* modot·te kuru hazu des*u*
彼はすぐ戻って くるはずです

shoulder kata
かた

shout (verb) sakebimas*u*
さけびます

show (in theatre) shō
ショー

could you show me? misete kuremasen ka?
見せてくれません か？

(direction) oshiete kuremasen ka?
おしえてくれません か？

shower (in bathroom) shawā
シャワー

(of rain) niwaka-ame
にわか雨

with shower shawā-tsuki (no)
シャワー付き（ の ）

shower gel bodī-sōp*u*
ボディーソープ

shrine jinja
神社

shut (verb) shimemas*u*
閉めます

when do you shut? koko wa nanji ni shimarimas*u* ka?
ここは何時に閉 まりますか？

when does it shut? its*u* shimarimas*u* ka?
いつ閉まりますか？

they're shut shimat·te imas*u*
閉まっています

I've shut myself out kagi o naka ni wasuremash*i*ta
かぎを中に忘れ ました

shut up! damare!
だまれ！

shutter (on camera) shat·tā
シャッター

(on window) amado
あまど

sick (ill) byōki (no)
病気（ の ）

I'm going to be sick (vomit)

hakisō desu
吐きそうです

side yoko
よこ

the other side of the street
tōri no mukōgawa
通りの向こう側

side street wakimichi
わき道

sidewalk hodō
歩道

on the sidewalk hodō de
歩道で

sight: the sights of ... ... no
meisho
…の名所

sightseeing: we're going
sightseeing kankō ni
dekakeru tsumori desu
観光にでかけるつも
りです

sightseeing tour kankōryokō
観光旅行

sign kamban
看板

(roadsign) hyōshiki
標識

signature shomei
署名

silk kinu
きぬ

silly baka (na)
ばか（な）

silver (noun) gin
銀

similar onaji yō (na)
同じような

simple (easy) kantan (na)
かんたん（な）

since: since last week senshū
kara
先週から

since I got here koko ni kite
irai
ここに来て以来

sing utaimasu
歌います

Singapore Shin·gapōru
シンガポール

singer kashu
歌手

single: a single to ... ... made
katamichi-kip·pu o
ichi-mai
…まで片道切符を一
枚

I'm single watashi wa
dokushin desu
私は独身です

single bed shin·guru-bed·do
シングルベッド

single room shin·guru
シングル

single ticket
katamichi-kip·pu
片道切符

sink (in kitchen) nagashi
ながし

sister (elder: one's own) ane
姉

(someone else's) onē-san
お姉さん
(younger: one's own) imōto
妹
(someone else's) imōto-san
妹さん
sister-in-law (elder: one's own)
giri no ane
義理の姉
(someone else's) giri no
onē-san
義理のお姉さん
(younger: one's own) giri no
imōto
義理の妹
(someone else's) giri no
imōto-san
義理の妹さん
sit: can I sit here? koko ni
suwat·te mo ī desu ka?
ここに座ってもいい
ですか？
is anyone sitting here? koko
ni wa dare ka suwat·te
imasu ka?
ここにはだれか座っ
ていますか？
sit down suwarimasu
座ります
sit down osuwari kudasai
お座りください
size saizu
サイズ
skin hifu
ひふ

skinny yaseta
やせた
skirt sukāto
スカート
sky sora
空
skyscraper kōsōbiru
高層ビル
sleep (verb) nemurimasu
眠ります
did you sleep well? yoku
nemuremashita ka?
よく眠れましたか？
sleeper (on train)
shindaisha
寝台車
sleeping bag nebukuro
寝袋
sleeping car shindaisha
寝台車
sleeping pill suimin·yaku
睡眠薬
sleeve sode
そで
slide (photographic) suraido
スライド
slippers surip·pa
スリッパ
slippery suberiyasui
すべりやすい
slow osoi
おそい
slow down! mot·to
yuk·kuri!
もっとゆっくり！

slowly yuk·kuri
ゆっくり

very slowly unto yuk·kuri
うんとゆっくり

small chīsai
ちいさい

smell: it smells (smells bad)
nioimasu ne
においますね

smile (verb) hohoemimasu
ほほえみます

smoke (noun) kemuri
けむり

do you mind if I smoke?
tabako o sut·te mo ī desu
ka?
たばこを吸っても
いいですか？

I don't smoke tabako wa
suimasen
たばこは吸いません

do you smoke? tabako o
suimasu ka?
たばこを吸います
か？

snack: just a snack chot·to
oyatsu
ちょっとおやつ

sneeze (noun) kushami o
shimasu
くしゃみをします

snow yuki
雪

it's snowing yuki ga fut·te
imasu
雪が降っています

so: it's so good totemo ī desu
とてもいいです

it's so expensive totemo
takai desu
とても高いです

not so much son·na ni
takusan ja naku
そんなにたくさん
じゃなく

not so bad son·na ni
waruku nai
そんなに悪くない

so am I watashi mo sō desu
私もそうです

so do I watashi mo sō desu
私もそうです

so-so māmā desu
まあまあです

soaking solution (for contact
lenses) hozon-eki
保存液

soap sek·ken
せっけん

soap powder kona-sek·ken
粉せっけん

sober shirafu (no)
しらふ（の）

sock sok·kusu
ソックス

socket (electrical) soket·to
ソケット

soda (water) sōda-sui
ソーダ水

sofa sofā

ソファー
soft (material etc) yawarakai
やわらかい
soft-boiled egg
hanjuk*u*-tamago
半熟たまご
soft drink sof*u*to-dorink*u*
ソフトドリンク
soft lenses sof*u*to-kontak*u*to
ソフトコンタクト
sole (of shoe) kuts*u* no soko
くつの底
(of foot) ashi no ura
足の裏
**could you put new soles on
these?** kuts*u* no soko o
harikaete kuremasen ka?
くつの底を張り替え
てくれませんか？
**some: can I have some
water/apples?** mizu/rin·go
o s*u*koshi moraemas*u* ka?
水／りんごをすこし
もらえますか？
can I have some? s*u*koshi
morat·te mo ī des*u* ka?
すこしもらって
もいいですか？
somebody, someone dare ka
だれか
something nani ka
何か
something to eat nani ka
taberu mono
何か食べるもの

sometimes tokidoki
ときどき
somewhere doko ka
どこか
son (one's own) mus*u*ko
息子
(someone else's) mus*u*ko-san
息子さん
song uta
歌
son-in-law (one's own) giri no
mus*u*ko
義理の息子
(someone else's) giri no
mus*u*ko-san
義理の息子さん
soon sug*u*
すぐ
I'll be back soon sug*u*
modot·te kimas*u*
すぐ戻ってきます
as soon as possible
narubek*u* hayak*u*
なるべくはやく
sore: it's sore itai des*u*
痛いです
sore throat nodo no itami
のどの痛み
I've got a sore throat nodo
ga itai des*u*
のどが痛いです
sorry: (I'm) sorry dōmo
sumimasen
どうもすみません
sorry? (didn't understand) nante

147

īmashita ka?
何て言いましたか？

sort: what sort of ...? dono
yōna ...?
どのような… ？

soup sūpu
スープ

sour (taste) sup·pai
すっぱい

south minami
南

in the south minami ni
南に

South Africa
Minami-Afurika
南アフリカ

South African (adj)
Minami-Afurika (no)
南アフリカ（の）

I'm South African watashi wa
Minami-Afurika-jin desu
私は南アフリカ人
です

southeast nantō
南東

South Korea Kankoku
韓国

southwest nansei
南西

souvenir omiyage
おみやげ

soya milk tōnyū
豆乳

Spain Supein
スペイン

Spanish (adj) Supein (no)
スペイン（の）

spare tyre yobi no taiya
予備のタイヤ

speak: do you speak English?
Eigo o hanasemasu ka?
英語を話せますか？

I don't speak ... ... wa
hanasemasen
…は話せません

dialogue

can I speak to Yoko?
Yōko-san wa
iras·shaimasu ka?
who's calling?
dochira-sama desu ka?
it's Patricia Patricia desu
I'm sorry, Yoko's not in,
can I take a message?
mōshiwake arimasen ga,
Yōko wa ima rusu ni
shite orimasu, nani ka
den·gon wa arimasu ka?
no thanks, I'll call back
later īe, kek·kō desu,
atode kakenaoshimasu
please tell her Patricia
called kanojo ni Patricia
kara denwa ga at·ta to
otsutae kudasai

spectacles megane
めがね

speed limit soku*do*seigen
速度制限

spend okane o tsukaimas*u*
お金をつかいます

spider kumo
クモ

spin-dryer das·suiki
脱水機

spoon spūn
スプーン

sport spōts*u*
スポーツ

sprain: I've sprained my ... ...
o kujiite shimaimash*i*ta
…をくじいてしまい
ました

spring (season) haru
春

(of car, seat) spuring*u*
スプリング

in the spring haru ni
春に

square (in town) hiroba
広場

stairs kaidan
階段

stale furui
ふるい

stamp (noun) kit·te
切手

dialogue

a stamp for England,
please Igiris*u* made no

kit·te o kudasai

what are you sending?
nani o yūso saremas*u* ka?

this postcard kono hagaki
des*u*

standby kyanseru-machi
キャンセル待ち

star hoshi
ほし

(in film) sut*ā*
スター

start (noun) sut*ā*to
スタート

(verb) hajimemas*u*
始めます

when does it start? its*u*
hajimarimas*u* ka?
いつ始まりますか？

the car won't start kuruma
no enjin ga kakarimasen
車のエンジンがかか
りません

starter (of car) shidōki
始動機

(food) zensai
前菜

station eki
駅

statue zō
像

stay: where are you staying?
doko ni tomat·te imas*u* ka?
どこに泊まってい
ますか？

I'm staying at ... … ni tomat·te imasu

…に泊まっています

I'd like to stay another two nights mō ni-haku shitai to omoimasu

もう二泊したいとおもいます

steak stēki

ステーキ

steal nusumimasu

盗みます

my bag has been stolen bag·gu o nusumaremashita

バッグを盗まれました

steep (hill) kewashī

けわしい

step: on the steps kaidan de

階段で

sterling Igirisu-pondo

イギリスポンド

steward (on plane) schuwādo

スチュワード

stewardess schūwādesu

スチュワーデス

still: I'm still here mada koko ni imasu

まだここにいます

(on the phone) hai, moshi-moshi

はい、もしもし

is he still there? kare wa mada soko ni imasu ka?

彼はまだそこにいま

すか？

keep still! ugokanaide kudasai!

うごかないでください！

sting: I've been stung hachi ni sasaremashita

ハチにさされました

stockings stok·kingu

ストッキング

stomach onaka

おなか

stomach ache fukutsū

腹痛

stone (rock) ishi

石

stop (verb) tomarimasu

止まります

please, stop here (to taxi driver etc) koko de tomete kudasai

ここで止めてください

do you stop near ...? … no chikaku de tomarimasu ka?

…の近くで止まりますか？

stop it! yamete kudasai!

やめてください！

stopover keiyu

経由

storm arashi

あらし

straight (whisky) storēto

ストレート

it's straight ahead mas·sugu

it·ta tokoro desu
まっすぐ行ったとこ
ろです

straightaway sugu ni
すぐに

strange (odd) hen (na)
へん（な）

stranger shiranai hito
知らないひと

I'm a stranger here koko wa
hajimete desu
ここは初めてです

strap (on watch) bando
バンド

(on dress, suitcase) storap·pu
ストラップ

strawberry ichigo
いちご

straw mat tatami
たたみ

stream kawa
川

street tōri
通り

on the street tōri de
通りで

streetmap dōrochizu
道路地図

string himo
ひも

strong tsuyoi
つよい

stuck tsukaeta
つかえた

it's stuck tsukaete
shimaimashita
つかえてしまい
ました

student gakusei
学生

stupid baka (na)
ばか（な）

suburb kōgai
郊外

subway (US: railway)
chikatetsu
地下鉄

suddenly totsuzen ni
突然に

suede suēdo
スエード

sugar satō
さとう

suit (noun) sūtsu
スーツ

it doesn't suit me (jacket etc)
watashi niwa niaimasen
私には似合いません

it suits you yoku niaimasu
よく似合います

suitcase sūtsukēsu
スーツケース

summer natsu
夏

in the summer natsu ni
夏に

sumo wrestling sumō
すもう

sun taiyō
太陽

in the sun hinata de
ひなたで

out of the sun hikage de
ひかげで

sunbathe nik·kōyoku
日光浴

sunblock (cream) hiyake-dome
ひやけ止め

sunburn hiyake
ひやけ

sunburnt hiyake shita
ひやけした

Sunday Nichiyōbi
日曜日

sunglasses san·gurasu
サングラス

sunny: it's sunny harete imasu
晴れています

sunset nichibotsu
日没

sunshade hiyoke
ひよけ

sunshine nik·kō
日光

sunstroke nis·shabyō
日射病

suntan hiyake
ひやけ

suntan lotion santan-rōshon
サンタンローション

suntanned hi ni yaketa
日にやけた

suntan oil san-oiru
サンオイル

super sugoi
すごい

supermarket sūpā
スーパー

supper yūshoku
夕食

supplement (extra charge) tsuikaryōkin
追加料金

supply (noun) takuwae
たくわえ

(verb) chōtatsu shimasu
調達します

sure: are you sure? tashika desu ka?
たしかですか？

sure! mochiron!
もちろん！

surface mail sarubin
サル便

surname myōji
名字

sweater sētā
セーター

sweatshirt torēnā
トレーナー

Sweden Suēden
スウェーデン

Swedish (adj) Suēden (no)
スウェーデン（の）

sweet (adj: taste) amai
あまい

sweets kyandī
キャンディー

swelling hare

腫れ

swim (verb) oyogimasu
泳ぎます

I'm going for a swim oyogi ni ikimasu
泳ぎにいきます

let's go for a swim oyogi ni ikimashō
泳ぎにいきましょう

swimming costume mizugi
水着

swimming pool pūru
プール

swimming trunks mizugi
水着

switch (noun) suit·chi
スイッチ

switch off (engine) tomemasu
止めます

(TV, lights) keshimasu
消します

switch on (engine) kakemasu
かけます

(TV, lights) tsukemasu
つけます

swollen hareta
腫れた

T

table tēburu
テーブル

a table for two futari-bun no

seki
二人分の席

tablecloth tēburu-kurosu
テーブルクロス

table tennis tak·kyū
卓球

table wine tēburu-wain
テーブルワイン

tailor shinshifuku-ten
紳士服店

Taiwan Taiwan
台湾

take (verb: lead a person) tsurete ikimasu
連れていきます

(object) mot·te ikimasu
持っていきます

(accept) torimasu
取ります

can you take me to the ...?
... made tsurete it·te kuremasen ka?
…まで連れていってくれませんか？

do you take credit cards?
kurejit·to-kādo wa tsukaemasu ka?
クレジットカードはつかえますか？

fine, I'll take it ja, sore ni shimasu
じゃ、それにします

can I take this? (leaflet etc)
kore o morat·te mo ī

desu ka?

これをもらって
もいいですか？

how long does it take? jikan
wa dono kurai kakarimasu
ka?

時間はどのくらいか
かりますか？

it takes three hours san-jikan
kakarimasu

三時間かかります

is this seat taken? kono seki
wa fusagat·te imasu ka?

この席はふさがっ
ていますか？

hamburger to take away
hambāgā o teiku·auto de

ハンバーガーをテイ
クアウトで

can you take a little off here?
(to hairdresser) koko o mō
sukoshi kit·te kuremasen ka?

ここをもうすこし切っ
てくれませんか？

talcum powder
tarukam-paudā

タルカムパウダー

talk (verb) hanashimasu

話します

tall (person) se ga takai

背が高い

(building) takai

高い

tampons tampon

タンポン

tan (noun) hiyake

ひやけ

to get a tan hiyake shimasu

ひやけします

tap jaguchi

じゃ口

tape (cassette) tēpu

テープ

taste (noun) aji

味

can I taste it? ajimi shite mo
ī desu ka?

味見してもいいです
か？

taxi takushī

タクシー

will you get me a taxi?
takushī o yonde kuremasen
ka?

タクシーを呼んでく
れませんか？

where can I find a taxi? doko
de takushī o
tsukamaeraremasu ka?

どこでタクシーをつ
かまえられますか？

dialogue

**to the airport/to the ...
Hotel, please** kūkō/...
hoteru made, onegai
shimasu

how much will it be? ikura
kurai kakarimasu ka?

about 2,500 yen daitai ni-sen-go-hyaku-en desu

that's fine right here, thanks sumimasen, koko de oroshite kudasai

taxi-driver takushī no untenshu
タクシーの運転手

taxi rank takushī-noriba
タクシー乗り場

tea (drink) kōcha
紅茶

green tea ocha
お茶

tea for one/two please kōcha o hitotsu/futatsu kudasai
紅茶をひとつ／ふたつください

teabags tībag·gu
ティーバッグ

teach: could you teach me? oshiete kuremasen ka?
教えてくれませんか？

teacher sensei
先生

teahouse kis·sa-ten
喫茶店

team chīmu
チーム

teaspoon tīsupūn
ティースプーン

tea towel fukin
ふきん

teenager tīn·eijā

ティーンエイジャー

telephone denwa
電話
see phone

television terebi
テレビ

tell: could you tell him ...? kare ni ... to tsutaete kuremasen ka?
彼に…と伝えてくれませんか？

temperature (weather) kion
気温
(fever) netsu
ねつ

temple (Buddhist) otera
お寺

tent tento
テント

term (at university, school) gak·ki
学期

terminus (rail) shūten
終点

terrible hidoi
ひどい

text (message) kētai mēru
携帯メール

terrific subarashī
すばらしい

than ... yorimo
…よりも
smaller than ... ... yorimo chīsai
…よりもちいさい

thank: thank you, thanks

arigatō
ありがとう

thank you very much hontō
ni arigatō gozaimasu
ほんとうにありがと
うございます

thanks for the lift nosete
kurete arigatō
乗せてくれてあり
がとう

no thanks īe kek·kō desu
いいえ、けっこう
です

dialogue

thanks arigatō
that's OK, don't mention it
īe, dō itashimashite

that (nearby) sore
それ
(further away) are
あれ
(adj: nearby) sono
その
(further away) ano
あの

that one (nearby) sore
それ
(further away) are
あれ

I hope that ... ... -tara ī desu
ne
…―たらいいですね

that's nice suteki desu
すてきです

is that ...? sore wa … desu
ka?
それは…ですか？

that's it (that's right) sono tōri
desu
そのとおりです

the* sono
その

theatre gekijō
劇場

their(s)* (male) karera no
彼らの
(female) kanojotachi no
彼女たちの

them* (things) sore
それ
(male) karera (o)
彼ら（を）
(female) kanojotachi (o)
彼女たち（を）

for them karera/kanojotachi
no tame ni
彼ら／彼女たちの
ために

with them karera/
kanojotachi to is·sho ni
彼ら／彼女たち
と一緒に

to them karera/kanojotachi
ni
彼ら／彼女たちに

who? – them dare desu ka? –
karera/kanojotachi desu

だれですか？—
彼ら／彼女たちです
then (at that time) sono toki
その時
(after that) sore kara
それから
there soko de
そこで
over there mukō ni
むこうに
up there asoko ni
あそこに
is there ...? ... ga arimasu
ka?
…がありますか？
are there ...? ... ga arimasu
ka?
…がありますか？
there is ... ... ga arimasu
…があります
there are ... ga arimasu
…があります
there you are (giving
something) hai, dōzo
はい、どうぞ
Thermos® flask mahōbin
魔法びん
these* korera
これら
(adj) kono
この
I'd like these kore ga ki ni
irimashita
これが気に入りまし
た

they* (things) sorera
それら
(male) karera
彼ら
(female) kanojotachi
彼女たち
thick atsui
厚い
(stupid) nibui
にぶい
thief dorobō
どろぼう
thigh momo
もも
thin (person) yaseta
やせた
(object) usui
うすい
thing mono
もの
my things watashi no
shibutsu
私の私物
think kan·gaemasu
考えます
I think so watashi wa sō
omoimasu
私はそうおもいます
I don't think so
watashi wa sō wa
omoimasen
私はそうはおもい
ません
I'll think about it sore ni
tsuite wa kan·gaete

okimasu
それについては考え
ておきます

third party insurance
daisansha-hoken
第三者保険

thirsty: I'm thirsty nodo ga
kawakimashita
のどがかわきました

this kore
これ
(adj) kono
この

this one kore
これ

this is my wife watashi no
tsuma desu
私の妻です

is this ...? kore wa ... desu
ka?
これは…ですか？

those arera
あれら
(adj) ano
あの

which ones? – those dore
desu ka? – are desu
どれですか？ーあれ
です

thread (noun) ito
いと

throat nodo
のど

throat pastilles torōchi
トローチ

through tōt·te
通って

does it go through ...? (train,
bus) ... o tōrimasu ka?
…を通りますか？

throw (verb) nagemasu
投げます

throw away sutemasu
捨てます

thumb oya-yubi
おやゆび

thunderstorm rai-u
雷雨

Thursday Moku·yōbi
木曜日

ticket ken
券
(for transport) kip·pu
切符

dialogue

a return to Sendai Sendai
made ōfuku-kip·p o
ichi-mai

coming back when? kaeri
wa itsu desu ka?

today/next Tuesday
kyō/tsugi no Kayōbi
desu

that will be 13,000 yen
ichi-man-san-zen-en ni
narimasu

ticket office kip·pu-uriba

切符売り場

tie (necktie) nek*u*tai
ネクタイ

tight (clothes etc) kitsui
きつい

it's too tight kitsu·sugimas*u*
きつすぎます

tights pantī–s*u*tok·king*u*
パンティーストッキ
ング

time* jikan
時間

what's the time? ima nanji
des*u* ka?
いま何時ですか？

this time konkai
今回

last time zenkai
前回

next time kondo
今度

three times san-kai
三回

timetable jikok*u*hyō
時刻表

tin (can) kan
缶

tin-opener kankiri
缶切り

tiny totemo chīsai
とてもちいさい

tip (to waiter etc) chip·p*u*
チップ

tired ts*u*kareta
つかれた

I'm tired ts*u*karemash*i*ta
つかれました

tissues tis·sh*u*
ティッシュ

to: to Tokyo/London Tōkyō/
Rondon e
東京／ロンドンへ

to Japan/Britain nip·pon/
Igiris*u* e
日本／イギリスへ

to the post office yūbin-
kyok*u* e
郵便局へ

toast (bread) tōs*u*to
トースト

today kyō
きょう

toe ts*u*masaki
つまさき

together is·sho ni
一緒に

we're together (in shop etc)
is·sho des*u*
一緒です

toilet toire
トイレ

where is the toilet? toire wa
doko des*u* ka?
トイレはどこです
か？

I have to go to the toilet
toire ni ikitai no
des*u* ga
トイレにいきたいの
ですが

toilet paper toiret·to-pēpā
トイレットペーパー

Tokyo Bay Tōkyō-wan
東京湾

tomato tomato
トマト

tomato ketchup kechap·pu
ケチャップ

tomorrow ashita
あした

tomorrow morning ashita no asa
あしたの朝

the day after tomorrow asat·te
あさって

tongue shita
舌

tonic (water) tonik·ku-uōtā
トニックウォーター

tonight komban
今晩

too (excessively) ... sugimasu
…すぎます

(also) mo
も

too hot atsu-sugimasu
あつすぎます

too much ōsugimasu
多すぎます

me too watashi mo
私も

tooth ha
歯

toothache haita

歯痛

toothbrush haburashi
歯ブラシ

toothpaste hamigakiko
歯みがき粉

top: on top of ... ... no ue ni
…の上に

at the top tep·pen ni
てっぺんに

top floor saijōkai
最上階

topless top·puresu
トップレス

torch kaichūdentō
懐中電灯

total gōkei
合計

tour (noun) tsuā
ツアー

is there a tour of ...? ... no tsuā ga arimasu ka?
…のツアーがありますか？

tour guide gaido
ガイド

tourist ryokōkyaku
旅行客

tourist information office kankō-an·naijo
観光案内所

towards ... ... no hō e
…のほうへ

towel taoru
タオル

town machi

町
in town machi de
町に
just out of town
machihazure
町はずれに
town centre hankagai
繁華街
toy omocha
おもちゃ
track (platform)
purat·to-hōmu
プラットホーム
which track is it for Nara?
Nara-iki wa dono
purat·to-hōmu desu ka?
奈良行きはどのプ
ラットホームですか？
tracksuit suet·t(o)-sūtsu
スエットスーツ
trade fair mihon-ichi
見本市
traditional dentō-teki (na)
伝統的（な）
traffic kōtsū
交通
traffic jam jūtai
渋滞
traffic lights shin·gō
信号
train densha
電車
by train densha de
電車で

dialogue

is this the train for Otaru?
kore wa Otaru-iki no
densha desu ka?
I am not sure sā, chot·to
wakarimasen
no, you want that platform
there īe, mukō no
purat·to-hōmu desu

trainers (shoes) sunīkā
スニーカー
train station eki
駅
tram romendensha
路面電車
translate hon·yaku shimasu
翻訳します
could you translate that?
sore o yaku shite
kuremasen ka?
それを訳してくれ
ませんか？
translation hon·yaku
翻訳
translator hon·yakusha
翻訳者
trash (waste) gomi
ごみ
trashcan gomibako
ごみ箱
travel ryokō shimasu
旅行します
we're travelling around

achikochi ryokō shite imasu

あちこち旅行して
います

travel agent's ryokōgaisha

旅行会社

traveller's cheque traberāzu–chek·ku

トラベラーズチェッ
ク

do you take traveller's cheques? traberāzu–chek·ku wa tsukaemasu ka?

トラベラーズチェッ
クはつかえますか？

tray obon

おぼん

tree ki

木

tremendous sugoi

すごい

trendy oshare (na)

おしゃれ（な）

trim: just a trim, please (to hairdresser) kesaki o soroeru teido ni onegai shimasu

毛先をそろえる程度
にお願いします

trip (excursion) kankōryokō

観光旅行

I'd like to go on a trip to ... ... o ryokō shite mitai desu

…を旅行してみたい
です

trolley (for luggage) nimotsu-yō

kāto

荷物用カート

trouble (noun) yak·kaigoto

やっかいごと

I'm having trouble with ... ... de komat·te imasu

…で困っています

trousers zubon

ズボン

true hontō (no)

ほんとう（の）

that's not true sore wa hontō ja arimasen

それはほんとうじゃ
ありません

trunk (US: of car) toranku

トランク

trunks (swimming) mizugi

水着

try (verb) tameshimasu

試します

can I try it? (food) ajimi shite mo ī desu ka?

味見してもいいです
か？

(at doing something) yat·te mite mo ī desu ka?

やってみてもいい
ですか？

try on shichaku shimasu

試着します

can I try it on? shichaku shite mo ī desu ka?

試着してもいいです
か？

T-shirt tī-shatsu
Tシャツ

Tuesday Kayōbi
火曜日

tuna maguro
まぐろ

tunnel ton·neru
トンネル

turn: turn left/right
hidari/migi e magat·te
kudasai
左／右へ曲がって
ください

turn off: where do I turn off?
doko de magarimasu ka?
どこで曲がります
か？

can you turn the heating off?
dambō o kit·te kuremasen
ka?
暖房を切ってくれ
ませんか？

turn on: can you turn the
heating on? dambō o
tsukete kuremasen ka?
暖房をつけてくれ
ませんか？

turning (in road) magarikado
曲り角

TV terebi
テレビ

tweezers kenuki
毛抜き

twice ni-kai
二回

twice as much ni-bai
二倍

twin beds tsuin-bed·do
ツインベッド

twin room tsuin
ツイン

twist: I've twisted my ankle
ashikubi o kujiite
shimaimashita
足首をくじいてし
まいました

type (noun) shurui
種類

another type of ... betsu no
shurui no ...
別の種類の…

typhoon taifū
台風

typical (dish etc) daihyō-teki
(na)
代表的（な）

tyre taiya
タイヤ

U

ugly minikui
みにくい

UK Igirisu
イギリス

ulcer kaiyō
かいよう

umbrella kasa
かさ

uncle (one's own) oji
おじ
(someone else's) oji-san
おじさん

unconscious muishiki (no)
無意識（の）

under (in position) … no shita ni
…のしたに
(less than) … ika
…以下

underdone (meat) namayake (no)
なまやけ（の）

underground (railway) chikatetsu
地下鉄

underpants pantsu
パンツ

understand: I understand
wakarimasu
わかります
I don't understand
wakarimasen
わかりません
do you understand?
wakarimasu ka?
わかりますか？

unemployed shitsugyō-chū
失業中

unfashionable ryūkō-okure (no)
流行おくれ（の）

United States Gas-shūkoku
合衆国

university daigaku
大学

unleaded petrol
muen-gasorin
無鉛ガソリン

unlimited mileage
sōkōkyori-museigen
走行距離無制限

unlock kagi o akemasu
かぎを開けます

unpack nihodoki shimasu
荷ほどきします

until: until 6 o'clock rokuji made
6時まで
until Saturday Doyōbi made
土曜日まで

unusual mezurashī
めずらしい

up ue ni
上に
up there asoko ni
あそこに
he's not up yet (not out of bed)
kare wa mada nete imasu
彼はまだ寝ています
what's up? (what's wrong?) dō ka shimashita ka?
どうかしましたか？

upmarket kōkyū (na)
高級（な）

upset stomach i no chōshi ga yoku nai
胃の調子がよくない
I have an upset stomach i no

chōshi ga yoku arimasen
胃の調子がよくあり
ません

upside down sakasama
さかさま

upstairs ue
上

up-to-date saishin (no)
最新（の）

urgent kinkyū (na)
緊急（な）

us* watashitachi (o)
私たち（を）

with us watashitachi to
私たちと

for us watashitachi no tame
ni
私たちのために

USA Amerika Gas·shūkoku
アメリカ合衆国

use (verb) tsukaimasu
つかいます

may I use ...? ... o tsukat·te
mo ī desu ka?
…をつかってもいい
ですか？

useful yaku ni tatsu
役にたつ

usual futsū (no)
ふつう（の）

the usual (drink etc) itsumono
いつもの

V

vacancy: do you have any
vacancies? (hotel) akibeya ga
arimas(u) ka?
空き部屋があります
か？

vacation yasumi
休み

on vacation yasumi de
休みで

vaccination yobōchūsha
予防注射

vacuum cleaner sōjiki
そうじ機

valid (ticket etc) yūkō (na)
有効（な）

how long is it valid for?
yūkōkikan wa dono kurai
des(u) ka?
有効期間はどの
くらいですか？

valley tani
たに

valuable (adj) kichō (na)
貴重（な）

can I leave my valuables
here? kichō-hin o
koko ni azukeraremasu
ka?
貴重品をここに
預られますか？

value (noun) kachi
価値

van ban
バン

vanilla banira
バニラ

a vanilla ice cream
banira-aisukurīmu
バニラアイスクリー
ム

vary: it varies bāi ni
yorimasu
場合によります

vase kabin
花びん

veal koushi no niku
仔牛の肉

vegetables yasai
野菜

vegetarian (noun)
saishoku-shugisha
菜食主義者

vending machine jidō-ham-
baiki
自動販売機

very totemo
とても

very little for me hon·no
sukoshi dake
ほんのすこしだけ

I like it very much totemo
suki desu
とても好きです

via keiyu de
経由で

video (noun: film) bideo-tēpu
ビデオテープ

(recorder) bideo-kamera
ビデオカメラ

view nagame
ながめ

village mura
村

vinegar su
酢

visa biza
ビザ

visit (verb) tazunemasu
訪ねます

I'd like to visit ... ... o
tazunetai desu
…を訪ねたいです

vital: it's vital that ... ... wa
totemo taisetsu desu
…はとてもたいせつ
です

vodka uok·ka
ウォッカ

voice koe
こえ

volcano kazan
火山

voltage den·atsu
電圧

vomit hakimasu
吐きます

W

waist uesto
ウェスト

waistcoat besto
ベスト

wait machimasu
待ちます

wait for me mat·te kudasai
待ってください

don't wait for me matanaide kudasai
待たないでください

can I wait until my wife gets here? tsuma ga kuru made mat·te mo ī desu ka?
妻が来るまで待ってもいいですか？

can you do it while I wait? mat·te iru aida ni yat·te kuremasen ka?
待っているあいだにやってくれませんか？

could you wait here for me? koko de chot·to mat·te ite kuremasen ka?
ここでちょっと待っていてくれませんか？

waiter uētā
ウェイター

waiter! chot·to sumimasen!
ちょっとすみません！

waitress uētoresu
ウェートレス

waitress! chot·to sumimasen!
ちょっとすみません！

wake: can you wake me up at 5.30? goji-han ni okoshite kuremasen ka?
５時半に起こしてくれませんか？

wake-up call mōningu-kōru
モーニングコール

Wales Uēruzu
ウェールズ

walk: is it a long walk? arukuto tōi desu ka?
歩くととおいですか？

it's only a short walk aruite sugu desu
歩いてすぐです

I'll walk aruite ikimasu
歩いていきます

I'm going for a walk sampo ni dekakemasu
散歩にでかけます

wall kabe
かべ

wallet saifu
さいふ

want: I want a ... ... ga hoshī desu
…が欲しいです

I don't want any ... ... wa irimasen
…はいりません

I want to go home uchi ni kaeritai desu
うちに帰りたいです

I don't want to sō shitaku nai desu

そうしたくないです

he wants to ... kare wa ...-tai desu

彼は…―たいです

what do you want? nani ga hoshī desu ka?

何が欲しいですか？

ward (in hospital) byōtō

病棟

warm atatakai

あたたかい

I'm so warm atsui desu

あついです

was* ... deshita

…でした

wash (verb) araimasu

洗います

can you wash these? kore o arat·te kuremasen ka?

これを洗ってくれ
ませんか？

washhand basin sem·mendai

洗面台

washing (clothes) sentakumono

せんたくもの

washing machine sentak·ki

せんたく機

washing powder senzai

洗剤

washing-up: to do the washing-up shok·ki o araimasu

食器を洗います

washing-up liquid shok·ki-yō senzai

食器用洗剤

wasp hachi

ハチ

watch (wristwatch) udedokei

腕時計

will you watch my things for me? watashi no nimotsu o mite ite kuremasen ka?

私の荷物を見ていて
くれませんか？

watch out! abunai!

あぶない！

watch strap tokei no bando

時計のバンド

water mizu

水

may I have some water? mizu o moraemasu ka?

水をもらえますか？

waterproof (adj) bōsui (no)

防水（の）

waterskiing suijō-sukī

水上スキー

way: it's this way kot·chi no hō desu

こっちのほうです

it's that way at·chi no hō desu

あっちのほうです

is it a long way to ...? ... made tōi desu ka?

…までとおいですか？

no way! dame des*u*!
だめです！

dialogue

> could you tell me the way
> to ...? ... ewa dō ikeba ī
> des*u* ka?
> go straight on until you
> reach the traffic lights
> shin·go ni ikiataru made
> mas·sug*u* des*u*
> turn left hidari e magat·te
> kudasai
> take the first on the right
> saisho no magarikado o
> migi ni magat·te kudasai

we* watashitachi
私たち
weak yowai
よわい
(tea) usui
うすい
weather tenki
天気

dialogue

> what's the weather
> forecast? tenkiyohō wa
> dō des*u* ka?
> it's going to be fine hareru
> yō des*u*
> it's going to rain ame ni

naru yō des*u*
it'll brighten up later ato
de hareru yō des*u*

wedding kek·kon-shiki
結婚式
wedding ring
kek·kon-yubiwa
結婚指輪
Wednesday Suiyōbi
水曜日
week (one, two, three etc) shūkan
週間
(this, last, next etc) shū
週
a week (from) today raishū
no kyō
来週のきょう
a week (from) tomorrow
raishū no ashita
来週のあした
weekend shūmats*u*
週末
at the weekend shūmats*u* ni
週末に
weight omosa
おもさ
weird hen (na)
へん（な）
weirdo henjin
変人
welcome: welcome to ... ... e
yōkoso
…へようこそ
you're welcome (don't

mention it) dō itashimash*i*te

どういたしまして

well: I don't feel well kibun ga yok*u* arimasen

気分がよくあり
ません

she's not well kanojo wa byōki des*u*

彼女は病気です

you speak English very well Eigo ga totemo jōz*u* des*u* ne

英語がとてもじょう
ずですね

well done! sugoi!

すごい！

this one as well kore mo des*u*

これもです

well well! (surprise) oya oya!

おやおや！

dialogue

> **how are you?** gokigen ikaga des*u* ka?
> **very well, thanks, and you?** hai, okagesama des*u* ga, sochira wa?

well-done (meat) uerudan

ウェルダン

Welsh (adj) Uēruz*u* (no)

ウェールズ

I'm Welsh watashi wa

Uēruz*u*-jin des*u*

私はウェールズ人
です

were* … desh*i*ta

…でした

West: the West Ōbei

欧米

west nishi

西

in the west nishi ni

西に

Western Ōbei (no)

欧米（の）

Westerner Ōbei-jin

欧米人

Western-style yōfū (no)

洋風（の）

wet nureta

ぬれた

whale kujira

くじら

what? nan des*u* ka?

なんですか？

what's that? sore wa nan des*u* ka?

それは何ですか？

what's happening? nani ga arundes*u* ka?

何があるんですか？

(**what's on?**) nani o yat·te imas*u* ka?

何をやっています
か？

(**what's wrong?**) dō shitandes*u* ka?

どうしたんですか？
what should I do? dō shitara ī deshō ka?

どうしたらいいでしょうか？
what a view! ī nagame desu ne!

いいながめですね！
what bus do I take? dono basu ni noreba ī desu ka?

どのバスに乗ればいいですか？

wheel sharin
車輪

wheelchair kuruma-isu
車いす

when? itsu?
いつ？

when we get back kaet·te kara
帰ってから

when's the train/ferry? res·sha/ferī wa nanji desu ka?
列車／フェリーは何時ですか？

where? doko?
どこ？

I don't know where it is doko daka shirimasen
どこだか知りません

dialogue

where is the railway station? eki wa doko desu ka?

it's over there mukō desu

could you show me where it is on the map? chizu de doko daka oshiete kuremasen ka?

it's just here koko desu

see way

which: which bus? dono basu?
どのバス？

dialogue

which one? dore?

that one? sore desu

this one? kore?

no, that one īe, sore desu

while: while I'm here koko ni iru aida ni
ここにいるあいだに

whisky uisukī
ウィスキー

white shiroi
しろい

white wine shiro-wain
白ワイン

who? dare?
だれ？

who is it? donata desu ka?
どなたですか？

the man who ... ... hito
…ひと

whole: the whole week maru is·shūkan

まる一週間

the whole lot zembu

ぜんぶ

whose: whose is this? kore wa dare no desu ka?

これはだれので
すか？

why? dōshite desu ka?

どうしてですか？

why not? dōshite desu ka?

どうしてですか？

wide hiroi

ひろい

wife (one's own) tsuma

妻

(someone else's) oku-san

奥さん

my wife watashi no tsuma

私の妻

will*: will you do it for me? sō shite kuremasen ka?

そうしてくれません
か？

wind (noun) kaze

風

window mado

まど

near the window mado no soba de

まどのそばで

in the window (of shop) shōuindō ni

ショーウィンドーに

window seat madogawa no seki

窓側の席

windscreen furonto-garasu

フロントガラス

windscreen wiper waipā

ワイパー

windsurfing uindosāfin

ウィンドサーフィン

windy: it's so windy kaze ga tsuyoi desu

風がつよいです

wine wain

ワイン

can we have some more wine? wain o mō sukoshi moraemasu ka?

ワインをもうすこし
もらえますか？

wine list wain no risuto

ワインのリスト

winter fuyu

冬

in the winter fuyu ni

冬に

wire waiyā

ワイヤー

(electric) kōdo

コード

with ... to is·sho ni

…と一緒に

I'm staying with ... ... no tokoro ni tomat·te imasu

…のところに泊まっ
ています

without nashi de
なしで

witness shōnin
証人

will you be a witness for me?
watashi no shōnin ni nat·te
kuremasen ka?
私の証人になってく
れませんか？

woman josei
女性

wonderful subarashī
すばらしい

won't*: it won't start dō shite
mo stāto shimasen
どうしてもスタート
しません

wood (material) zaimoku
材木

woods (forest) mori
森

wool ūru
ウール

word kotoba
ことば

work (noun) shigoto
仕事

it's not working ugokimasen
動きません

I work in ... ... de hataraite
imasu
…で働いています

world sekai
世界

worry: I'm worried shimpai

desu
心配です

worse: it's worse nao warui
desu
なおわるいです

worst sai-ak (no)
最悪（の）

worth: is it worth a visit? it·te
miru kachi ga arimasu ka?
行って見る価値が
ありますか？

**would: would you give this to
...?** kore o ... ni watashite
kuremasen ka?
これを…にわたし
てくれませんか？

wrap: could you wrap it up?
tsutsunde kuremasen ka?
包んでくれませんか？

wrapping paper hōsōshi
包装紙

wrestler resurā
レスラー

sumo wrestler rikishi
力士

wrestling resuringu
レスリング

sumo wrestling sumō
すもう

wrist tekubi
手首

write kakimasu
書きます

could you write it down?
kaite kuremasen ka?

書いてくれませんか？
how do you write it? dō kakimasu ka?
どう書きますか？
writing paper binsen
びんせん
wrong: it's the wrong key kagi ga aimasen
かぎが合いません
this is the wrong train kore wa chigau densha desu
これはちがう電車です
the bill's wrong okanjō ga machigat·te imasu
お勘定がまちがっています
sorry, wrong number sumimasen, ban·gō o machigaemashita
すみません、番号をまちがえました
sorry, wrong room sumimasen, heya o machigaemashita
すみません、部屋をまちがえました
there's something wrong with ... ... wa doko ka okashī desu
…はどこかおかしいです
what's wrong? dō ka shimashita ka?
どうかしましたか？

X

X-ray rentogen
レントゲン

Y

yacht yot·to
ヨット
yard yādo
ヤード
year toshi
年
yellow kīroi
きいろい
yen en
円
yes hai
はい
yesterday kinō
きのう
yesterday morning kinō no asa
きのうの朝
the day before yesterday ototoi
おととい
yet mada
まだ

dialogue

is it here yet? mō tsukimashita ka?

no, not yet īe, mada des*u*
**you'll have to wait a little
longer yet** mō shibarak*u*
kakarimas

yoghurt yōgur*u*to
ヨーグルト
you* (sing) anata
あなた
(pl) anatatachi
あなたたち
this is for you kore wa anata
ni agemas
これはあなたに
あげます
with you anata to is·sho ni
あなたと一緒に
young wakai
わかい
your(s)* (sing) anata no
あなたの
(pl) anatatachi no
あなたたちの
youth hostel yūs*u*–hosteru
ユースホステル

Z

Zen Buddhism Zen
禅
Zen garden Zentei
禅庭
Zen priest Zensō
禅僧

Zen sect Zenshū
禅宗
Zen temple Zendera
禅寺
zero zero
ゼロ
zip fas*u*nā
ファスナー
could you put a new zip on?
atarashī fas*u*nā ni kaete
kuremasen ka?
あたらしいファス
ナーに替えてくれま
せんか？
zip code yūbimban·gō
郵便番号
zoo dōbutsu·en
動物園

Zo

175

Japanese

→

English

Colloquialisms

The following are words you may well hear. You shouldn't be tempted to use any of the stronger ones unless you are sure of your audience.

aho! fool!
baka! you fool!, stupid bastard!
bakamitai stupid
bakayarō! damn fool!
bijin beautiful woman
charinko bicycle
chikushō! damn!, hell! (literally: beast)
chot·to! hey!
damare! shut up!
dōmo thanks; hi
gaijin foreigner
ja nē bye, cheerio
kak·ko ī trendy; cool; handsome
kireru blow one's top
konoyarō! damn fool!
kuso! shit!
maji de honestly; really
mansatsu ten-thousand yen note
mashi better
meshi meal
shinjiran·nai unbelievable
subarashī! fantastic!
sugoi! great!, super!; well done!
tondemo nai! no way!
urusai! shut up!
uso! that's a lie!
usotsuki! liar!
yada! no!; yuk!
yokat·ta! good!

A

abek·ku lovers, a couple
abunai dangerous
at·chi e it·te! go away!
agemasu to give
ago chin; jaw
aibeya ni narimasu to share (room)
aimasu to meet
aiseki shimasu to share (table)
aji taste; flavour
Ajia Asia
Ajia (no) Asian
akachan baby
akai red
akemasu to open
akemashite omedetō goza-imasu! Happy New Year!
aki autumn, (US) fall
akiraka (na) clear, obvious
akuseru accelerator
amai sweet (taste)
amari not very much
  amari ōku nai not many
ame candies, sweets; rain
Amerika Gas·shūkoku USA
ana hole
anata (ga) you (sing)
anata no your; yours
anata o you (sing)
anata wa you (sing)
  anata wa ... desu you are
anatatachi (ga) you (pl)
anatatachi no your; yours (pl)
anatatachi o you (pl)
anatatachi wa you (pl)
ane sister (one's own: older)

ani brother (one's own: older)
an·naisho information desk
ano that; those (further away)
anzen (na) safe
aoi blue
apāto apartment, flat
araimasu to wash
arashi storm
aratamat·ta formal
are that; that one; those (further away)
arigatō thank you, thanks
arimasen: sore ja arimasen not that one
  ... ga arimasen no ...
aruite walk; on foot
arukōru alcohol
arukōru-nuki (no) non-alco-holic
asa morning
asat·te the day after tomor-row
asayū-nishoku-tsuki half board
ashi leg; foot
ashikubi ankle
ashita tomorrow
ashita no asa tomorrow morning
ashita no gogo tomorrow afternoon
asobiba playground
asoko ni up there; over there
as·sat·te the day after tomorrow
atama head
atama ga ī intelligent
atamakin deposit (as part pay-ment)

atarashī new

atatakai warm; mild

at·chi: at·chi e it·te! go away!
at·chi no hō desu it's that
  way

ato de after; afterwards, later,
  later on

atsumemasu to collect

atsui thick; hot

azayaka (na) bright

B

baka (na) silly; stupid
  baka! you fool!

bakageta ridiculous

bak·kin fine (punishment)

ban van

ban·gō number

ban·gō o machigaemashita
  wrong number

ban·gumi programme

bansōkō plasters, Bandaid®

basu-ryokō coach trip

basu-tāminaru coach station,
  bus station

basu-tei bus stop

basu-tsuki no heya with a
  private bathroom

bed·do bed (Western-style)

ben·goshi lawyer

benri (na) convenient

beruto belt

besuto waistcoat

betsubetsu (no) separate

betsu no another, different

bijinesu-hoteru business hotel

bijutsu art

bijutsu-kan art gallery

bimbō poor

bim·mei flight number

bin jar; bottle

binīru-bukuro carrier bag,
  plastic bag

binsen writing pad

biru building

bīru beer

biyōin hairdresser's (women's)

biza visa

bochi cemetery

bōi porter (in hotel)

boku (ga) I (fam, m)

boku no my; mine (fam, m)

boku o me (fam, m)

bokushi priest (Christian)

boku wa I (fam, m)

bon·net·to bonnet, (US)
  hood

bōru ball

bōrupen ballpoint pen

bōshi cap, hat

bōto boat

brajā bra

bubun part, bit
  ōkī bubun a big bit

buchō director, head of
  department

budō martial arts

Buk·kyō Buddhism

Buk·kyō (no) Buddhist

Buk·kyōto Buddhist

bunraku traditional puppet
  theatre

butsudan house altar

byō second (of time)

byōbu screen

byōin hospital

byōki illness; disease
byōki (no) sick, ill
byōtō ward

C

cha-iro (no) brown
-chan diminutive suffix added to child's name or familiar suffix used between friends and family
chanto properly
chawan bowl (porcelain)
chek·ku-in shimasu to check in
chibusa breast
chichi father (one's own)
chigai difference
chigau different
chihō region, district
chikai near, nearby
chikatetsu underground, (US) subway
chīki area
chīmu team
chip·pu tip
chirashi leaflet
chīsai small
chizu map
chō area
chōdo koko de right here
chōka-tenimotsu excess baggage
chokusetsu (no) direct
chokutsū direct
chōkyori-basu coach, bus
chōkyori-denwa long-distance call

chōme area of a few square blocks
chōshi ga okashī faulty
chōshoku breakfast
chōshoku-tsuki yado bed and breakfast
chot·to! hey!
   chot·to mat·te kudasai! just a minute!
   chot·to sumimasen! excuse me!
Chūgoku China
Chūgoku (no) Chinese
chūibukai careful
chūko (no) second-hand
chūkurai (no) medium, medium-sized
chūmon order
chūmon shimasu to order
chūsha injection
chūshajō car park, parking lot
chūshin centre
chūshoku lunch
   chūshoku-go after lunch

D

daburu double; double room; double whisky
-dai classifier for machines, cars, bikes and stereos
daidokoro kitchen
daigaku college; university
daihyō representative
daihyō-teki (na) typical
daijōbu all right, OK; no problem
daisuki desu to love

daitai roughly, approximately

daitōryō president (of country)

daiyaru shimas*u* to dial

dake only, just

dambō heater, heating

dame! don't!

dame des*u*! certainly not!

sore wa dame des*u* it's no good

dandan gradually

dansei men

dansei-yō toire gents' toilet, men's room

dantai party, group

dare? who?

dare ka anybody; somebody, someone

dare mo ...-masen nobody, no-one; none

das·shimen cotton wool, absorbent cotton

de by, by means of; with; at; on; in

deguchi exit, way out

dekakemas*u* to go away

dekimas can

dekimasen cannot

dekireba hopefully

dekirudake ... as ... as possible

dekirudake hayak*u* as soon as possible

demo but; even the

... demo ... demo nai neither ... nor ...

den·ats*u* voltage

denchi battery

den·gon message

denki electricity; light

denki (no) electric

denki-kamisori shaver

denki-kamisori-yō konsento shaving point

denki-seihin electrical appliances

denki-ya electrician; electrical goods shop

denkyū light bulb

densensei (no) infectious

densha train

denshi-renji microwave (oven)

dentō-teki (na) traditional

denwa telephone, phone

denwaban·gō phone number

denwaban·gō-an·nai directory enquiries

denwachō phone book

denwa shimas*u* to call, to phone

depāto department store

des*u* be; am; is; are; it is

anata wa ... des*u* you are ...

watashi wa ... des*u* I am ...

... des*u* ka? is it ...?

desh*i*ta were; was; it was

dewa mata see you again

dīzeru-sha diesel

do degree

dō? how?

dō shimash*i*ta ka? what's the matter?

dō itashimash*i*te don't mention it, you're welcome

doa door

doabōi doorman

dōbuts*u* animal

dōbuts*u*-en zoo

dochira which; who
  dochira demo nai neither (one) of them
dochiraka either of them
dochira-sama des*u* ka? who's calling?
Doits*u* Germany
Doits*u* (no) German
dōkan des*u* I agree; all right
dōka yamete kudasai please don't
doko? where?
  doko des*u* ka? where is it?
doko demo everywhere; anywhere
doko ka somewhere
doku*shin* single, not married
dōmo thanks; hi
  dōmo arigatō thanks
  dōmo sumimasen sorry
dono? which?
dore? which one?
dore mo …-masen none
doro mud
dorobō thief
dōrochizu road map; streetmap
dōshite des ka? why?; why not?
Doyōbi Saturday
dōzo I don't mind, please go ahead; here you are
  dōzo osaki ni after you
  dōzo yoroshik*u* pleased to meet you

E

e to; towards; until; painting, picture; drawing
ē yes
ehagaki postcard
eiga film, movie
eigakan cinema, movie theater
Eigo English (language)
  Eigo de in English
eigyō-chū open
eigyōjikan opening times
Eikok*u* Britain
Eikok*u* (no) British
eizu AIDS
eki train station
empits*u* pencil
em-saiz*u* medium
en circle; yen
erabimas*u* to choose
erebētā lift, elevator
eri collar
eru-saiz large
eya-kon air-conditioning

F

fak·kus*u* fax
fak·kus*u* o okurimas*u* to fax
fas*u*nā zip
Frans*u* (no) French
Frans*u*-go French (language)
f*u*ronto reception desk (in hotel)
f*u*ronto-gakari receptionist (in hotel)

furonto-garas**u** windscreen
fu city
fuben (na) inconvenient
fūfu married couple
fujinfuku-uriba ladies' wear
fukai deep
fukanō(na) impossible
fukin tea towel
Fuk·katsu·sai Easter
fukumimasu to include
fukutsū stomachache
fukuro bag, paper bag
fūmi flavour
fumoto bottom
fun minute
fune boat, ship
funsui fountain (ornamental)
furui old; stale
fusuma sliding door (patterned)
futa cap; lid
futatsu two; a couple
fūtō envelope
futon mattress; bedding
futot·ta fat
futsuka two days
futsukayoi hangover
futsū local intercity train
futsū(no) ordinary, usual
fuyu winter
fuyukai (na) unpleasant

G

ga subject particle that emphasizes the subject
... ga arimasu there is ...; there are ...

... ga arimasen no ...; there's no ...; there are no ...
gaido guide
gaijin foreigner
gaikoku abroad
gaikoku (no) foreign
gaikoku-go foreign language
gaikoku-jin foreigner
gaishutsu shimasu to go out
gaku amount
gake cliff
gak·kari shita disappointed
gak·ki term (at university, school)
gak·kō school
gakusei student
Gantan New Year's Day
garakuta rubbish
garasu glass
gasorin petrol, (US) gas
gasorin-sutando petrol station, (US) gas station
geijutsu-ka artist
gekijō theatre
genkan doorway, entrance, porch
genki? how are you?
 genki de ne take care, bye, see you
genkin cash
genkin-jidō-shiharaiki cash dispenser, ATM
genkin ni kaemasu to cash
genzō film processing
genzo shimasu to develop
geta wooden sandals
gēto gate (at airport)
getsu month (this, last, next etc)

Gets*u*yōbi Monday
gezai laxative
gin silver
ginkō bank (money)
giri no imōto sister-in-law (one's own: younger)
giri no mus*u*ko son-in-law (one's own)
giri no musume daughter-in-law (one's own)
giri no okā-san mother-in-law (someone else's)
giri no onē-san sister-in-law (someone else's: older)
giri no onī-san brother-in-law (someone else's: older)
giri no otō-san father-in-law (someone else's)
giri no otōto brother-in-law (one's own: younger)
go five
go- polite prefix
-go after
gochisō-sama desh*i*ta it was delicious (literally: it was a feast)
gogak*u*-kōs*u* language course
Gogats*u* May
gogo afternoon, pm
　kyōno gogo ni this afternoon
go-hyak*u* five hundred
go-jū fifty
gojūsho address
　gojūsho wa? what's your address?
gōkei total
gokigen: gokigen ikaga des*u*

ka? how are you?
　gokigen·yō! have a nice day!
gom*u* rubber (material)
gomen·nasai excuse me, sorry
gomi rubbish, trash; waste
gomibako bin; dustbin, trashcan
goro about, approximately
goryōshin parents (someone else's)
goshujin husband (someone else's)
gozen am
　gozen shichiji ni at 7am
gun county
gurīnsha first-class carriage
gurīnsha-jōshaken first-class train ticket
gyōrets*u* queue

H

ha tooth
haburashi toothbrush
hachi eight; wasp
Hachigats*u* August
hachi-jū eighty
hae fly
haguki gum (in mouth)
haha mother (one's own)
hai yes; lungs
-hai classifier meaning glassful or cupful
hai-iro (no) grey
hai-ok*u* unleaded petrol
hairimas*u* to come in
haisha dentist

haita toothache
haitatsu delivery
haitatsu shimasu to deliver
haizara ashtray
hajimarimasu to begin
hajime beginning
hajimemasu to start
hajimemashite how do you do?, pleased to meet you
hajimete the first time
hakubutsukan museum
hakike nausea
hako box
hamabe beach
hamaki cigar
hambun half
hamigakiko toothpaste
hana nose; flower
hanabi fireworks
hanashi-chū engaged, (US) occupied
hanashimasu to speak; to talk
hana-ya florist's
han-dāsu (no) half a dozen
handobag·gu bag, handbag, (US) purse
hanemasu to knock over
hangaku half fare
hangaku (no) half-price
hanjikan half an hour
hankagai city centre, downtown
hanko personal seal
han·nama (na) not cooked
han·rit·toru half a litre
hantai opposite
to hantai (no) against,

opposed to
hap-pyaku eight hundred
harai-modoshi refund
hareta fine (weather); swollen
harete imasu it's sunny; it's swollen
hari needle
haru spring
hasami scissors
hashi bridge (over river); chopsticks
hashirimasu to run
hata flag
hatake field
hayai fast, quick; early
hayaku quickly
hei fence
heikin-teki average (not good)
hempi (na) secluded
hen (na) weird, strange, odd
heya accommodation; room
hi fire; day
hidari left
 hidari e to the left
 hidari ni on the left
hidari-kiki (no) left-handed
hidoi bad; dreadful; nasty
hidoku badly
hifu skin
higaeri-ryokō day trip
higashi east
hiji elbow
hijōguchi fire escape; emergency exit
hikage shade
hikari light
-hiki classifier for animals
hikidashi drawer
hikimasu to pull; to play

(instrument)
hikinobashi enlargement
hik·kuri kaeshimasu to knock over
hikō flight
hikōki plane, airplane
hikui low
himo string
hinata sun
hi ni yaketa suntanned
hinshitsu quality
hiraita open
hiroba square
hiroi wide
hīru heel (of shoe)
hisho secretary
hitai forehead
hito person; people
hito-ban ni tsuki per night
hitogomi crowd
hito-hako packet
hito-kire piece
hito-kumi pair
hito-pak·ku pack
hitori alone
hitotsu piece; one
  hitotsu mo ...-masen no
  mō hitotsu another, one more
hitotsu (no) a, an
hitsuyō (na) necessary, essential
hiyake tan, suntan; sunburn
hiyake-dome sunblock
hiyake shimasu to get a tan
hiyo ga kakarimasu to cost
hiza knee
hō cheek (on face)
hodō pavement, sidewalk

hodo ... nai less ...than
hohoemimasu to smile
hoka the rest
hoka hoka bentō lunch box shop
hoka ni nani ka something else, anything else
hoka niwa nai desu nothing else
hoka no other
hoken insurance
hōki brush
hōkō direction
hokori dust
hokusei northwest
hokutō northeast
hom·mono (no) real, genuine
homo (no) gay
hon book
-hon classfier for pens, cigarettes and other cylindrical objects
hone bone
hone ga oreta broken
hon no sukoshi just a little
hontō (ni) really
  hontōdesu ka? really?
hontō(no) true
hon·ya bookshop, bookstore
hon·yaku translation
hon·yaku shimasu to translate
honyūbin baby's bottle
hōritsu law
hōseki jewellery
hōseki-ten jeweller's
hoshi star
hoshīdesu to want
hoshō guarantee

HO

hoshōkin deposit
hōsōshi wrapping paper
hos·sa fit, attack
hōtai bandage; dressing
hoteru hotel
hoteru no heya hotel room
hotoke-sama Buddha
hotondo almost, nearly
hotondo ...-masen hardly
hyaku hundred
hyaku man million
hyōshiki sign

ī good
 ī desu that's good; that's
 fine
ichi one
ichiba market
ichiban suki (na) favourite
ichi-dāsu (no) dozen
Ichigatsu January
ichinichi-jū all day
ichiryū (no) excellent
ie house
īe no
igai dewa apart from
igai wa except
Igirisu Britain
Igirisu (no) British
Igirisu-jin British person
Igirisu-pondo sterling
ijō over, more than
 sore ijō more than that
ika less than, under
ikebana flower arrangement
iki-iki shita lively

ikikata route
ikimasu to go
ikimashō! let's go!
ikitai desu I'd like to
ik·kai ground floor, (US) first
 floor; once
ik·kaibun dose
ikura desu ka? how much is
 it?
ikutsu? how many?; how
 old?
ikutsuka (no) several
ima now; just, only just
 ima wa dame desu not just
 now
 ima nanji desu ka? what
 time is it?
imamade ni ever
īmasu to say; to call
ī-meiru e-mail
imōto sister (one's own:
 younger)
inaka country; countryside
Indo (no) Indian
inryōsui drinking water
intāchenji interchange (on
 motorway)
inu dog
ip·pai full; a glass of
ip·pai ni shimasu to fill up
ip·paku (no) overnight
ip·pan-teki (na) general
iraira suru annoying
iras·shaimase may I help
 you
ireba dentures
iriguchi entrance, way in
iro colour
iseki ruins

isha doctor
ishi stone, rock
isogashī busy
isogimasu to hurry
is·sho ni together
  ... to is·sho ni with ...
is·soku pair; pair of
  shoes/socks
isu chair
Isuramukyo (no) Muslim
itadakimasu! enjoy your
  meal!, bon appetit!
itai hurt; painful
itai desu it's sore
itami pain, ache
itamidome painkillers
itamimasu to hurt
Itaria Italy
Itaria (no) Italian
ito thread
itoko cousin
itsuka fifth
itsumo always
itsu? when?
itsutsu five
it·tan ...-tara once, as soon as
iwa rock
iya (na) disgusting, nasty
izaka-ya pub

J

ja well
jaguchi tap, faucet
jama shimasu to disturb
ja mata see you later
jā ne bye, cheerio
ji o'clock

jibun de myself; by myself
jidō automatic
jidō-hambaiki vending
  machine
jidōsha-hoken green card (car
  insurance)
jikan time; hour
jiko accident
jikokuhyō timetable, (US)
  schedule
jimen ground
jimoto no local
jimusho office
jinja shrine
jishin earthquake
jitensha bicycle, bike
jitensha-okiba bicycle park
jōdan joke
jōhin (na) posh
jōhō information
jōkyaku passenger
josei woman; lady
jū ten; gun; rifle
jūbun enough
jūdai (na) serious
Jūgatsu October
jū-go fifteen
jugyō lesson
jū-hachi eighteen
jū-ichi eleven
Jūichigatsu November
jūjiro crossroads, intersection
jukushita ripe
jū-kyū nineteen
jū-ni twelve
Jūnigatsu December
jū-roku sixteen
jū-san thirteen
jū-shichi seventeen

jūsho address
jūshoroku address book
jūtai traffic jam
jūtan carpet
jū-yon fourteen

K

ka mosquito
  ... ka ... ka either ... or ...
ka? question particle
kaban bag
kabe wall
kabin vase
kachō section chief
kādo card
kādo-denwa cardphone
kaerimasu to go back, to return
kaeshimasu to give back
kagu furniture
kagami mirror
kagetsu month (one, two, three etc)
kagi key; lock
kagi o akemasu to unlock
kago basket
kai floor, storey
kaichūdentō torch
kaidan steps, stairs
kaigan coast
kaigi meeting (business); conference
kaigishitsu conference room
kaikaishiki opening ceremony
kaikei cash desk
kaimasu to buy

kaisha company, business
kaisoku local train with limited stops
kaji fire (blaze)
kakebuton duvet
kakejiku scroll (hanging)
kakemasu to switch on (engine); to play (music)
kakimasu to write
kakitome-yūbin de by registered mail
kakunin shimasu to confirm
kamban sign
kamera-ya camera shop
kami paper; hair
kami-omutsu disposable nappies/diapers
kami-sama God
kamisori razor
kampai! cheers!
kampeki (na) perfect
kanari fairly, pretty, quite; a bit
  kanari takusan quite a lot
kanari (no) fair (amount)
kanashī sad
kanemochi (no) rich (person)
kan·gae idea
kan·gaemasu to think
kan·geikai reception (for guests)
kan·gofu nurse (woman)
kan·goshi nurse (man)
kanji character (written); Chinese character
kanjimasu to feel
kankiri can-opener, tin-opener
kankō-an·naijo tourist infor-

mation office
Kankoku South Korea
Kankoku (no) Korean
kankōryokō trip, excursion, sightseeing tour
kan·nushi Shinto priest
kanō(na) possible
kanojo (ga) she
kanojo no her; hers
kanojo o her
kanojo wa she
kanojotachi (ga) they (f)
kanojotachi no their; theirs (f)
kanojotachi o them (f)
kanojotachi wa they (f)
kanpai! cheers!
kanrishoku executive
kansen infection
kansha (no) grateful
kantan (na) simple, easy
kanzen ni completely
kanzō liver (in body)
kanzume can
kao face
kap·pu cup
kap·puru couple
kara from; since
kara (no) empty
karada body
karada ni ī healthy
karai hot, spicy
kare he
kare ga he
kare no his
kare o him
kare wa he
karera (ga) they (m)
karera no their; theirs (m)

karera o them (m)
karera wa they (m)
karimasu to rent, to hire; to borrow
karui light (not heavy)
kasa umbrella
kashimasu to lend
kashikoi clever
kashu singer; pop singer
kata shoulder
katahō one end; one side
katai hard
katamichi-kip·pu single ticket, one-way ticket
kat·to cut
kawa leather; river
kawaita dry
kawari ni instead
kawase-tegata banker's draft
kawat·ta odd, strange, peculiar
Kayōbi Tuesday
kazan volcano
kaze wind
kazoku family
kazu number, figure
kega o shita injured
keiba race (for horses)
keieisha manager (in business)
keikan policeman
keisatsu police
keisatsu-sho police station
keitai-denwa mobile phone
keiyaku contract
keiyu stopover
keiyu de via
kek·kō desu all right, fine
īe kek·kō desu no thanks
kek·kon marriage

kek·kon shita married
kek·kon shite imasu I'm married
kek·kon shite imasu ka? are you married?
kek·kon-kinen-bi wedding anniversary
kek·kon-shiki wedding
kek·kon-yubiwa wedding ring
kek·kyoku after all
kemuri smoke
ken ticket; prefecture
kendō Japanese fencing
ken·eki quarantine
kenka fight
kenkō (na) healthy
keredomo although
kesa this morning
keshiki scenery
keshimasu to switch off
keshō make-up
keshōhin cosmetics
keshōshitsu ladies' toilets, ladies' room
kes·shite ...-masen never
ketsu·eki blood
kewashī steep
ki tree; mind; heart
kibako wooden box
kibō hope
kibun feeling
kichō(na) valuable
kiete iru off (lights)
kigaemasu to get changed
kiji material (fabric)
kikai machine
kikan period (of time)
kiken (na) risky

kikimasu to listen
kikoemasu to hear
kimasu to come
kimemasu to decide
kimi (ga) you (sing, fam)
kimi no your; yours (sing, fam)
kimi o you (sing, fam)
kimi wa you (sing, fam)
kimochi no ī pleasant
kimono kimono; Japanese clothes
kimpatsu (no) blond
kin gold
kinen-hi monument
kin·en-koshitsu nonsmoking compartment
kin·gyo goldfish
kinkyū emergency
kinkyū (na) urgent
kinō yesterday
kinō no asa yesterday morning
kinu silk
Kin·yōbi Friday
kinyūshimasu to fill in
kinzoku metal
kion temperature (weather)
ki o tsukete! look out!
kip·pu ticket
kip·pu-uriba box office; ticket office
kirai desu hate
kirei (na) beautiful; pretty; nice; clean
kirei ni shimasu to clean up
kiri mist, fog
kirimasu to cut
kīroi yellow

kis*u* kiss
kishibe shore (of lake)
kis·sa-ten teahouse; café
kis shimas*u* to kiss
kita north
Kita-Chōsen North Korea
kitai hazure (no) disappoint-
    ing
kitai shimas*u* to look for-
    ward to
kitanai dirty
kitsui tight
kit·te stamp
-ko classifier for fruit, cakes,
    eggs and small chunky
    objects
kōban police box
kōcha tea (drink)
kōdo wire; lead
kodomo child; children
kodomo-yō (no) children's
koe voice
kōen park
kogai open air
kōgai suburb
Kōgō-Heika Empress of
    Japan
kohei (na) fair, impartial
kōhī coffee
koi carp
koin-randorī launderette,
    laundromat
kōjo factory
kōka coin
kōkan-rēto exchange rate
kok·kyō border (of country)
kok*u*naisen domestic flight
koko here
  koko des*u* right here, just
    here
  ... wa koko des*u* here is/are
    ...
  masa ni koko de just here
  koko ni over here
  koko no kore des*u* this one
    here
kokonoka ninth
kokonots*u* nine
kok*u*rits*u* (no) national
kok*u*sai-teki (na)
    international
kok*u*seki nationality
kōkūbin de by airmail
kōkūbin·yō fūtō airmail enve-
    lope
kōkyū (na) upmarket
komban tonight, this
    evening
komban wa good evening
kome rice (uncooked)
komichi path
komori child minder
kona-sek·ken soap powder
konda crowded
konde iru busy
kondo next time
kon-iro (no) navy (blue)
konkai this time
konkūru contest
kon·nichi wa hello
kono this; these
konoha leaf
konosaki down the road
kono shita des*u* down here
konsento power point
kop·p*u* glass
kore this; this one; these
  kore des*u* ka this one here

kore kara in future
kore wa ... desu this is ...
korekuto-kōru reverse charge call, collect call
kōri ice
korobimasu to fall
koruku-nuki corkscrew
kōsu course
kōsaten junction
koshō breakdown
kōshūbenjo public toilets
kōshūdenwa phone box, payphone
kōsōbiru skyscraper
kōsokudōro motorway, freeway, highway
kos·setsu fracture
kōsui perfume
kotatsu footwarmer
kot·chi this; this way; here
kōto coat
kotoba word, language
kōtsū traffic
kōtsūjiko road accident
kot·tōhin antique
kot·tōhin-ten antique shop
kowareta damaged; broken
kowarete imasu out of order
kowashimasu to break, to damage
kōza bank account, account
kozeni change, money
kōzui flood
kozutsumi parcel, package
kusa grass
kusuri drug, medicine
kusuri-ya pharmacy
ku ward, area of a city
kubi neck

kuchi mouth
kuchibeni lipstick
kuchibiru lips
kudaketa informal
kudamono fruit
Kugats September
kuishimbō (no) greedy
kujira whale
kujō complaint
kujō īmas to complain
kūki air
kūkō airport
kumo spider
kumori (no) cloudy, dull
-kun suffix used when addressing a young person
kuni country, nation
kurabemasu to compare
kurai about, approximately
kuremasu to give
... o kuremasen ka? could I have ...?
...-te kuremasen ka? could you ...?
kurikaeshimasu to repeat
Kurisumasu-Ibu Christmas Eve
kuro black
kuroi dark
kurōku cloakroom
kuruma car
kushami o shimasu to sneeze
kushi comb
kutsu shoe
kutsu-himo shoelaces
kutsunaoshi shoe repairer
kutsu no soko sole (of shoe)
kutsuzumi shoe polish
kuzushimasu to change

(money)
kyaku customer
kyakusha coach, carriage
kyakushitsu compartment
kyakushitsu-gakari maid
kyanseru-machi standby
kyō today
kyōdai brother
kyōdo-keiei-sha partner (in business)
kyoka permit
kyōkai church
kyoku-dome-yūbin poste restante
kyori distance
kyōryoku help
kyū nine
kyūden palace
kyūgyō closed
kyū-hyaku nine hundred
kyū-jū ninety
kyūka holiday, vacation
kyūkei-jikan interval
kyūkō express train
kyūkyūbako first-aid kit
kyūkyūbyōtō casualty department
kyūkyūsha ambulance
kyūreki lunar calendar
kyūsuiki fountain (for drinking)

M

mabushī bright
machi town; area
machi-awase-basho meeting place

machigai error, mistake
machigat·ta false, not true
machimasu to wait
mada still; only; yet
  īe, mada desu not yet
made to; up to; until; as far as
  Mok·yōbi made ni by Thursday
mado window
madogawa no seki window seat
mae ago; front
  ichijikan mae an hour ago
  sono mae no hi the day before
mae mot·te in advance
mae ni in front, at the front; formerly, in the past; before
magarikado turning (in road)
magomusuko grandson (one's own)
magomusume granddaughter (one's own)
mahōbin Thermos® flask
-mai classifier for pieces of paper, tickets and other thin, flat objects
mainichi (no) daily
majime (na) serious
makura pillow
makura-kabā pillow case
mama mum
māmā desu not bad, so-so
man·ga comic book
manikyua nail varnish
man·naka middle
manshon apartment block
Marē-hantō (no) Malay

maroyaka (na) mild

masaka! oh no!

-masen not

-masen deshita didn't

mata again

mata wa or

matsu pine

mat·taku chigaimasu definitely not

mat·taku sono tōri desu definitely

mawari-michi diversion, detour

mayaku drugs (narcotics)

mayonaka midnight

mayonaka ni in the middle of the night; at midnight

me eye

megane spectacles, eyeglasses

mei niece (one's own)

meishi business card

meisho the sights

menkyo licence

menrui noodles

menzei(hin) duty-free (goods)

menzeihin-ten duty-free shop

met·ta ni not often

met·ta ni ...-masen hardly ever

mezurashī rare, uncommon, unusual

miatarimasen missing

michi road

midori (no) green

midori no madoguchi ticket counter

migi right

migi e to the right

migi ni on the right

mihon-ichi fair; trade fair

mijikai brief, short

mik·ka third

mimasu to look at; to see

mimi ear

mimi ga kikoenai deaf

minami south

o minami in the south

minato harbour, port

min·geihin-ten craft shop

minikui ugly

min·na everyone; all

... wa min·na all the ...

minshuku guesthouse

miryoku-teki (na) attractive

mise shop

mitsukemasu to find

mit·tsu three

mizu water

mizugi swimming trunks; swimming costume

mizūmi lake

mizusashi jug

mo also, too; even; both ... and; neither ... nor

mō already

mō hitotsu another, one more

mochimasu to have; to carry; to hold

mochinushi owner

mochiron of course

mochiron chigaimasu of course not

mochite handle

modorimasu to get back, to return

modot·te ikimasu to go back

modot·te kimasu to come back

mōfu blanket

mokutekichi destination

Moku·yōbi Thursday

momen cotton

momo thigh

mon gate

mondai problem

mono thing

more leak

mori woods, forest

moshi if

　moshi ... demo even if ...

moshi-moshi hello; I'm still here

mōsukoshi some more, a little bit more

mot·te kimasu to bring; to fetch

mot·to more

mot·to ī better

mot·to sukunaku less

mot·to takusan a lot more

mot·to tōku further

moyō pattern

muchū(na) crazy

muen-gasorin unleaded petrol

muika sixth

muishiki (no) unconscious

muji (no) plain

mukai no opposite

mukashi-fū (no) old-fashioned

mukō there; over there

　mukō desu, mukō ni over there

mukōgawa across

mune chest, breast

mura village

murasaki (no) purple, violet

muryō free of charge

mushi insect

mushi-atsui humid

mushi-sasare insect bite

musuko son (one's own)

musume daughter (one's own)

mut·tsu six

muzukashī hard, difficult

myōji surname

N

nadare avalanche

nagai long

　nagai aida a long time

nagame view

nagashi sink

nagemasu to throw

naisen telephone extension

naka inside

naka e hairimasu to go in

nakai-san maid

naka ni inside

-nakereba narimasen I must ...

nakimasu to cry

nakunarimasu to disappear

nakushimasu to lose

nama (no) raw

namae name; first name, given name

namake-mono lazy

nana seven

nana-hyaku seven hundred

nana-jū seventy
nanatsu seven
nani? what?
 nani desu ka? what?
 sore wa nani desu ka?
 what's that?
 nani demo ī desu it doesn't
 matter
nani ka something, anything
 nani ka ... ka? would you
 like anything ...?
nani mo ...-masen nothing
nani mo nai desu nothing
 else
nanoka seventh
nansei southwest
nante īmashita? pardon
 (me)?, sorry?
nantō southeast
naorimasu to cure
naoshimasu to mend
nao warui desu it's worse;
 much worse
naraimasu to learn
narubeku hayaku as soon as
 possible
naruhodo I see; indeed
nashi de without
natsu summer
nazenara because
ne? isn't it?, haven't we?,
 haven't you? etc
nedan cost, price
nedoko bed (Japanese-style)
nega negative (film)
neko cat
nemurimasu to sleep
nen·gajō New Year's card
nenkin-seikatsu·sha pensioner

netsu fever; temperature
netsup·poi feverish
nezumi mouse; rat
ni two; to; in; at; into; on;
 indirect object particle
ni-bai (no) double; twice as
 much
ni-bam·me (no) second
nibui stupid
nichibotsu sunset
Nichiyōbi Sunday
nigai bitter
Nigatsu February
nihodoki shimasu to unpack
Nihon Japan
Nihon (no) Japanese
Nihon·go Japanese (language)
 Nihon·go de in Japanese
Nihon-jin Japanese (person)
ni-hyaku two hundred
ni-jū twenty
niku meat
ni-kai first floor, (US) second
 floor; twice
nik·ki diary (for personal experiences)
nik·kō sunshine
niku-ya butcher's
nimotsu luggage, baggage
nimotsu o tsumemasu to
 pack
-nin classifier for people
nin·gyō doll
nin·gyō-geki puppet show
ninki no aru popular
ninshin-chū (no) pregnant
Nip·pon Japan
nise (no) fake
nishi west

nishūkan fortnight

ni-tō second class (train etc)

niwa garden

niwaka-ame shower (of rain)

no of; possessive particle

no aida ni between; during

nodo throat

nodo no itami sore throat

no hōe towards

nōjō farm

nok·ku shimasu to knock

nomi flea

nomimasu to drink

nomimono drink

no mukōni beyond

norikaemasu to change (trains etc)

norimasu to get on (train etc)

no shita ni under (in position)

no soba near; by

  umi no soba by the sea

  no soba ni beside

no soko ni at the bottom of

no soto ni outside

no tame ni because of; for

no tonari next to

no ue on

no ushiro ni behind

nuimasu to sew

nunoji cloth, fabric

nureta wet

nusumimasu to steal

nyūjōryō admission charge

O

o object particle

o- polite prefix

o-ai-dekite ureshīdesu nice to meet you

ōbā overcoat

oba-san aunt

obā-san grandmother (someone else's)

Ōbei the West

Ōbei (no) Western

Ōbei-jin Westerner

obi sash

oboete imasu to remember

obon tray

ocha green tea

ōdōri main road; avenue

odorimasu to dance

odoroku-hodo (no) astonishing

ōfuku-kip·pu return ticket, round-trip ticket

ofuro bath

ofuro-ba bathroom

ofuro-tsuki de ... ... with bathroom

ogenki desu ka? how are you?

ohayōgozaimasu good morning

oi nephew (one's own)

oishī delicious

oji-san uncle

ojī-san grandfather

ojō-san daughter (someone else's)

ōku much

  ōku nai not a lot

oka hill

okagesama de fine; well

okane money

okane o tsukaimasu to spend

okanjō bill, (US) check

okā-san mother

okashī funny, strange

ōkī big, large

okimasu to get up; to leave; to keep; to put

okiwasuremasu to leave behind

okorimasu to happen

okot·ta angry

oku-san wife (someone else's)

okugai outdoor

okunai indoor

okure delay

okurimasu to send

okurimono gift

okyaku-sama guest

ōkyū-teate first aid

omago-san grandchild (someone else's)

omatase sorry to keep you waiting

omatsuri festival

omawari-san policeman

omedetō! congratulations!

Ōmisoka New Year's Eve

omiyage souvenir

omo (na) main

omocha toy

omoi serious, grave; heavy

omoimas to think

omosa weight

omoshiroi exciting; interesting; funny, amusing

omutsu nappy, diaper

onaji the same

onaji yō (na) similar

onaka stomach

onaka ga suita hungry

onegai shimasu please; thank you

hai, onegai shimasu yes, please

onē-san sister

on·gaku music

on·gak-ka musician

onī-san brother

on·na no ko girl

onsen hot spring

Oranda Holland

Oranda (no) Dutch

orenji-iro (no) orange

origami paper folding

orikaeshi denwa shimasu to ring back

orimasu to get out; to get off

oroshimasu to let off

osake alcoholic drink

osaki ni good night; goodbye; see you

osenkō joss stick

oshare (na) trendy, fashionable

oshibori moistened hand towel

oshikomi-gōtō burglary

oshimasu to push

oshīre cupboard, closet

oshiri hip; bottom

Oshōgatsu New Year

osoi slow; late

osoku slowly

osoraku probably

osoroshī horrible, awful

osōshiki funeral

ōsugi too many, too much

ōsugimas*u* that is too much

osuwari kudasai sit down

otanjōbi omedetō gozaimas*u*! happy birthday!

otera Buddhist temple

otoko no hito man

otoko no ko boy

otona adult

otō-san father; dad

otoshiyori old person

otōto brother (one's own: younger)

ototoi the day before yesterday

owan bowl

owari end

owarimas*u* to finish

owarimash*i*ta it's finished

oyasuminasai good night

oya-yubi thumb

oyogimas*u* to swim

P

pachinko pinball

pak·k*u*-ryokō package holiday

pan bread

panf*u*ret·to brochure

pank*u* puncture

pantī–s*u*tok·king*u* tights, pantyhose

pants*u* underpants; shorts

pan-ya baker's

piru contraceptive pill

pop·pus*u* pop music

pos*u*to letterbox, mailbox

purasu*t*ik·k*u* plastic

purat·to-hōm*u* platform; track

pūru swimming pool

R

raishū next week

raishū no ashita a week tomorrow

raishū no kyō a week today

rai-u thunderstorm

regyurā regular unleaded petrol

rei example

reitōshita frozen

reizōko fridge

rek·kāsha breakdown service

renji cooker

renta-kā rented car; car rental

rentaru (no) to rent, for hire

renzu lens; camera lens; contact lens

reshīto receipt

rimujin-bas*u* airport bus

rins*u* conditioner (for hair)

roji lane

rok*u* six

rōka corridor

Rok*u*gats*u* June

rok*u*-jū sixty

romendensha tram

rop·pyak*u* six hundred

rosenzu network map

rōsok*u* candle

ryō amount (quantity)

ryōgae-jo bureau de change

ryōgae-rēto exchange rate

Ry

ryōhō both
ryōjikan consulate
ryokan Japanese traditional inn
ryōkin charge; fare; rental
ryōkinbako fare box
ryokō journey
  sore dewa tanoshī ryokō o! have a good journey!
ryokōgaisha travel agent's
ryokōkyaku tourist
ryokōshimasu to travel
ryōri food; dish (meal)
ryōri shimasu to cook
ryōshin parents (one's own)
ryūkōokure (no) unfashionable

S

sābisu-ryō service charge
sagashimasu to search, to look for
sai-aku (no) worst
saifu purse; wallet
saigai disaster
saigo (no) final, last
saijitsu public holiday
saijōkai top floor
saikin recently
saikō(no) best
saishin (no) latest, most recent, up-to-date
saisho (no) first
  saisho ni at first
saishoku-shugisha vegetarian
saizu size
sakana fish

sakana-ya fishmonger's
sakasama upside down
sakazuki sake cup
saki first
sakihodo earlier
sakura cherry blossom
sakura no ki cherry tree
-sama Mr; Mrs; Ms; Miss
sambashi jetty
sam-byaku three hundred
samonaito otherwise
sampatsu haircut (man's)
samui cold
san three
-san Mr; Mrs; Ms; Miss
San-gatsu March
san-jū thirty
san-kai second floor, (US) third floor; three times
san-shoku-tsuki full board
sara plate
sararī-man businessman; salaried worker
sarubin surface mail, overland mail
satō sugar
-satsu classifier for books
sawagashī loud
sayōnara goodbye
se ga takai tall
seifu government
seihin product
seijō(na) normal
seika net price
seikaku (na) accurate
seikyūsho bill, (US) check; invoice
seiri period (menstruation)
seiri-yōnapukin sanitary nap-

kins/towels
seishiki (na) formal
seiyō(no) Occidental
sekai world
seki seat; cough
sek·ken soap
semai narrow (street)
-semasu to let, to allow
sem·mendai washhand basin
sempūki fan (electrical)
sen thousand; line; plug (in sink)
senaka back (of body)
senaka no itami backache
senchi centimetre
sen·nuki bottle-opener
se no hikui short
sensei teacher; polite form of address for teachers, doctors, dentists etc
senshitsu cabin
senshū last week
senshūkara since last week
senshūno Kin·yōbi last Friday
sensu fan
sentak-ki washing machine
sentaku-mono washing, laundry
sentaku-ya laundry (place)
sentō public baths
sen·yōno basu-toire private bathroom
senzai washing powder
serotēpu Sellotape®, Scotch tape®
ses·shi centigrade
sētā pullover, sweater
setomono china
setsubi equipment

setsumei shimasu to explain
setsuzoku connection (in travelling)
setsuzokubin connecting flight
sewa o shimasu to look after
shachō managing director, president (of company)
shako garage (for parking)
shareta posh
sharin wheel
shasen lane (on motorway)
shashin photo; picture
shatsu shirt
shawā-tsuki (no) with shower
shi death; city; four
shiai game, match
shibafu lawn
shibai play (in theatre)
shibutsu belongings
shichaku shimasu to try on
shichaku-shitsu fitting room
shichi seven
Shichigatsu July
shigai-kyokuban dialling code, area code
Shigatsu April
shigoto business; job, work
shihainin manager
shiharai payment
shiharaimasu to pay
shihei banknote, (US) bill
shijō market (in business)
shiken exam
shiki-buton mattress
shikiten ceremony
shik·ki lacquerware
shima island
shimarimasu to close

shimasu to do; to play; to give; to make; to work (as); to taste; to smell; to feel; to sound; to cost

shimat·ta closed

shimbun newspaper, paper

shimbun·ya newsagent's

shimemasu to shut

shimet·ta damp

shimo frost

shimpai worried

shinai: … shinai hō ga ī desu you shouldn't …

shincho height

shinda dead

shindaisha sleeper, sleeping car

shin·gō traffic lights

shin·gu bedding (Western-style)

shin·guru single room

shin·guru-bed·do single bed

shinimasu to die

shinjiran·nai unbelievable

shinkansen bullet train

shinsen (na) fresh

shinsetsu (na) friendly, nice; kind; generous

shinshifuku-uriba menswear

shinshitsu bedroom

shintai-shōgai-sha disabled person; the disabled

shinzō heart

shirabemasu to find out; to check

shirafu (no) sober

shirimasen I don't know

shiro castle

shiroi white

shita downstairs; tongue

shita (ni) below

shita e ikimasu to go down

shite: … shite kuremasen ka? could you please …?

shi-teki (na) private

shitsugyō-chū unemployed

shitsumon question

shitsurei (na) rude

shitsurei shimasu excuse me

shit·te imasu to know

shiyō-chū engaged, occupied

shizen (na) natural; peaceful, quiet

shizuka ni! quiet!

shōbōsho fire brigade

shōdoku-zai antiseptic

shōgi Japanese chess

shōgo midday, noon

shohōsen prescription

shōji sliding door (wooden lattice and paper)

shōka-furyō indigestion

shōkai shimasu to introduce

shōkaki fire extinguisher

shokbutsu plant

shokudōsha restaurant car, buffet car

shokuji meal

shokuji o shimasu to have dinner

shok·ki o araimasu to do the washing-up

shok·ki-yōsenzai washing-up liquid

shokuryōhin food (in shop)

shokuryōhin-ten food shop/store

shomei signature

shōmeisho certificate
shōnin witness
shōrai future
shorui document
shōtai invitation
shōtai shimasu to invite
shōtsu pants, panties
shū week (this, last, next etc)
shujin husband (one's own)
shūkai meeting
shūkan custom; week (one, two, three etc)
shūkyō religion
shūmatsu weekend
shumi hobby
shup·patsu departure
shup·patsu-raunji departure lounge
shup·patsu shimasu to leave, to depart
shūri shimasu to repair
shurui type, make, brand name
shut·chō business trip
shūten terminus
sukoshi a little bit, not much; little; some
sukoshi no a few
sukunaku-tomo at least
sō so
  sō desu that's right
sōbi equipment
sōin monastery
sōjiki vacuum cleaner
soko (de) there
sōkō-kyori-museigen unlimited mileage
sokutatsu express (mail)
somatsu (na) poor (quality)

son·na such; so; like that
son·na ni takusan ja naku not so much
son·na ni waruku nai not so bad
sono the; that (nearby)
  sono tōri desu that's it
sono toki then, at that time
sō-on noise
sora sky
sore it; that (nearby); that one (nearby); those; them (objects)
sore dake desu that's all
sore de ī desu ka? is that OK?
sore desu that one
sore wa ... des it is ...
sore zembu all of it
sorekara and then
sorera (ga) they (inanimate objects)
sorera no their; theirs (inanimate objects)
sorera o them (inanimate objects)
sorera wa they (inanimate objects)
sorezore (no) each, every
sōridaijin prime minister
sōryo Buddhist priest
soshite and
soto ni outside
sōzai-ya delicatessen
sutando lamp
suteki (na) lovely
sutemasu to throw away
subarashī beautiful; excellent, great, wonderful

subete everything
subete no every
sugu at once, immediately; soon
  sugu ni straightaway; in a minute
-sugimasu too
sugoi super, great
  sugoi! well done!
suichū-yokusen hydrofoil
suidō-ya plumber
suijō-skī waterskiing
suit·chi switch
Suiyōbi Wednesday
sūjitsu mae the other day
suki: ... ga suki desu ka? do you like ...?
  suki desu I like it
  suki ja arimasen I don't like it
sumi corner
  sumi ni in the corner
sumimasen thanks; sorry; may I?
suna sand
sunde imasu to live
sunīkā trainers
sūpā supermarket
sup·pai sour
suwarimasu to sit down
suzushī cool

T

tabako cigarette
tabemasu to eat
tabemono food
tabitabi (no) frequent

tabun perhaps, maybe
  tabun chigau deshō perhaps not
tada free of charge
tadashī correct, right
taifū typhoon
Taiheiyō Pacific Ocean
taikutsu bored
taikutsu (na) boring
taira (na) flat
taisetsu (na) important
taishikan embassy
taitei most; mostly, most of the time
  taitei no most
taiyō sun
takai high; expensive; tall
takasa height
take bamboo
tak·kyū table tennis
tako kite
tako-age kite-flying
takusan a lot, lots
takusan (no) much; many; a lot, lots
  takusan no ... plenty of ..., a lot of ...
takushī-noriba taxi rank
takushī no unten-shu taxi-driver
takuwae supply
tambo paddy field
tameshimasu to try
tana shelf
tani valley
tanjōbi birthday
tanomimasu to ask
tanoshimimasu to enjoy oneself

tansha moped

taoru flannel; towel

tarimasen there's not enough

tashika certain, sure

tashika desu ka? are you sure?

tashika ni certainly

tasukete! help!

tatami straw mat

tatoeba for example

tatoe ...-temo even if

tazunemasu to visit

te hand

tebukuro gloves

techō notebook; diary

tegami letter

tegoro (na) reasonable; inexpensive

tehai shimasu to arrange

teiki-bin scheduled flight

teikiken rail pass

teinei (na) polite

tekubi wrist

tenchō manager (in shop)

te ni iremasu to get, to fetch

tenimots baggage; hand luggage

tenimotsu-azukari-jo left luggage (office), baggage checkroom

tenimotsu-uketori-jo baggage claim

tenjikan pavilion

tenki weather

Ten·nō-Heika Emperor of Japan

tenrankai exhibition

tenso-saki forwarding address

tento tent

tep·pen ni at the top

terebi television

tēru-rampu rear lights

tetsudaimasu to help

tetsudō railway

tis·shu (pēpā) tissues, Kleenex®

to with, accompanying; and; door (of house: Japanese-style)

-to metropolis

tō pagoda; ten

tobimasu to fly

tōchaku arrival

tōchaku shimasu to arrive, to get in

todana cupboard

tōi far

toire toilet, rest room

tōjiki crockery

tojikomemasu to lock in

tōjōken boarding pass

tōku (no) distant

tōka tenth

tokei clock, watch

tōki pottery

tokidoki sometimes

tok·kyū super express train

toku ni especially

tokonoma alcove

tokoro place; someone's house

toko-ya barber's

Tōkyōwan Tokyo Bay

tomarimasu to stop; to stay

tōmei (no) clear

tomemasu to switch off (engine)

tomodachi friend
ton·neru tunnel
toranku boot (of car), (US) trunk
torēnā sweatshirt
tori bird
tōri street
toridashimasu to get out, to take out
torihiki deal (business)
torikaemasu to change, to replace
torikeshimasu to cancel
torimasu to take, to accept
tōrokuban·gō registration number, license number
toshi age; city; year
toshi o tot·ta old (person)
totemo quite; very; extremely; so; a lot
totemo oishī delicious, excellent
totsuzen ni suddenly
tot·te handle
tōt·te through
tot·te okimasu to keep
tōyō(no) Oriental, Eastern
tozan mountaineering
tsugi (no) next
    sono tsugi no hi the day after
tsugōno ī convenient (time)
tsukaeta stuck
tsukaimasu to use
tsukamaemasu to fetch; to catch
tsukaremashīta I'm tired
tsukareta tired
tsukemasu to switch on (TV, lights)

tsuki moon
tsukiatari end of a road
tsukimasu to arrive
tsukurimasu to make
tsuma wife (one's own)
tsumaranai dull, uninteresting
tsumasaki toe
tsume nail (finger)
tsumetai cold
-tsū classifier for letters
tsuā tour
tsuika-ryōkin supplement, extra charge
tsuin twin room
tsui ni eventually
tsuitach first
tsuite no about, concerning
tsūjite imasu to lead
tsurete ikimasu to take, to lead
tsūrogawa no seki aisle seat
tsuyadashi polish
tsūyaku interpreter
tsuyu rainy season
tsuyoi strong

U

ubaguruma buggy
uchi home
uchimashō deal
    sore de te o uchimashō it's a deal
ude arm
udedokei wristwatch
ue upstairs; above
    ... no ue ni on top of ...

ue ni up
ugokashimasu to move
uketorimasu to accept
uketsuke reception desk
 uketsuke de at reception
uketsuke-gakari receptionist
uketsukemasu to accept
ukezara saucer
uma horse
umi sea
umibe shore
un luck
untem·menkyoshō driving licence
unten shimasu to drive
untenshu driver
un·yoku fortunately
ura back
ureshī happy, glad
uridashi-chū for sale
urimasu to sell
ūru wool
urusai noisy
 urusai! shut up!
ushiro ni at the back
uso o tsukimasu to lie, to tell untruth
usu-... pale (colour)
usui weak; thin; light, pale
uta song
utaimasu to sing
utsukushī beautiful

W

wa subject particle
wafū Japanese-style
wakai young

wakarimasu to understand
 wakarimasu ka? do you understand?
 wakarimasen I don't understand
wakimichi side street
wan bay
waraimasu to laugh
waribiki discount
warikan going Dutch
warui bad; ill
waruku badly
washi paper
wasuremasu to forget
watakushi (ga) I (pol)
watakushi no my; mine (pol)
watakushi o me (pol)
watakushi wa I (pol)
watashi (ga) I
 watashi mo me too
 watashi mo sō desu so am I, so do I
watashi no my; mine
 watashi no desu it's mine
watashi o me
watashi wa I
 watashi wa ... desu I am
watashitachi (ga) we
watashitachi no our; ours
watashitachi o us
watashitachi wa we
waza to deliberately
winkā indicator

Y

yakan kettle
yakedo burn

yakedo shimasu to burn
yak·kai-goto trouble
yak·kyoku pharmacy
yaku ni tatsu helpful; useful
yakusō herbs (medicinal)
yakyū baseball
yama mountain
yamagoya cabin (in mountains)
yamete kudasai! stop it!
yane roof
yao-ya greengrocer's
yasai vegetables
yasashī easy
yaseta thin, skinny
yasui cheap, inexpensive;
  low
yasumi holiday, vacation
yat·tsu eight
yawarakai soft
yoake dawn
yōfū(no) Western-style
yōfuku clothes (Western)
yogore dirt
yogoreta polluted
yōi ga dekita ready
yoku often
yōka eighth
yokat·ta! good!
yokubari (na) greedy
yok·ka fourth
yoku kireru sharp
yoko side
yoko ni narimasu to lie down
yokusō bath, bathtub
yom-bun no ichi quarter
yomimasu to read
yōmoku foreign cigarettes
yon four
yon-hyaku four hundred

yon-jū forty
yop·parat·ta drunk
yorimasu: bāi ni yorimas it
  depends
yorimo than
yoru night
yōshi form, document
yoshinasai! don't do that!
yotei schedule
yot·tsu four
yowai weak
yoyaku reservation; appointment
yoyaku shimasu to book, to
  reserve
yūbe last night
yubi finger
yūbimban·gō postcode, zip
  code
yūbin post, mail
yubi-nin·gyō puppet
yūbinkyoku post office
yūbinkyoku no honkyoku
  main post office
yubiwa ring (on finger)
yūdoku (na) poisonous
yūen four-star petrol
yūenchi fair, funfair
yūgata evening
yuka floor (of room)
yukata cotton dressing gown
yuki snow
yuk·kuri slowly
yūkō(na) valid (ticket etc)
yūmei (na) famous
yurui loose
yūshoku evening meal
yūsōshimasu to post, to mail
yut·tari shita comfortable

Z

zabuton floor cushion
zan·nen (des)! what a shame!, it's a pity!
zas·shi magazine
zeikan Customs
zeitaku (na) luxurious
zembu the whole lot, all of them
 sore zembu all of it
zembu de altogether
Zen-dera Zen temple
zenkai last time
zensai starter, appetizer
Zen-sō Zen priest
Zen-tei Zen garden
zenzen not in the least
zet·tai chigaimasu! certainly not!
zō statue
zubon trousers, (US) pants
zutsū headache
zut·to much, a lot more

Japanese

→

English
Signs and
Notices

Contents

General Signs

大人 otona adult

子供 kodomo child

危険 kiken danger

飲み水 nomimizu drinking water

・・・お断り … okotowari … forbidden

案内 an·nai information

芝生に入らないでください shibafu ni hairanaide kudasai keep off the grass

立ち入り禁止 tachiiri-kinshi keep out

禁漁区 kinryōku no fishing

禁煙 kin·en no smoking

故障 koshō out of order

ゴミ gomi litter

ゴミ捨てるな gomi suteruna no litter

横断歩道 ōdanhodō pedestrian crossing

静かに shizukani quiet, please

Airport, Planes

空港 kūkō airport

空港バス kūkō-basu airport bus

航空便 kōkūbin flight

便名 bim·mei flight number

到着 tōchaku arrival(s)

出発 shup·patsu departure(s)

行き先 ikisaki destination

・・・行き … iki bound for …

経由 keiyu via

搭乗口 tōjōguchi boarding gate

搭乗券 tōjōken boarding pass

ゲート gēto gate

東口 higashi-guchi east exit (or entrance)

北口 kita-guchi north exit (or entrance)

南口 minami-guchi south exit (or entrance)

西口 nishi-guchi west exit (or entrance)

航空 kōkū airline

航空券 kōkūken airline ticket

全日空 Zen-Nik·kū All Nippon Airways

国内線 kokunai-sen domestic airlines

国際線 kokusai-sen international airlines

日本航空 Nihon-Kōkū Japan Airlines

予約 yoyaku reservations

案内 an·nai information

案内係 an·nai-gakari information desk

手荷物受取所 tenimotsu-uketori-jo baggage claim

215

チェックイン chek·ku·in check-in

免税店 menzei-ten duty-free shop

Banks, Money

銀行 ginkō bank

外国為替公認銀行 gaikoku-kawase-kōnin-ginkō authorized foreign exchange bank

両替所 ryōgaejo bureau de change, foreign exchange

外国為替 gaikoku-kawase foreign exchange

窓口 madoguchi counter

為替レート kawase-rēto exchange rate

振替 furikae transfer

為替手形 kawase-tegata banker's draft

トラベラーズチェック traberāzu-chek·ku traveller's cheque

クレジットカード kurejit·to-kādo credit card

カード可 kādo-ka credit cards accepted

口座番号 kōzaban·gō account number

口座 kōza bank account

料金 ryōkin fee

有料 yūryō fee charged

無料 muryō no charge

消費税 shōhi-zei VAT, (US) consumption tax

円 en yen

¥ yen

ドル doru dollar

ポンド pondo pound sterling

Bus Travel

バス basu bus

バスセンター basu-sentā bus station

バス停 basu-tei bus stop

バス乗り場 basu-noriba bus boarding point

バスターミナル basu-tāminaru bus terminal

・・・行き ... iki bound for ...

市バス shi-basu municipal bus

都営バス toei-basu municipal bus (in Tokyo)

切符売り場 kip·pu-uriba ticket office

切符 kip·pu ticket

回数券 kaisūken book of tickets

運賃表 unchin-hyō table of fares

有効 yūkō valid

乗車は前扉から jōsha wa mae tobira kara enter at

front door

降車は後扉から kōsha wa ushiro tobira kara exit at rear door

運賃箱 unchim-bako fare box

料金箱 ryōkin-bako fare box

回送 kaisō out of service

次は停車 tsugi-wa-teisha stopping at the next stop

精算所 seisanjo excess fare office

Countries, Nationalities

アメリカ Amerika America; American

オーストラリア Ōsutoraria Australia; Australian

英 Ei Britain; British; England; English

英国 Eikoku Britain; British; England; English

カナダ Kanada Canada; Canadian

中国 Chūgoku China; Chinese

デンマーク Dem·māku Denmark; Danish

オランダ Oranda Holland; Dutch

イギリス Igirisu England; English; Britain; British

ヨーロッパ Yōrop·pa Europe; European

フランス Fransu France; French

仏 Futsu France; French

ドイツ Doitsu Germany; German

独 Doku Germany; German

インド Indo India; Indian

イタリア Itaria Italy; Italian

日 Nichi Japan; Japanese

日本 Nihon Japan; Japanese

マレーシア Marēshia Malaysia; Malay

ニュージーランド Nyū-Jīrando New Zealand

北朝鮮 Kita-Chōsen North Korea; North Korean

ノルウェー Noruē Norway; Norwegian

・・・人 ...-jin person

フィリピン Firipin Philippines; Filipina

ロシア Roshia Russia; Russian

韓国 Kankoku South Korea; South Korean

スペイン Spein Spain; Spanish

スウェーデン Suēden Sweden; Swedish

米 Bei USA

米国 Beikoku USA

217

Customs

税関 zeikan Customs

税関審査 zeikan-shinsa Customs check

税関告知書 zeikan-kokuchi-sho Customs declaration form

税関申告用紙 zeikan-shinkoku-yōshi Customs declaration form

出国 shuk·koku departure from a country

入国 nyūkoku entry into a country

入国カード nyūkoku-kādo entry card, landing card

入国審査 nyūkoku-shinsa entry examination

外国人 gaikoku-jin foreigners

出入国管理 shutsunyūkoku-kanri immigration

日本人 Nihon-jin Japanese nationals

検疫 ken·eki quarantine

Days

月曜日 Getsuyōbi Monday

火曜日 Kayōbi Tuesday

水曜日 Suiyōbi Wednesday

木曜日 Mokuyōbi Thursday

金曜日 Kin·yōbi Friday

土曜日 Doyōbi Saturday

日曜日 Nichiyōbi Sunday

Emergencies

救急車 kyūkyū-sha ambulance

119番 hyaku-jū-kyū-ban ambulance; fire brigade

病院 byōin hospital

救急病院 kyūkyū-byōin emergency hospital

応急手当て ōkyū-teate first aid

救急箱 kyūkyū-bako first-aid box

救急セット kyūkyū-set·to first-aid kit, emergency kit

110番 hyaku-tō-ban police

警察 keisats police

火災報知器 kasai-hōchiki fire alarm

消防署 shōbōsho fire brigade

消火器 shōkaki fire extinguisher

避難口 hinan·guchi emergency exit

非常口 hijōguchi emergency exit

故障 koshō breakdown

非常呼び出し hijō-yobidashi emergency call

非常電話 hijō-denwa emergency telephone

Entertainment

映画館 eigakan cinema, movie theater

映画 eiga film, movie

成人映画 seijin-eiga adult film

アニメーション animēshon cartoon

洋画 yōga Western film

字幕 jimaku subtitles

ロードショー rōdoshō special release

上映中 jōei-chū now showing

会場時間 kaijō-jikan opening time

前売券 maeuri-ken advance booking

劇場 gekijō theatre

切符 kip·pu ticket

切符売場 kip·pu-uriba ticket office, box office

席 seki seat

座席 zaseki seat

座席番号 zaseki-ban·gō seat number

指定席 shiteiseki reserved seat

指定券 shitei-ken reserved seat ticket

満席 manseki all seats taken

満員 man·in full

劇 geki play, drama

時代劇 jidai-geki historical play or film

帝国劇場 Teikoku-Gekijō Imperial Theatre

歌舞伎座 Kabuki-za kabuki theatre

国立劇場 Kokuritsu-Gekijō National Theatre

文楽 Bunraku traditional puppet theatre

能 Nō Noh play

狂言 Kyōgen traditional comic drama

歌舞伎 Kabuki traditional drama from the Edo period

ディスコ disuko disco

ナイトクラブ naito-kurabu nightclub

ホステスバー hosutesu-bā hostess bar

カラオケ karaoke karaoke bar

未成年お断り miseinen-okotowari minors not admitted

未成年者入場無効 miseinensha-nyūjō-mukō minors not admitted

パチンコ pachinko pinball

ゲームセンター gēmu-sentā amusement arcade

ターキッシュ・バス takis·shu basu Turkish bath

219

Ferry, Boat Services

救命ボート kyūmei-bōto lifeboat

フェリー ferī ferry; ferry service

ホバークラフト hobā-kurafuto hovercraft

水中翼船 suichū-yokusen hydrofoil

Forms

用紙 yōshi form

アンケート ankēto questionnaire

ボールペンで御記入ください bōrupen de gokinyū kudasai write in ink

氏名 shimei full name

お名前 onamae name

住所 jūsho address

滞在住所 taizaijūsho address during stay

連絡先 renrakusaki contact address

年齢 nenrei age

生年月日 seinen-gap·pi date of birth

国籍 kokuseki nationality

職業 shokugyō occupation

パスポート番号 pasupōto-ban·gō passport number

旅券番号 ryoken-ban·gō passport number

外国人登録証明書 gaikoku-jin-tōroku-shōmeisho foreign resident's ID card, alien registration card

身分証明書 mibun-shōmeisho ID card

出発予定日 shup·patsu-yoteibi intended date of departure

滞在日数 taizai-nis·sū length of stay

泊数 hakusū length of visit

訪日目的 hōnichi-mokuteki purpose of visit

御署名 go-shomē signature

サイン sain signature

Garages

ガソリンスタンド gasorin-sutando petrol station, (US) gas station

ガソリン gasorin petrol, (US) gas

石油 sekiyu petrol, (US) gas

軽油 keiyu diesel

ハイオク hai-oku high octane

スーパー sūpā super, premium

レギュラー regyurā

regular unleaded

オイル oiru oil

灯油 tōyu paraffin, kerosene

自動車整備工場 jidōsha-seibi-kōjō auto repairs

洗車 sensha car wash

料金 ryōkin fee, charge

有料 yūryō fee, charge

無料点検 muryōtenken free inspection

無料 muryō no charge

点検サービス tenken-sābisu service

タイヤチェック taiya-chek·ku tyre check, (US) tire check

水 mizu water

エア eya air

Geographical Terms

岬 misaki cape, promontory

国 kuni country

森 mori forest

温泉 onsen hot spring

島 shima island

湖 mizūmi lake

地図 chizu map

山 yama mountain

山脈 sam·myaku mountain range

半島 hantō peninsula

川 kawa river

海 umi sea

頂上 chōjō summit

谷 tani valley

火山 kazan volcano

滝 taki waterfall

市 shi town, city

村 mura village

県 ken prefecture

東 higashi east

北 kita north

地方 chihō region, area

南 minami south

西 nishi west

関西 Kansai Kansai Region (Osaka etc)

関東 Kantō Kanto Region (Tokyo etc)

Hairdresser's, Beauty Salon

美容院 biyōin hairdresser's, beauty salon

床屋 tokoya barber's shop

理髪店 rihatsu·ten barber's shop

ビューティーサロン byūtī-saron beauty salon

ブロードライ burō-dorai blow dry

カット kat·to cut

調髪 chōhatsu cut

ヘアスタイル heya-sutairu hairstyle

ヘアセット heya-set·to set
シャンプーセット shampū-set-to shampoo and set
洗髪 sempatsu wash
マニキュア manikyua manicure
マッサージ mas·sāji massage

Health

医者 isha doctor
歯医者 haisha dentist
医院 īn (small) hospital
病院 byōin hospital
診療所 shinryōjo clinic
保健所 hokenjo public health centre
診療 shinryō consultation
診療時間 shinryō-jikan consultation hours

Hiring, Renting

貸し・・・ kashi-... ... hire, ... rental
貸し自転車 kashi-jitensha bicycle hire
貸しボート kashi-bōto boat hire
貸し自動車 kashi-jidōsha car rental
レンタカー rentakā car rental

貸し部屋 kashibeya room to let
時間貸し jikan-gashi hourly rental
頭金 atama-kin deposit
手付金 tetsukekin deposit
距離払い kyori-barai payment by distance
時間払い jikan-barai payment by the hour
レンタルサービス rentaru-sābisu rental service
2 D K ni-dī-kē two rooms and dining kitchen

Hotels

ホテル hoteru hotel
民宿 minshuku guesthouse
ビジネスホテル bijinesu-hoteru business hotel
カプセルホテル kapuseru- hoteru capsule hotel
旅館 ryokan traditional inn
会計係 kaikei-gakari cashier
フロント furonto reception
受付 uketsuke reception
ロビー robī lobby
日本交通公社（JTB） Nihon-Kōtsū-Kōsha Japan Travel Bureau
団体 dantai group

予約 **yoyaku** reservations
部屋 **heya** room
和室 **washitsu** Japanese-style room
洋室 **yōshitsu** Western-style room
冷房 **reibō** air-conditioning
お風呂 **ofuro** bath
ダイニングルーム **dainingu-rūmu** dining room
食堂 **shokudō** dining room
飲料水 **inryōsui** drinking water
飲み水 **nomimizu** drinking water
クリーニング **kurīningu** dry-cleaning
暖房 **dambō** heating
温泉 **onsen** hot spring
ラウンジ **raunji** lounge
ルームサービス **rūmu-sābisu** room service
電話 **denwa** telephone
自動販売機 **jidō-hambaiki** vending machine

Japanese Culture and Festivals (see also Public Holidays)

寺院 **jīn** temple
寺 **tera** temple
神社 **jinja** shrine
相撲 **sumō** traditional Japanese wrestling
正月 **Shōgatsu** New Year
節分 **Setsubun** Bean-Throwing Festival (3 February)
雛祭 **Hina-matsuri** Girls' Festival, Doll Festival (3 March)
花見 **Hanami** Cherry Blossom Viewing
花祭 **Hana-matsuri** Buddha's Birthday (8 April)
七夕 **Tanabata** Star Festival (7 July)
お盆 **Obon** Bon Festival, Buddhist festival celebrated in summer
七五三 **Shichigosan** Festival for 3, 5 and 7 year olds (15 November)
クリスマス **Kurisumasu** Christmas
美術館 **bijutsukan** art gallery
博物館 **hakbutsukan** museum
温泉 **onsen** hot spring
お風呂 **ofuro** public bath

Lifts (Elevators)

エレベーター **erebētā** lift, elevator
階 **...-kai** floor, storey

223

地階 chikai basement
一階 ik·kai ground floor, (US) first floor
二階 ni·kai first floor, (US) second floor
定員 tē·in capacity
満員 man·in full
閉 hei close
開 kai open
上 ue up
下 shita down
非常停止 hijōteishi emergency stop
非常電話 hijōdenwa emergency telephone
故障 koshō out of order

Medicines

1日・・・錠 ichinichi ...-jō ... tablets a day
1日・・・回 ichinichi ...-kai ... times a day
食後 shokugo after meals
就寝前 shūshinzen before going to bed
食前 shokuzen before meals
食間 shok·kan between meals
服用方法 fūku·yōhōhō directions for oral use
適量 tekiryō dosage
匙 saji spoonful(s)
錠剤 jōzai tablets
アスピリン asupirin aspirin
鎮痛剤 chintsū-zai painkiller
非ピリン系鎮痛剤 hi-pirin-kei-chintsū-zai paracetamol
咳止めドロップ sekidome-dorop·pu throat lozenges

Months

一月 Ichigatsu January
二月 Nigatsu February
三月 San·gatsu March
四月 Shigatsu April
五月 Gogatsu May
六月 Rokgatsu June
七月 Shichigatsu July
八月 Hachigatsu August
九月 Kugatsu September
十月 Jūgatsu October
十一月 Jūichigatsu November
十二月 Jūnigatsu December

Notices on Doors

入口 iriguchi entrance, way in
出口 deguchi exit, way out
自動ドア jidō-doa automatic door
引く hiku pull
押す osu push

営業中 eigyōchū open
開く hiraku to open
開 kai open
閉 hei closed
閉じる tojiru to close, to shut
休日 kyūjitsu closed
営業中 eigyōchū open for business
年中無休 nenjū-mukyū open all year round
月曜定休日 Getsu-yō-teikyūbi closed on Mondays
日祭日休み nichi-saijitsu-yasumi closed on Sundays and National Holidays
本日休業 honjitsu-kyūgyō closed today
定休日 teikyūbi closed for holidays
非常出口 hijōdeguchi emergency exit
非常口 hijōguchi emergency exit
避難口 hinan·guchi emergency exit
開放厳禁 kaihō-genkin keep closed
入場お断り nyūjō okotowari no admittance
関係者以外の立ち入り禁止 kankeisha igai no tachiiri kinshi no admittance for unauthorized personnel
立ち入り禁止 tachiiri-kinshi no entry

Phones

電話 denwa phone
公衆電話 kōshūdenwa public phone
電話ボックス denwa-bok·ksu phone booth
国際電信電話 Kokusai-Denshin-Denwa Overseas Telecommunications Service
テレホンカード terehon-kādo phonecard
電話代 denwadai call charge
通話料 tsūwaryō call charge
交換手 kōkanshu operator
電話帳 denwachō directory
内線 naisen extension
電話番号 denwaban·gō phone number
国際電話 kokusai-denwa international call
市内電話 shinai-denwa local call
長距離電話 chōkyori-denwa long-distance call
市外電話 shigai-denwa out-of-town call
ファックス fak·kusu fax; fax machine

Place Names

箱根 Hakone
広島 Hiroshima
北海道 Hok·kaidō

本州 Honshū
伊勢 Ise
鎌倉 Kamakura
神戸 Kōbe
京都 Kyōto
九州 Kyūshū
長崎 Nagasaki
名古屋 Nagoya
奈良 Nara
日光 Nik·kō
大阪 Ōsaka
四国 Shikoku
東京 Tōkyō
横浜 Yokohama

Post Office

郵便局 yūbinkyoku post office

yūbinkyoku no māku symbol for Japanese post office

窓口 madoguchi counter
切手 kit·te stamp
手紙 tegami letter
小包 kozutsumi parcel, package
航空書簡 kōkū-shokan aerogramme
航空便 kōkūbin airmail
速達 sokutatsu express mail
書留 kakitome registered mail
船便 funabin sea mail
サル便 sarubin surface

mail, overland mail
住所 jūsho address
宛名 atena addressee
印刷物 insatsubutsu printed matter
留置 tomeoki poste restante, general delivery
為替 kawase money order
地方 chihō out of town
外国向け gaikoku-muke overseas mail
都区内 tokunai to other parts of Toyko
他府県 tafuken to other prefectures

Public Holidays

祝日 shukujitsu public holiday
元日 Ganjitsu New Year's Day
成人の日 Sējin-no-hi Coming-of-Age Day (2nd Monday in January)
建国記念日 kenkoku-kinem·bi National Foundation Day (11 February)
春分の日 shum-bun·no-hi Vernal Equinox
みどりの日 midori-no-hi The Greenery Day (29 April)
憲法記念日 kempōkinem·bi Constitution Day (3 May)

子供の日 kodomo-no-hi
Boys' Festival, Children's
Day (5 May)

海の日 Sea Day (20 July)

敬老の日 keirō-no-hi
Respect the Aged Day (15
September)

秋分の日 shūbun-no-hi
Autumnal Equinox

体育の日 tai-iku-no-hi
Sports Day (2nd Monday in
October)

文化の日 bunka-no-hi
Culture Day (3 November)

勤労感謝の日
kinrōkansha-no-hi Labour
Thanksgiving Day (23
November)

天皇誕生日 Ten·nō-tanjōbi
The Emperor's Birthday (23
December)

Restaurants, Cafés and Bars

食堂 shokudō restaurant

料理屋 ryōri-ya restaurant

レストラン restoran
restaurant

割烹 kap·pō upmarket
restaurant

料亭 ryōtei upmarket
restaurant

和食 washoku Japanese
restaurant

中華料理 chūka-ryōri
Chinese restaurant

天ぷら tempura restaurant
specializing in deep-fried
food

小料理屋 koryōri-ya small
restaurant usually serving
local dishes

飯屋 meshi-ya small local
restaurant

寿司処 sushi-dokoro sushi
restaurant

精進料理屋 shōjin-ryōri-ya
vegetarian restaurant

食事処 shokji-dokoro very
small local restaurant

営業中 eigyō-chū meals
being served

定食 teishoku set meal

蕎麦 soba noodles

ラーメン rāmen Chinese
noodles

お会計 okaikei cashier

喫茶店 kis·saten coffee shop

軽食喫茶 keishoku-kis·sa
coffee shop serving light meals

軽食 keishoku snackbar

スナック snak·ku
snackbar

スナックバー snak·kubā
snackbar

バー bā bar

居酒屋 izaka-ya bar,
serving local cuisine

227

飲み屋 nomi-ya bar, serving food, often from a mobile stall

Road Signs

左折禁止 sasetsu-kinshi no left turn

右折禁止 usetsu-kinshi no right turn

停車禁止 teisha-kinshi no stopping

通行禁止 tsūkō-kinshi no through traffic

通行止め tsūkō-dome no through traffic

スピードを落とせ spīdo o otose reduce speed

最高速度 saikō-sokudo maximum speed

道路工事 dōrokōji road under construction

工事中 kōji-chū road works

急カーブ kyūkābu sharp bend

徐行 jokō slow

一旦停止 it·tan-teishi stop

一旦停車 it·tan-teisha stop

止まれ tomare stop

この先百メートル kono saki hyaku-mētoru 100 metres ahead

事故 jiko accident

注意 chūi caution

危険 kiken danger

回り道 mawari-michi diversion, detour

高速道路 kōsokudōro expressway

国道 kokudō national motorway/highway

有料道路 yūryōdōro toll road

料金 ryōkin fee

有料 yūryō fee charged

無料 muryō no charge

交差点 kōsaten junction, intersection

本線 honsen lane for through traffic

踏切 fumikiri level crossing, railroad crossing

駐車場 chūshajō car park, parking lot

非常駐車帯 hijō-chūsha-tai emergency parking area

一時預かり ichiji-azukari short-term parking

駐車禁止 chūsha-kinshi no parking

満車 mansha car park/parking lot full

Shopping

・・・屋 ...-ya
… shop/store

・・・店 ...-ten
… shop/store

レジ reji cash desk, cashier

会計 kaikei cashier

お勘定 okanjō pay here

骨董品店 kot·tōhin-ten antique shop, curiosity shop

オーディオ製品 ōdio-seihin audio and hi-fi equipment

パン屋 pan-ya baker's

本屋 hon-ya bookshop, bookstore

書店 shoten bookshop, bookstore

肉屋 niku-ya butcher's

ケーキ屋 kēki-ya cake shop

カメラ屋 kamera-ya camera shop

子供服（売場） kodomofuku(-uriba) children's wear

陶器 tōki china

瀬戸物屋 setomono-ya china shop

喫茶店 kis·saten coffee shop

お菓子屋 okashi-ya confectioner's, candy store

化粧品 keshōhin cosmetics

デパート depāto department store

クリーニング店 kurīningu-ten dry cleaner's

電気製品 denki-seihin electrical goods

電気屋 denki-ya electrical goods shop

魚屋 sakana-ya fishmonger

花屋 hana-ya florist

食品 shokuhin food

果物屋 kudamono-ya fruit shop

八百屋 yao-ya greengrocer's

食料品店 shokuryōhin-ten grocer's

金物屋 kanamono-ya hardware store

着物 kimono kimonos

売店 baiten kiosk

台所用品 daidokoro-yōhin kitchen goods

婦人服（売場） fujin-fuku(-uriba) ladies' wear department

コインランドリー koin-randorī launderette, laundromat

市場 ichiba market

紳士服（売場） shinshifuku(-uriba) menswear department

酒屋 saka-ya off-licence, liquor store

メガネ（店） megane(-ten) optician

香水 kōsui perfumery

薬屋 kusuri-ya pharmacy

薬局 yak·kyoku pharmacy

写真屋 shashin-ya photography shop

レコード店 rekōdo-ten record shop, music store

古本屋 furuhon-ya second-hand bookshop/bookstore

靴屋 kutsu-ya shoe shop

土産店 miyage-ten souvenir shop

スポーツ用品店 spōtsu-yōhin-ten sports shop

文房具屋 bumbōgu-ya stationery shop

スーパー sūpā supermarket

おもちゃ売場 omocha-uriba toy department

おもちゃ屋 omocha-ya toy shop

旅行代理店 ryokōdairi-ten travel agency

旅行会社 ryokōgaisha travel agency

下着売場 shitagi-uriba underwear department

お手を触れないでください ote o furenaide kudasai please do not touch

バーゲン bāgen bargains

大売り出し ōuridashi bargains, sale

セール sēru sale

セール実施中 sēru-jis-shi-chū sale now on

特別価格 tokubetsu-kakaku special price

お歳暮 oseibo year-end gifts

歳末売り出し saimatsu-uridashi year-end sale

お中元 ochūgen mid-summer presents

エスカレーター esukarētā escalator

・・・階 ...-kai floor

屋上 okjō roof

Streets and Roads

路線 rosen lane

道路 dōro road

幹線道路 kansen-dōro arterial road, trunk road

高速道路 kōsoku-dōro motorway, highway

追い越し線 oikoshi-sen lane for overtaking

広場 hiroba square

Taxis

タクシー takushī taxi

個人タクシー kojin-takushī mini-cab

タクシー乗場 takushī-noriba taxi rank

空車 kūsha for hire, free

料金メーター ryōkin-mētā fare meter

夜間割り増し料金 yakan-warimashi-ryōkin late-night fare

回送 **kaisō** out of service
自動ドア **jidō-doa**
automatic door

Timetables

時刻表 **jikokhyō** timetable,
schedule
到着 **tōchak** arrival
出発 **shup·pats** departure
発車 **has·sha** departure
方面 **hōmen** direction
行き先 **ikisaki** destination
乗場 **noriba** boarding
platform/track
・・・行き **… iki** bound
for …
経由 **keiyu** via
・・・線 **… sen** … line

Toilets

公衆便所 **kōshū benjo**
public toilet
化粧室 **keshōshits** toilet,
rest room
お手洗い **otearai** toilet(s),
rest room(s)
トイレ **toire** toilet, rest room
便所 **benjo** toilet, rest room
男子用 **danshi-yō** gents'
toilet, men's room
女子用 **joshi-yō** ladies'
toilet, ladies' room
紳士用 **shinshi-yō** gents'
toilet, men's room
婦人用 **fujin-yō** ladies'
toilet, ladies' room
男 **otoko** men
女 **onna** women
使用中 **shiyō-chū**
occupied, engaged
空 **aki** vacant

Train Types

電車 **densha** train
列車 **res·sha** train
新幹線 **shinkansen** bullet
train
急行 **kyūkō** express
ひかり **hikari** fastest bullet
train
普通 **futsū** local slow train
stopping at all stations
準急 **junkyū** semi-express
こだま **kodama** slower
bullet train
特別急行 **tokbets-kyūkō**
super express with limited
stops only
特急 **tok·kyū** super express
with limited stops only
グリーン車 **gurīn-sha**
green car (first class)

Train and Underground Travel

鉄道 **tetsdō** railway, railroad

私鉄 **shitets** private railway

駅 **eki** station

・・・券 **...-ken** ... ticket

切符 **kip·p** ticket

回数券 **kaisūken** book of tickets

定期券 **teiki-ken** season ticket

前売券 **maeuri-ken** advance sale tickets

予約 **yoyak** reservations

指定席（券）**shiteiseki (-ken)** reserved seat (ticket)

自由席 **jiyūseki** unreserved seat

切符売場 **kip·p-uriba** ticket office; ticket vending machine

窓口 **madoguchi** ticket window

出札口 **shus·sats-guchi** ticket window

みどりの窓口 **midori no madoguchi** first-class ticket window

料金表 **ryōkinhyō** table of charges

運賃表 **unchinhyō** table of fares

大人 **otona** adult

子供 **kodomo** child

団体 **dantai** group

個人 **kojin** individual

改札口 **kaisats-guchi** ticket barrier

入場券 **nyūjōken** platform ticket

ホーム **hōm** platform, (US) track

・・・番線 **...-bansen** platform ..., (US) track ...

座席 **zaseki** seat

席 **seki** seat

有効 **yūkō** valid

無効 **mukō** not valid

・・・円区間行き **...-en-kukan-yuki** for destinations within the ...-yen zone (eg 200-yen zone)

下車前途無効 **gesha-zento-mukō** after alighting, not valid for further travel

発売当日限り有効 **hatsbai-tōjits-kagiri-yūkō** valid only on day of purchase

精算所 **seisanjo** excess fare office

到着 **tōchak** arrival(s)

発車 **has·sha** departure(s)

出発 **shup·pats** departure(s)

乗り換え口 **norikae-guchi** this way for changing trains

車掌 **shashō** conductor

・・・号車 **...-gō-sha**

carriage …

食堂車 **shokdō-sha** dining car

満員 **man·in** full

回送 **kaisō** out of service

荷物 **nimots** luggage, baggage

コインロッカー **koin-rok·kā** coin-operated locker

一時預かり所 **ichiji-azkari-jo** left luggage office, baggage checkroom

遺失物取扱所 **ishitsbuts-toriatskai-jo** lost property office, lost and found

お忘れ物 **owasure-mono** lost property, lost and found

待合室 **machiai-shits** waiting room

地図 **chizu** map

左側通行 **hidarigawa-tsūkō** keep to the left

右側通行 **migigawa-tsūkō** keep to the right

東口 **higashi-guchi** east exit (or entrance)

北口 **kita-guchi** north exit (or entrance)

南口 **minami-guchi** south exit (or entrance)

西口 **nishi-guchi** west exit (or entrance)

地下鉄 **chikatets** underground, (US) subway

Youth Hostels

ユースホステル **yūs-hosteru** youth hostel

台所 **daidokoro** kitchen

キッチン **kit·chin** kitchen

コインランドリー **koin-randorī** launderette, laundromat

売店 **baiten** shop

シャワー **shawā** shower

Menu Reader: Food

Contents

Essential Terms

bowl chawan 茶碗
chopsticks hashi はし
cup kap·p カップ
dessert dezāto デザート
fork fōk フォーク
fried rice chāhan チャーハン
glass kop·p コップ
knife naif ナイフ
menu menyū メニュー
noodles menrui めん類
plate sara さら
rice (boiled) gohan ごはん
soup sūp スープ
soy sauce shōyu しょうゆ
spoon spūn スプーン
table tēburu テーブル

excuse me!
chot·to sumimasen!
ちょっとすみません！

could I have the bill, please?
okanjō o onegai shimas
お勘定をお願いします

Basic Foods

パン **pan** bread
バター **batā** butter
みそ **miso** fermented soybean paste
ケチャップ **kechap·pu** ketchup
油 **abura** oil
こしょう **koshō** pepper
しお **shio** salt
しょうゆ **shōyu** soy sauce
さとう **satō** sugar

Basic Preparation and Cooking Methods

バーベキューした **bābekyū shita** barbecued
ゆでた **yudeta** boiled
土鍋で煮た **donabe de nita** casseroled
煮た **nita** cooked
揚げた **ageta** deep-fried
干した **hoshita** dried
焼いた **yaita** grilled
漬けた **tsuketa** pickled
ローストした **rōsto shita** roast
蒸した **mushita** steamed
煮込んだ **nikonda** stewed
炒めた **itameta** stir-fried
詰めものした **tsumemono shita** stuffed

Basic Set Meals

定食 **teishoku** set meal with rice, soup, pickles and main dish of meat or fish
日替り定食 **higawari-teishoku** set meal of the day
てんぷら定食 **tempura-teishoku** set meal with deep-fried prawns
うなぎ定食 **unagi-teishoku** set meal with eel
焼魚定食 **yakizakana-teishoku** set meal with fried fish
焼肉定食 **yakiniku-teishoku** set meal with grilled meat
とんかつ定食 **tonkatsu-teishoku** set meal with pork
刺身定食 **sashimi-teishoku** set meal with raw fish

Bean Curd Dishes

豆腐 **tōfu** bean curd
油揚げ **abura-age** deep-fried bean curd
田楽 **dengaku** grilled bean curd on a wooden skewer

Beef and Beef Dishes

牛肉 gyūniku beef

ビーフ bīfu beef

すきやき sukiyaki beef and vegetables cooked with soy sauce in a pot at the table

鉄板焼き tep·pan·yaki beef and vegetables grilled at the table

牛しょうが焼き gyūshōgayaki beef cooked in soy sauce with ginger

牛照り焼き gyūteriyaki beef cooked in soy sauce and sake

ビフテキ bifuteki beef steak

焼肉 yakiniku fried beef marinated in soy sauce

ローストビーフ rōsto-bīfu roast beef

サーロイン sāroin sirloin

しゃぶしゃぶ shabushabu sliced beef with vegetables boiled at the table

ステーキ stēki steak

Biscuits, Cakes, Crackers and Sweets

ビスケット bisuket·to biscuits, cookies

クッキー kuk·kī biscuits, cookies

ケーキ kēki cake

わたあめ wata-ame candy floss, cotton candy

チーズケーキ chīzu-kēki cheesecake

チョコレート chokorēto chocolate

お菓子 okashi confectionery

シュークリーム shūkurīmu cream puff

ドーナッツ dōnat·tsu doughnut

エクレア ekurea éclair

和菓子 wagashi Japanese-style confectionery

おこし okoshi popped rice confectionery

ぜんざい zenzai rice cake with sweet bean sauce

もち mochi rice cakes

塩せんべい shio-sembei rice crackers flavoured with salt

せんべい sembei rice crackers flavoured with soy

sauce

まんじゅう **manjū** rice-flour cakes with sweet bean paste

ようかん **yōkan** soft, sweet bean paste

ショートケーキ **shōto-kēki** sponge cake with fresh cream and strawberries

カステラ **kasutera** sponge cake

おしるこ **oshiruko** sweet bean soup with rice cake

くずもち **kuzumochi** triangles of arrowroot jelly in brown sugar syrup

もなか **monaka** wafers filled with sweet bean paste

Chicken, Poultry etc

鶏肉 **toriniku** chicken

鶏料理 **tori-ryōri** poultry dishes

やきとり **yakitori** barbecued chicken on a skewer

ささみ **sasami** breast

がちょう **gachō** goose

きじ **kiji** pheasant

うずら **uzura** quail

ローストチキン **rōsto-chikin** roast chicken

七面鳥 **shchimenchō** turkey

Chinese Food

中華料理 **Chūka-ryōri** Chinese-style cuisine

麻婆豆腐 **mābōdōfu** bean curd in spicy sauce

かに卵 **kanitama** crab omelette

からあげ **kara-age** deep-fried pieces of pork or chicken

はるまき **harumaki** deep-fried spring rolls

ぎょうざ **gyōza** fried dumplings stuffed with minced pork

八宝菜 **hap-pōsai** fried pork with vegetables

チャーハン **chāhan** fried rice

野菜炒め **yasai-itame** fried vegetables

肉団子 **nikudango** meatballs

やきそば **yakisoba** noodles fried in a wok

ラーメン **rāmen** noodles in bouillon

チャーシューメン **chāshūmen** noodles in bouillon with slices of pork

みそラーメン **miso-rāmen** noodles in bouillon with fermented soybean paste

タンメン **tam·men** noodles in bouillon with vegetables

ワンタンメン **wantam·men** pork dumplings, served in bouillon with noodles

シューマイ **shūmai** steamed pork meatballs in thin pastry

すぶた **subuta** sweet and sour pork

Condiments, Herbs, Spices and Pickles

梅干し **umeboshi** dried, pickled sour Japanese plums

納豆 **nat·tō** fermented soybeans

しょうが **shōga** ginger

みつば **mitsuba** Japanese coriander

しそ **shiso** Japanese basil

マヨネーズ **mayonēzu** mayonnaise

からし **karashi** mustard

パセリ **paseri** parsley

こしょう **koshō** pepper

ドレッシング **dores·shingu** salad dressing

しお **shio** salt

しょうゆ **shōyu** soy sauce

とんかつソース **tonkatsu·sōsu** thick sweet fruity sauce

酢 **su** vinegar

たくあん **taku·an** yellow radish pickles

Desserts

デザート **dezāto** desserts

アップルパイ **ap·puru-pai** apple pie

チョコレートアイスクリーム **chokorēto-aisu-kurīmu** chocolate ice cream

チョコレートムース **chokorēto-mūsu** chocolate mousse

チョコレートサンデー **chokorēto-sandē** chocolate sundae

コーヒーゼリー **kohī-zerī** coffee-flavoured jelly

クレープ **kurēpu** crepe

宇治氷 **uji-gōri** crushed ice with green tea syrup

宇治金時 **uji-kintoki** crushed ice with green tea syrup and sweet bean paste

氷レモン **kōri-remon** crushed ice with lemon

syrup

氷メロン **kōri-meron**
crushed ice with melon
syrup

氷いちご **kōri-ichigo**
crushed ice with
strawberry syrup

氷あずき **kōri-azki**
crushed ice with sweet
bean paste

フルーツサラダ **frūtsu-sarada** fruit cocktail, fruit
salad

フルーツゼリー **frūtsu-zerī** fruit jelly

みつまめ **mitsumame**
gelatin cubes and sweet
bean paste with pieces of
fruit

あんみつ **am·mitsu**
gelatin cubes with sweet
bean paste and pieces of
fruit

アイスクリーム **aisu-kurīmu** ice cream

ゼリー **zerī** jelly

レモンパイ **remon-pai**
lemon pie

レモンスフレ **remon-sufure** lemon soufflé

ムース **mūsu** mousse

シャーベット **shābet·to**
sorbet

ストロベリーアイス
クリーム **storoberī-aisu-**

kurīmu strawberry ice cream

ストロベリーサンデ
ー **storoberī-sandē**
strawberry sundae

プリン **purin** caramel
custard

バニラアイスクリー
ム **banira-aisu-kurīmu**
vanilla ice cream

ヨーグルト **yōguruto**
yoghurt

Eggs and Egg Dishes

卵 **tamago** egg

かに卵 **kanitama** crab
omelette

めだまやき **medama-yaki**
fried egg

ゆでたまご **yude-tamago**
hard-boiled egg

オムレツ **omuretsu**
omelette

たまごやき **tamago-yaki**
Japanese-style omelette

オムライス **omuraisu**
omelette with rice

おとしたまご **otoshi-tamago** poached egg

茶碗蒸し **chawam·mushi**
savoury custard with egg
and fish

半熟たまご **hanjuku-**

tamago soft-boiled egg

たまごスープ tamago-sūpu soup with egg

たまご豆腐 tamago-dōfu steamed egg

Fish

あわび awabi abalone
赤貝 akagai ark shell
ふぐ fugu blowfish
みる貝 mirugai boiled round clams
かつお katsuo bonito, tunny
こい koi carp
はまぐり hamaguri clams
たら tara cod
たらこ tarako cod roe
あなご anago conger eel
しじみ shijimi corbicula
かに kani crab
からすみ karasumi dried mullet roe
うなぎ unagi eel
ひらめ hirame flatfish
とびうお tobi-uo flying fish
きんめだい kim·me-dai gold-eyed bream
にしん nishin herring
かずのこ kazunoko herring roe
あじ aji horse mackerel
くらげ kurage jellyfish

たらばがに taraba-gani king crab
どじょう dojō loach
いせえび ise-ebi lobster
さば saba mackerel
中トロ chū-toro medium fatty tuna
あんこう ankō monkfish
ムール貝 mūru-gai mussels
たこ tako octopus
かき kaki oyster
さんま sam·ma Pacific saury
かます kamasu pike, barracuda
くるまえび kuruma-ebi prawns
にじます nijimasu rainbow trout
刺身 sashimi raw fish
たいらぎ tairagi razor shell ligament
さけ sake salmon
イクラ ikura salmon roe
いわし iwashi sardines
たちうお tachi-uo scabbard fish
ほたて貝 hotategai scallops
貝柱 kai-bashira scallops
すずき suzuki sea bass
たい tai sea bream
はも hamo sea eel
きす kisu sea smelt
うに uni sea urchin

さめ **same** shark

あさり **asari** short-necked clam

えび **ebi** shrimps, prawns

ししゃも **shishamo** smelt

スモークサーモン **sumōku-sāmon** smoked salmon

トロ **toro** soft, fatty pink belly of tuna

したびらめ **shita-birame** sole

いか **ika** squid

あゆ **ayu** sweet smelt

かじき **kajiki** swordfish

さざえ **sazae** top-shell

なまこ **namako** trepang

ます **masu** trout

まぐろ **maguro** tuna

かれい **karei** turbot

すっぽん **sup·pon** turtle

ふか **fuka** type of shark

くじら **kujira** whale

しらす **shirasu** whitebait

ぶり **buri** yellowtail

Fish Dishes

ふぐ料理 **fugu-ryōri** blowfish cuisine

かばやき **kabayaki** broiled eel

うな重 **unajū** broiled eel on rice

うな丼 **unadon** broiled eel on rice in a bowl

炉ばた焼き **robata-yaki** charcoal-grilled fish and vegetables

あじのたたき **aji no tataki** chopped raw horse mackerel, mild ginger and herbs

てんぷら **tempura** deep-fried seafood and vegetables

たこやき **takoyaki** dumplings with small pieces of octopus

鍋物 **nabemono** fish and vegetables cooked in a pot at the table

寄せ鍋 **yosenabe** fish and vegetables cooked in a pot at the table

刺身 **sashimi** raw fish

すし **sushi** raw fish on rice balls

ふぐ刺し **fugu-sashi** raw sliced blowfish

鉄火丼 **tek·kadon** rice in a bowl topped with slices of raw tuna

ふぐちり **fugu-chiri** shredded blowfish in vegetable chowder

おでん **oden** vegetables and fish dumplings stewed in a thin soy soup, served hot

Fruit, Nuts and Seeds

くだもの kudamono fruit
フルーツ frūtsu fruit
アーモンド āmondo almonds
りんご rin·go apple
バナナ banana banana
さくらんぼ sakurambo cherries
くり kuri chestnuts
ココナッツ kokonat·tsu coconut
いちじく ichijiku figs
ぎんなん gin·nan gingko nuts
グレープフルーツ grēpu-frūtsu grapefruit
ぶどう budō grapes
うめ ume Japanese plum
レモン remon lemon
メロン meron melon
オレンジ orenji orange
もも momo peach
ピーナッツ pīnat·tsu peanuts
なし nashi pear
かき kaki persimmon, sharon fruit
パイナップル painap·puru pineapple
すもも sumomo plum
ざくろ zakuro pomegranate
ごま goma sesame seeds
いちご ichigo strawberries
みかん mikan tangerine
くるみ kurumi walnuts
すいか suika watermelon

Lunch Boxes

弁当 bentō boxed lunch
幕の内弁当 makunouchi-bentō boxed lunch with rice, meat and vegetables

Meat and Meat Dishes (see also beef, chicken, poultry etc and pork)

肉 niku meat
ベーコン bēkon bacon
バーベキュー bābekyū barbecue
ロールキャベツ rōru-kyabetsu cabbage rolls filled with minced meat
あばら肉 abaraniku chops
コロッケ korok·ke croquettes
カツレツ katsuretsu cutlets
串揚げ kushi-age deep-fried meat on skewers
ヒレ肉 hireniku fillet
ハム ham ham
ハンバーグ hambāgu

hamburger

腎臓 jinzō kidney

ラム ramu lamb

レバー rebā liver

肉団子 nikudango meat-filled dumplings

ひき肉 hikiniku minced beef, pork or chicken

マトン maton mutton

骨付き honetsuki on the bone

ソーセージ sōsēji sausage

仔羊肉の串焼き ramu-no-kushiyaki skewered lamb

スペアリブ speyarib spare ribs

ちゃんこ鍋 chanko-nabe thick meat and vegetable stew

タン tan tongue

モツ motsu tripe

仔牛肉 koushi-niku veal

Menu Terms

メニュー menyū menu

並 nami cheaper selection

本日のおすすめ品 honjitsu no osusume-hin chef's speciality of the day

中華料理 Chūka-ryōri Chinese-style cuisine

デザート dezāto desserts

上 jō expensive selection

フランス料理 Fransu-ryōri French-style cuisine

くだもの kudamono fruit

イタリア料理 Itaria-ryōri Italian-style cuisine

日本料理 Nihon-ryōri Japanese-style cuisine

壊石料理 kaiseki-ryōri Japanese haute cuisine

メインコース mein-kōsu main course

肉 niku meat

郷土料理 kyōdo-ryōri regional specialities

定食 teishoku set meal

スープ sūpu soups

オードブル ōdoburu starters, appetizers

野菜 yasai vegetables

精進料理 shōjin-ryōri vegetarian cuisine

西洋料理 seiyō-ryōri Western-style cuisine

Noodles

そば soba buckwheat noodles

うどん udon thick noodles made from wheatflour

しらたき shirataki translucent, thin noodles made from potato flour

そうめん sōmen very

thin wheatflour vermicelli
served cold with soy-sauce
dipping sauce

やきそば yakisoba
Chinese noodles fried in a
wok

ラーメン rāmen Chinese
noodles in bouillon

チャーシューメン
chāshūmen Chinese
noodles in bouillon with
slices of pork

みそラーメン miso-
rāmen Chinese noodles in
bouillon with fermented
soybean paste

チャンポン champon
Chinese noodles in salted
bouillon with vegetables

天ざる ten-zaru cold
noodles served with deep-
fried shrimps

冷し中華 hiyashi-chūka
cold noodles with slices of
meat and vegetables in
vinegary sauce

ざるそば／うどん
zaru-soba/udon cold
noodles with sweet soy
sauce for dipping

かきたま kakitama
noodles and egg in fish
soup

五目そば gomoku-soba
noodles in bouillon with

vegetables and meat

カレー南蛮 karē-namban
noodles in curry-flavoured
soup with pork or beef

とろろそば tororo-soba
noodles in fish bouillon
garnished with grated yam

月見そば／うどん
tsukimi-soba/udon noodles
in fish bouillon with a raw
egg

鴨南蛮 kamo-namban
noodles in fish bouillon
with chicken

きつねそば／うどん
kitsune-soba/udon noodles
in fish bouillon with deep-
fried bean curd

てんぷらそば tempura-
soba noodles in fish
bouillon with deep-fried
shrimps

おかめそば／うどん
okame-soba/udon noodles
in fish bouillon with fish
dumplings

なめこそば／うどん
nameko-soba/udon noodles
in fish bouillon with
Japanese small mushrooms

肉南蛮 niku-namban
noodles in fish bouillon
with pork or beef

たぬきそば／うどん
tanuki-soba/udon noodles in

fish bouillon with small pieces of deep-fried batter

あんかけそば／うどん ankake-soba/udon noodles in thick bouillon with fish dumplings and vegetables

Pork and Pork Dishes

豚肉 butaniku pork

ポーク pōku pork

とんかつ tonkatsu deep-fried pork cutlets

かつ丼 katsudon deep-fried pork on rice

骨付き豚肉 honetsuki-butaniku pork chop

豚しょうが焼き buta-shōgayaki pork cooked in soy sauce with ginger

カツカレー katsukarē pork cutlets with curry

豚照り焼き buta-teriyaki pork cooked in soy sauce and sake

ローストポーク rōsto-pōku roast pork

バター焼き batāyaki sliced pork (or beef) fried in butter

Rice and Rice Dishes

ごはん gohan rice

ライス raisu rice

うな重 unajū broiled eel on rice

丼物 dom·mono bowl of rice with something on top

親子丼 oyakodon dom·mono with chicken and egg

かつ丼 katsudon dom·mono with deep-fried breaded pork cutlet

天丼 tendon dom·mono with deep-fried shrimps

卵丼 tamagodon dom·mono with soft scrambled eggs and onions

うな丼 unadon dom·mono with broiled eel

中華丼 chūkadon dom·mono with pork and vegetables

牛丼 gyūdon dom·mono with sliced beef

チャーハン chāhan fried rice

おにぎり onigiri riceballs

もち mochi rice cakes

お茶づけ ochazuke rice in tea or fish bouillon

釜飯 kamameshi rice steamed in fish bouillon

with pieces of meat, fish
and vegetables

チキンライス **chikin-rais**
rice with chicken, cooked
in tomato sauce

カレーライス **karērais**
rice with curry-flavoured
stew

オムライス **omurais** rice
wrapped in a plain
omelette

ハヤシライス **hayashi-rais** diced beef in gravy on
rice

Salads

サラダ **sarada** salad

生野菜 **nama-yasai** salad

ミックスサラダ
mik·kus-sarada mixed salad

ポテトサラダ **poteto-sarada** potato salad

ドレッシング
dores·shingu salad dressing

Snacks

チーズバーガー **chīzu-bāgā** cheeseburger

ポテトフライ **poteto-frai** chips, French fries

ポテトチップ **poteto-chipu** crisps, (US) potato
chips

ハンバーガー **hambāgā**
hamburger

ハムサンド **hamusando**
ham sandwich

ホットドッグ
hot·todog·gu hotdog

とうもろこし **tōmorokoshi**
roasted corn on the cob

サンドイッチ **sandoit·chi**
sandwich

スパゲッティ **spaget·ti**
spaghetti

トースト **tōsto** toast

ツナサンド **tsunasando**
tuna sandwich

Soups

スープ **sūpu** soups (usually
Western-style)

汁物 **shirumono** soups
(Japanese-style)

吸物 **suimono** clear fish
bouillon with meat, fish or
vegetable

すまし汁 **sumashi-jiru**
clear fish bouillon with
meat, fish or vegetable

コンソメスープ
konsome-sūpu consommé

野菜のクリームスー
プ **yasai no kurīmu-sūpu**
cream of vegetable soup

オニオングラタン
スープ **onion-guratan-**

sūpu onion soup au gratin
味噌汁 misoshiru soup with bean paste
ポタージュ potāju thick soup
トマトスープ tomato-sūpu tomato soup
そば soba buckwheat noodles in bouillon
うどん udon thick noodles made from wheatflour in bouillon
ラーメン rāmen Chinese noodles in bouillon

Starters and Appetizers

オードブル ōdoburu starters, appetizers
おつまみ otsumami Japanese-style starter/appetizer
アスパラガス asuparagasu asparagus
キャビア kyabia caviar
セロリ serori celery
はまぐり hamaguri clams
かに kani crab
フルーツジュース frūtsu-jūsu fruit juice
ハム ham ham
にしん nishin herring
いせえび ise-ebi lobster
メロン meron melon

マッシュルーム mashrūmu mushrooms
かき kaki oysters
くるまえび kuruma-ebi prawns
魚の卵 sakana no tamago roe
サラダ sarada salad
サラミ sarami salami
さけ sake salmon
ソーセージ sōsēji sausage
小えび ko-ebi shrimps
まぐろ maguro tuna

Sushi Dishes

すし sushi raw fish on riceballs
握りずし nigiri-zushi raw fish on seasoned riceballs
五目ずし gomoku-zushi mixed fish and vegetables on rice
ちらしずし chirashi-zushi mixed raw fish on rice
押しずし oshi-zushi sushi cut in squares
さばずし saba-zushi sushi with vinegared mackerel
かっぱ巻き kap·pa-maki cucumber and seasoned rice wrapped in seaweed
お新香巻き oshinko-maki

pickles and seasoned rice
wrapped in seaweed
茶巾ずし **chakin-zushi**
seasoned rice wrapped in
egg crepe
いなりずし **inari-zushi**
seasoned rice wrapped in
deep-fried bean curd
のり巻き **norimaki** sliced
roll of rice, vegetables or
cooked gourd wrapped in
seaweed
鉄火巻き **tek·ka-maki**
tuna and seasoned rice
wrapped in seaweed
わさび **wasabi** very spicy
horseradish served with
sushi

Vegetables

野菜 **yasai** vegetables
あずき **azuki** adzuki beans
アスパラガス
asuparagasu asparagus
なす **nasu** aubergine,
eggplant
アボカド **abokado**
avocado
やきいも **yaki-imo** baked
yam
たけのこ **takenoko**
bamboo shoots
しなちく **shinachiku**
bamboo shoots cooked in

soy sauce, sugar and sesame
oil
まめ **mame** beans
もやし **moyashi** bean
sprouts
ビーツ **bītsu** beet
てんさい **tensai** beetroot
えだまめ **edamame**
boiled green soybeans
おひたし **ohitashi** boiled
spinach with seasoning
そらまめ **soramame**
broad beans
ブロッコリ **burok·kori**
broccoli
しめじ **shimeji** brown
button mushrooms
芽キャベツ **mekyabetsu**
Brussels sprouts
ごぼう **gobō** burdock root
キャベツ **kyabetsu**
cabbage
にんじん **ninjin** carrot
カリフラワー **karifrawā**
cauliflower
セロリ **serori** celery
プチトマト **puchi-tomato**
cherry tomatoes
チコリ **chikori** chicory
白菜 **hakusai** Chinese
cabbage
春菊 **shun·giku** chrysanth-
emum greens
とうもろこし
tōmorokoshi corn on the

cob

ズッキーニ zuk·kīni courgette, zucchini

きゅうり kyūri cucumber

かんぴょう kampyō dried gourd shavings

しいたけ shītake dried mushrooms

のり nori dried seaweed

なめこ nameko edible fungus

きくらげ kikurage edible tree fungus

エンディーブ endību endive

きんぴら kimpira fried burdock root and carrot

にんにく nin·niku garlic

ししとう shishitō green chilli pepper

ピーマン pīman green pepper

さやいんげん saya-ingen haricot beans

わさび wasabi Japanese green horseradish

まつたけ matsutake Japanese mushrooms, with a distinctive aromatic flavour

いんげんまめ ingem·mame kidney beans

小松菜 komatsuna leafy cabbage

ねぎ negi leeks

レタス retasu lettuce

れんこん renkon lotus root

かぼちゃ kabocha pumpkin, squash

マッシュルーム mash-rūmu mushrooms (Western)

きのこ kinoko mushrooms (general term)

からし菜 karashina mustard greens

おくら okura okra

たまねぎ tamanegi onion

えんどうまめ endōmame peas

ポテト poteto potato

じゃがいも jagaimo potato

はつかだいこん hatsuka-daikon radish

ひじき hijiki seaweed cooked in soy sauce and sugar

ごま goma sesame seeds

だいず daizu soybeans

ほうれんそう hōrensō spinach

にら nira spring onions

わけぎ wakegi spring onions

コーン kōn sweetcorn

さつまいも satsumaimo sweet potato

さといも satoimo taro potato

トマト **tomato** tomato
かぶ **kabu** turnip
わかめ **wakame** type of
seaweed
こんぶ **kombu** type of
seaweed
クレソン **kureson**
watercress
ふき **fuki** wild butterbur
(green vegetable stalk)
やまいも **yamaimo** yam
えのきだけ **enokidake**
yellow button mushrooms

Menu Reader:
Drink

Contents

Essential Terms

beer bīru ビール
bottle bin びん
coffee kōhī コーヒー
cup kap·pu カップ
glass kop·pu コップ
milk miruku ミルク
mineral water mineraru-uōtā ミネラルウォーター
orange juice orenji-jūsu オレンジジュース
red wine aka-wain 赤ワイン
rice wine sake 酒
soft drink sofuto-dorinku ソフトドリンク
sugar satō さとう
tea kōcha 紅茶
 (green) ocha お茶
water mizu 水
white wine shiro-wain 白ワイン
wine wain ワイン
whisky uiskī ウィスキー

a cup of ..., please
... o hitotsu kudasai
…をひとつください

another beer, please
bīru o mō hitotsu onegai shimasu
ビールをもうひとつお願いします

a glass of sake
sake o ip·pai
酒を一杯

Beer, Spirits, Wine etc

ビール **bīru** beer
ブランディー **brandī** brandy
シャンペン **shampen** champagne
日本酒冷や **Nihonshu hiya** chilled rice wine
生ビール **nama-bīru** draught beer
辛口 **karakuchi** dry
ジン **jin** gin
ジントニック **jin-toniku** gin and tonic
ジンフィズ **jin-fizu** gin fizz
日本酒熱燗 **Nihonshu atsukan** heated rice wine
リキュール **rikyūru** liqueur
マティーニ **matīni** martini
ポートワイン **pōto-wain** port
赤ワイン **aka-wain** red wine
酒 **sake** rice wine
地酒 **jizake** rice wine (local variety)
升酒 **masuzake** rice wine served in wooden box cup
ラム **ramu** rum
オンザロック **onza-rok·ku** scotch on the rocks
スパークリング **spākuringu** sparkling
甘口 **amakuchi** sweet
トニックウォーター **toniku-uōtā** tonic
ベルモット **berumot·to** vermouth
焼酎 **shōchū** very strong, transparent, colourless spirit
ウォッカ **uok·ka** vodka
ウィスキー **uiskī** whisky
水割り **mizuwari** whisky with water
白ワイン **shiro-wain** white wine
ワイン **wain** wine

Coffee, Tea etc

お飲物 **o-nomimono** beverages
玄米茶 **gem·mai-cha** ban-cha tea with roasted rice
抹茶 **mat·cha** bitter green tea made of fine tea powder
ブラックコーヒー **buraku-kōhī** black coffee
紅茶 **kōcha** black tea, similar to English tea
ウーロン茶 **ūron-cha** Chinese tea
コーヒー **kōhī** coffee

259

お茶 **ocha** green tea

ココア **kokoa** hot chocolate

アイスティー **ais-tī** iced tea

アイスコーヒー **ais-kōhī** iced coffee

番茶 **ban-cha** inexpensive tea with large leaves

レモンティー **remon-tī** lemon tea

煎茶 **sencha** medium-grade green tea

ミルク **miruk** milk

お砂糖 **osatō** sugar

ほうじ茶 **hōjicha** tea made with roasted ban-cha leaves

ミルクティー **miruk-tī** tea with milk

ミルクコーヒー **miruk-kōhī** white coffee, coffee with milk

Soft Drinks

りんごジュース **rin·go-jūs** apple juice

コーヒー牛乳 **kōhī-gyūnyū** coffee-flavoured milk

コカコーラ **kōka-kōra** Coke®

コーラ **kōrā** cola

ファンタ **fanta** Fanta®

グレープフルーツジュース **gurēp-frūts-jūs** grapefruit juice

グレープジュース **gurēp-jūs** grape juice

ソーダ水 **sōdā-sui** green, sweet soda pop

お冷や **ohiya** iced water

レモネード **remonēdo** lemonade

レモンスカッシュ **remon-skash** lemon squash

メロンジュース **meron-jūs** melon juice

ミルク **miruk** milk

ミネラルウォーター **mineraru-uōtā** mineral water

オレンジジュース **orenji-jūs** orange juice

オレンジスカッシュ **orenji-skash** orange squash

ペプシ **Pepusi** Pepsi®

パインジュース **pain-jūs** pineapple juice

サイダー **saidā** soda pop

いちご牛乳 **ichigo-gyūnyū** strawberry milk

トマトジュース **tomato-jūs** tomato juice

みず **mizu** water

氷水 **kōrimizu** water with ice

How the
Language
Works

Pronunciation

Throughout this book, Japanese words have been transliterated into romanized form so that they can be read as though they were English, bearing in mind the notes on pronunciation given below.

a   as in r**a**ther

e   as in b**e**d; **e** is always pronounced, even at the end of a word

i   like the **ee** in f**ee**t, but slightly shorter

o   as in n**o**t

u   as in p**u**t

ae   separate **a** followed by **e**, pronounced **ah-eh**

ai   as in Th**ai**

ei   as in w**ei**ght

ie   separate **ee** followed by **e**, pronounced **ee-eh**

ue   separate **u** followed by **e**, pronounced **oo-eh**

g   hard **g** as in **g**irl

s   always as in ma**ss** (never **z**)

y   as in **y**et

A bar over a vowel means that it is twice as long as a vowel without a bar.

A dot (·) between two letters indicates a slight pause.

Note that ing in Japanese is pronounced more strongly than in English.

In spoken Japanese the sounds u and i, in certain contexts, are shortened and can become barely audible. In this book we show *u* and *i* in italics to mean that their pronunciation is clipped. For example, des*u* is pronounced as **des**.

Japanese is generally evenly stressed, with all syllables having the same emphasis.

Abbreviations

f	feminine	pol	polite
m	masculine	pl	plural
ob. part.	object particle	sing	singular
part.	particle	sub. part.	subject particle

General

The Japanese language has a number of characteristics which are very different from European languages, the most important of these being that there are no changes for case, number or gender and that verbs do not change according to the person or number. Also, pronouns, both personal and impersonal, are often omitted.

Another distinctive feature of Japanese is that small words known as postpositional particles are used after a noun or pronoun to indicate whether it is the subject, object or indirect object of a sentence. See pages 269.

Articles

There is no equivalent in Japanese for either the definite article 'the' or the indefinite articles 'a' and 'an'. The exact meaning of a word or phrase will be clear from the context. Therefore, **zas·shi** (magazine) can mean 'a magazine' or 'the magazine'.

If you want to be more precise, you can use the demonstrative adjectives **sono/ano** (that) or **kono** (this) with the appropriate word (see page 282).

The number **hitots** (one) (see page 286) can also be used to translate 'a/an', but generally this is not necessary:

bīru hitots, onegai shimas
['beer one please']
a beer, please

Nouns

Japanese nouns only have one form. Singular and plural forms of nouns are the same and there are no distinctions for gender (masculine/feminine/neuter). Therefore:

hon can mean 'a book', 'the book', 'books', 'some books' or 'the books'

bīru can mean: 'a beer', 'the beer', 'beers', 'some beers' or 'the beers'

Usually, what you mean will be perfectly clear from the context. Where necessary, you can be more specific by using numbers (see Counting, page 286).

Although the form of the noun itself does not change, grammatical particles placed after the noun indicate whether it is the subject, object or indirect object of a sentence:

watashi no fak·ku*su* wa todokimash*i*ta ka?
['I' + possessive part. 'fax' + sub. part. + 'arrived' + question part.]
has my fax arrived yet?

fak·ku*su* o okurimash*i*ta ka?
['fax' + ob. part. + 'sent' + question part.]
did you send the fax?

Wa and **o** are known as postpositional particles (see page 273).

One interesting aspect of many nouns is that they can be changed into verbs by just adding **suru** (to do) or **shimas** (polite form of 'to do'). Thus, **dokusho** is the Japanese word for 'reading', and **doksho suru** is the equivalent of 'to read'.

Pronouns

Generally, pronouns are omitted in Japanese whenever possible, but occasionally it might be necessary to use them for emphasis or to avoid misunderstanding. It should be remembered that, on the whole, use of pronouns does not show respect and should be avoided, especially when addressing one's superiors. If it does become necessary to use a personal pronoun, the words listed in the sections that follow can be used.

Personal Pronouns

watashi	I
bok	I (m, fam)
watakshi	I (pol)
anata	you (sing)
kimi	you (sing, fam, to a subordinate)
kare	he
kanojo	she
watashitachi	we
anatatachi	you (pl)
kimitachi	you (pl, fam, to subordinates)
karera	they (m)
kanojotachi	they (f)
sorera	they (inanimate objects)

watashi wa Igiris-jin des
['I' + sub. part. + 'English am']
I'm English

The subject of the sentence above is followed by the subject particle **wa** (see page 270).

Care should also be taken not to address Japanese using **anata**, the direct translation of 'you'. The best way to say, for example, 'where are you going?' in Japanese, is to use the person's name plus **-san**, instead of the word for 'you'. Another acceptable way to say this is to omit both 'you' and the name in Japanese.

Eigo o hanasemas ka?
['English' + ob. part. + 'speak can' + question part.]
do you speak English?

Nakada-san wa Frans-go o hanasemas ka?
['surname Mr' + sub. part. + 'French' + ob. part. + 'speak' + question part.]
Mr Nakada, do you speak French?

The form of the pronoun does not change, but there is a change in the postpositional particle that is placed after the pronoun; for direct object pronouns, use **o** instead of **wa**:

watashi o	me
bok o	me (m, fam)
watakshi o	me (pol)
anata o	you (sing)
kimi o	you (sing, fam, to a subordinate)
kare o	him
kanojo o	her
watashitachi o	us
anatatachi o	you (pl)
kimitachi o	you (pl, fam, to subordinates)
karera o	them (m)
kanojotachi o	them (f)
sorera o	them (inanimate objects)

kare o yonde kimashō
['he' + ob. part. + 'fetch']
I'll get him

'It'

Japanese has no word that is equivalent to the English pronoun 'it'; 'it' will be understood in phrases like the following:

doko des*u* ka?
['where is' + question part.]
where is it?

tōi des*u* ka?
['far is' + question part.]
is it far?

ame ga fut·te imas*u*
['rain' + sub. part. + 'fall is']
it's raining

If you really need to emphasise 'it', you can use **sore**, but this is a demonstrative pronoun rather than a personal pronoun, and actually means 'that':

sore wa kare no kuruma des
['that' + sub. part. + 'he' + possessive part. + 'car is']
it's his car

Demonstrative Pronouns

kore	this (one); these (ones)
sore	that (one); those (ones) (nearby or just mentioned)
are	that (one); those (ones) (further away)

kore wa watashi no des
['this' + sub. part. + 'I of am']
this is mine

sore dewa nak, kore des
['that as for not this is']
not that one, this one

are wa takai des
['that' + sub. part. + 'expensive is']
that one is expensive

See Demonstrative Adjectives, page 282.

Possessives

Possessive adjectives and pronouns are the same in Japanese.
To form the possessive, add the particle **no** to the pronoun:

watashi no	my; mine
bok no	my; mine (m, fam)
watakshi no	my; mine (pol)
anata no	your; yours (sing)
kimi no	you (sing, fam, to a subordinate)
kare no	his
kanojo no	her; hers
watashitachi no	our; ours
anatatachi no	your; yours (pl)
kimitachi no	you (pl, fam, to subordinates)
karera no	their; theirs (m)
kanojotachi no	their; theirs (f)
sorera no	their; theirs (inanimate objects)

watashi no des*u*

['I' + possessive part. + 'be']

it's mine

watashi no heya de

['I' + possessive part. + 'room in']

in my room

The possessive is generally omitted if the meaning is clear from the context:

handobag·g*u* o nak*u*shimash*i*ta

['handbag' + ob. part. + 'lost']

I've lost my handbag

In phrases like the one below, it's more respectful to use the possessive particle with the person's name or job title:

shachō no kuruma

['director' + possessive part. + 'car']

the director's car

rather than:

kare no kuruma

['he' + possessive part. + 'car']

his car

even if the English phrase doesn't use the name or title.

Postpositional Particles

Postpositional particles are small words that always follow the word they relate to. They have two main functions:

a) They indicate whether a noun or pronoun is the subject, object or indirect object of a sentence.

b) They are the equivalent of certain English grammatical elements, for example, prepositions (to, from, with etc), constructions such as 'and', 'because', 'also', and they are also used to indicate a question.

The following list shows the meanings of the various particles in brief; for further information and examples, see the text that follows this list.

ga	follows the subject of a sentence, emphasises the subject
wa	follows the subject of a sentence
o	follows the object of a sentence
ni	follows the indirect object of a sentence; or means on, in, to, at (referring to time and location)
e	to (indicates motion towards); towards; until
made	to; up to; until; as far as
kara	from; since
de	by, by means of; with; at; on; in (referring to location)
to	with, accompanied by; and, that
mo	too, also; even; both … and; neither … nor
no	of; possessive
ka?	question particle
ne?	question tag: isn't it?, haven't we?, haven't you? etc

Subject Particles

To indicate that a word is the subject of a sentence, the particles **ga** or **wa** are used:

> **onaka ga sukimash/ta ka?**
> ['stomach' + sub. part. + 'empty' + question part.]
> are you hungry?

The particle **ga** can indicate that the subject of the sentence is more important than the text that follows. In English this distinction can be achieved by tone of voice:

> **watashi ga ikimas***u*
> ['I' + sub. part. + 'will go']
> I will go, it's me who's going (not anyone else)

> **watashi ga haraimas***u*
> ['I' + sub. part. + 'pay']
> I'll pay (nobody else has to pay)

If **wa** is used instead of **ga**, this gives less emphasis to the subject and more to the rest of the text:

watashi wa Amerika-jin desu
['I' + sub. part. + 'American am']
I'm American

watashi wa gakusei desu
['I' + sub. part. + 'student am']
I'm a student

Ga is often used if the verb is **arimasu** or **imasu**:

kyō wa sumō ga arimasu
['today' + sub. part. + 'sumo' + sub. part. + 'is']
there's a sumo match today

and **wa** is often used when the verb is **des** or a negative:

sore wa totemo omoshiroi desu
['that' + sub. part. + 'very interesting is']
that's very interesting

watashi wa Igirisu-jin desu
['I' + sub. part. + 'English am']
I'm English

watashi wa ikimasen
['I' + sub. part. + 'go' + negative]
I'm not going

kono hon wa omoshiroku nai desu
['this book' + sub. part. + 'interesting not is']
this book is not interesting

Object Particle

The object particle **o** is placed after the object of the verb:

yoyaku o shite arimasu
['reservation' + ob. part. + 'made']
I have a reservation

Eigo o hanasemasu ka?
['English' + ob. part. + 'speak can' + question part.]
can you speak English?

Indirect Object Particle

The particle **ni** is used to indicate an indirect object:

sensei ni wain o agemash*i*ta
['teacher' + ind. ob. part. + 'wine' + ob. part. + 'gave']
I gave the teacher a bottle of wine

Other Particles

The particle **e** indicates motion towards something:

Kōbe e ikimas*u*
['Kobe to go']
I'm going to Kobe

The particle **made** means 'to', 'up to', 'until' or 'as far as':

kūkō made, onegai shimas*u*
['airport to please']
to the airport, please

... made nan-kiro arimas*u* ka?
['... to how many kilometres is' + question part.]
how many kilometres is it to ...?

Doyōbi made
['Saturday until']
until Saturday

The particle **kara** means 'from' or 'since':

Rondon kara Tōkyō made   **senshū kara**
['London from Tokyo to']   ['last week since']
from London to Tokyo   since last week

The particle **ni** (as well as being the indirect object particle) means 'on', 'in', 'to' or 'at', referring to time or location:

Doyōbi ni
['Saturday on']
on Saturday

Hiruton hoteru ni tomat·te imasu
['Hilton Hotel at staying']
I'm staying at the Hilton Hotel

Tōkyō ni oba ga sunde imasu
['Tokyo in aunt' + sub. part. + 'lives']
my aunt lives in Tokyo

The particle **de** can mean 'by', 'by means of' or 'with':

kuruma de   **basu de**
['car by']   ['bus by']
by car   by bus

kurejit·to-kādo de haraemasu ka?
['credit card by can pay' + question part.]
can I pay by credit card?

de can also mean 'at', 'on' or 'in', referring to location:

bā de suwat·te imashita
['bar at was sitting']
he was sitting at the bar

depāto no naka de aimashō
['department store of inside in meet let's']
I'll see you in the department store

The particle **to** means 'with', 'accompanying':

haha to kaimono shimasu
['mother with shopping do']
I go shopping with my mother

See page 284 for when to use **to** meaning 'and'.

The particle **mo** can mean 'too', 'also' or 'even':

kimi mo heya ni itano ka?   **watashi mo**
['you too room in were' + question part.]   me too
were you in the room too?

mo can also be used to translate 'both ... and' (in a positive statement) and 'neither ... nor' (with a negative verb, see page 278):

bīru mo sake mo nomimash/ta
['beer both sake and drank']
I drank both beer and sake

bīru mo sake mo nomimasen desh/ta
['beer both sake and not drank']
I drank neither beer nor sake

The particle **no** means 'of' or corresponds to the 's or the possessive in English:

ane no hon	**kurabu no membā**
['sister of book']	['club of member']
my sister's book	a member of the club

watashi no kuruma
['I of car']
my car

The particle **ka** is added to the end of a statement to change it into a question:

kip·pu wa takai desu
['ticket' + sub. part. + 'expensive']
the tickets are expensive

kip·pu wa takai desu ka?
['ticket' + sub. part. + 'expensive' + question part.]
are the tickets expensive?

The particle **ne** is the equivalent of English tag questions like 'isn't it?', 'haven't we?' and so on:

Keiko-san, kore wa anata no desu ne?
['Keiko' + polite form + 'this' + sub. part. + 'you of is' + question tag]
it's yours, Keiko, isn't it?

koko ni kita koto ga arimas*u* ne?

['here in that came' + sub. part. 'be'+ question tag]

we've been here, haven't we?

Verbs

Unlike English verbs, Japanese verbs do not change their form according to first, second, or third person subjects, singular or plural. Therefore, **ikimas*u*** means:

to go	he/she/it goes
I go	we go
you go	they go

However, Japanese verbs do change their form according to various other criteria, for example, the degree of politeness required, the tense, or whether the verb indicates 'wanting' or 'necessity'.

Polite Verb Forms

The form of Japanese verbs is changed to indicate different levels of politeness. As a general rule, longer verb forms denote courtesy:

yomimas*u* to read

shimbun yom*u* ka? (basic form)

shimbun yomimas*u* ka? (polite)

shimbun yomaremas*u* ka? (very polite)

do you read the paper?

It is more straightforward for beginners in Japanese to stick to the second form given above (**yomimas*u***). This is the verb form we have generally given in the English-Japanese section of this book and it is polite enough for most situations.

Present Tense

To express the simple present, use the basic form of the verb ending in **-mas*u***:

ikimas*u* to go	**swarimas*u*** to sit down
I go	I sit down
you go	you sit down`
he/she/it goes	he/she/it sits down
we go	we sit down
they go	they sit down

To express a continuing action in the present ('he is going', 'I am walking' etc), the **-mas*u*** ending is removed from the verb and replaced with **-te** or **-de**, and **imas*u*** is placed after the verb:

nani o yonde imas*u* ka?

['what' + ob. part. + 'reading' + question part.]

what are you reading?

karera wa tabete imas*u*

['they' + sub. part. + 'eating']

they are eating

kare wa tabako o sut·te imas*u*

['he' + sub. part. + 'cigarette' + ob. part. + 'inhale']

he is smoking

Past Tense

The ending **-mash*i*ta** indicates the past tense. Replace the **-mas*u*** ending of the verb with **-mash*i*ta**:

ikimas*u* to go	**mimas*u*** to see; to watch
ikimash*i*ta I went	**mimash*i*ta** I've seen
you went	you've seen
he/she/it went	he/she/it has seen
we went	we have seen
they went	they have seen

ts*u*kimas*u* to arrive	**tabemas*u*** to eat
kyō ts*u*kimash*i*ta	**watashitachi wa mō tabemash*i*ta**
['today arrived']	['we' + sub. part. + 'already have eaten']
we arrived today	we've already eaten

Future Tense

There is no real future tense in Japanese; instead the present tense is used to express the future:

mata ashita kimas*u*
['again tomorrow come']
I'll come back tomorrow

rainen Kyōto ni ikimas*u*
['next year Kyōto to go']
I'm going to Kyoto next year

Asking Permission

Asking permission to do something is indicated by the verb ending **-te** followed by **... ī des*u* ka?** (literally: is it allowed?):

anata ni tegami o kaite ī des*u* ka?
['you to letter' + ob. part. + 'write is is allowed' + question part.]
can I write to you?

Indicating Necessity

Necessity is indicated by the verb ending **-nakereba nari-masen**:

ikimas*u* to go
mō ikanakereba narimasen
['already go must']
I have to go now

kakimas*u* to write
tegami o kakanakereba narimasen
['letter' + ob. part. + 'write must']
I have to write a letter

Indicating Wanting

Wanting to do something is indicated by the verb ending **-tai**:

okurimas*u* to send
kore o Igiris*u* ni okuritai no des*u* ga
['this' + ob. part. + 'England to send want request please']
I want to send this to England

karimas*u* to rent

kuruma o karitai no des*u* ga

['car' + ob. part. + 'buy want request please']

I'd like to rent a car

Negatives

There is no simple equivalent to 'not' in Japanese. Instead the form of the verb changes to indicate the negative. The -mas*u* ending changes to **-masen** and the **-tai** (wanting) ending changes to **-tak*u* nai**:

kono gak·kō e ikimas*u*

['this school to go']

I go to this school

kono gak·kō e wa ikimasen

['this school to' + sub. part. + 'go' negative']

I don't go to this school

Igiris*u* ni ikitai des*u*

['England to want go' + polite ending]

I want to go to England

Igiris*u* ni ikitak*u* nai des*u*

['England to want go' + negative + polite ending]

I don't want to go to England

Japanese has no words like 'nobody', 'no-one', 'never', 'none', 'neither', 'nor', '(not) any'; these must be expressed in Japanese by a negative verb construction:

dare mo kimasen desh*i*ta

['somebody even come' + negative]

nobody came

dare mo hakbutskan e ikitagarimasen

['somebody even museum to want to go' + negative]

nobody wants to visit the museum

Kōbe niwa ichido mo it·ta koto ga arimasen
['Kobe to' + sub. part. + 'not once even that' + sub. part. + negative]
I've never been to Kobe

mō hitots mo arimasen
['already one even exist' + negative]
there's none left

hoshik arimasen
['want' + negative]
I don't want any

Adjectives

Japanese 'adjectives' are a special category of words, many of which behave in a way quite unlike their English counterparts. Many, indeed, are more like verbs since they have separate forms for present and past tenses and for positive and negative use. For example, the adjective for 'red' **akai** really means 'is red'.

There are two types of adjectives in Japanese. The first type end in **-ai**, **-ī**, **-oi** or **-ui**:

akai	is red
oishī	is delicious
omoshiroi	is interesting
warui	is bad

The final **-i** or **-ī** indicates the present positive form of the adjective, which is the basic form given in the English-Japanese section of this book; to make the past positive form, remove the **-i** or **-ī** to obtain the stem and add **-kat·ta**:

present positive	past positive
akai is red	**akakat·ta** was red
oishī is delicious	**oishikat·ta** was delicious
omoshiroi is interesting	**omoshirokat·ta** was interesting
warui is bad	**warukat·ta** was bad

These are all plain forms which generally would not be used by themselves; to make them polite forms, add **desu**:

nimotsu wa omokat·ta desu
['luggage' + sub. part. + 'was heavy' + polite ending]
the luggage was heavy

To form the present negative, remove **-i** or **-ī**, and add **-k nai**; for the past negative add **-ku nakat·ta** to the stem:

present negative	past negative
akaku nai is not red	**akaku nakat·ta** was not red
oishiku nai is not delicious	**oishiku nakat·ta** was not delicious
omoshiroku nai is not interesting	**omoshiroku nakat·ta** was not interesting
waruku nai is not bad	**waruku nakat·ta** was not bad

To make the above polite forms (as used in speech), change **-ku nai** to **-ku arimasen**:

kono suika wa amaku arimasen
['this watermelon' + sub. part. + 'sweet' + negative]
this watermelon is not sweet

Adjectival Nouns

The second type of Japanese adjective is more like an English adjective in that it does not change its ending and is not a form of verb. This type of adjective does not end in **-ai**, **-ī**, **-oi** or **-ui**, but consists of a noun followed by **na**:

shizuka (na)
quiet

Adjectival nouns are used with the following to form the present and past tenses (positive and negative):

positive	present	**des**
	past	**deshta**
negative	present	**dewa arimasen**
	past	**dewa arimasen deshta**

If the adjectival noun is followed by **des**, **na** can be omitted:

hoteru wa shizka des
['hotel' + sub. part. + 'quiet is']
the hotel is quiet

kono hon wa tekitō dewa arimasen
['this book' + sub. part. + 'suitable' + negative]
this book is not suitable

chit·toma shimpai dewa arimasen deshta
['not at all worried' + negative]
I wasn't worried at all

Comparatives and Superlatives

To form the comparative, put **mot·to** (more) in front of the adjective:

        mot·to hayak   **mot·to omoshiroi**
           faster   more interesting

To form the superlative, put **ichi·ban** (literally: number one) or **mot·tomo** (most) in front of the adjective:

ichi·ban omoshiroi toshi
['most is interesting city']
the most interesting city

mot·tomo takai hoteru
['most is expensive hotel']
the most expensive hotel

To express 'more ... than ...', '...-er than', use **yori** (than):

kono hoteru wa ryokan yori takai des*u*
['this hotel' + sub. part. + 'Japanese inn than expensive']
this hotel is more expensive than a Japanese inn

densha wa bas*u* yori hayai des*u*
['train' + sub. part. + 'bus than fast is']
the train is faster than the bus

To express 'as ... as ...' use to **onaji kurai** (about the same as):

Rondon wa Nagano to onaji kurai samui desu
['London' + sub. part. + 'Nagano as cold as is']
London is as cold as Nagano

To express 'not as ... as ...', use **hodo ... nai**:

Nippon wa Amerika hodo ōkiku nai desu
['Japan' + sub. part. + 'America not as big as is']
Japan is not as big as America

Demonstrative Adjectives

There are three demonstrative adjectives: **kono**, **sono** and **ano**:

kono	this; these
sono	that; those (nearby or just mentioned)
ano	that; those (further away)

kono densha	this train
sono tomodachi	that friend (of yours, that you mentioned)
ano basu	that bus (over there)

Adverbs

To form an adverb from the first type of adjective (ending in -ai, -ī, -oi or -ui), change the final -i to -k:

hayai	quick	**hayaku**	quickly
osoi	slow	**osoku**	slowly
yasashī	easy	**yasashiku**	easily
warui	bad	**waruku**	badly
yasui	cheap	**yask**	cheaply

To form the adverb from the second type of adjective (shown with **(na)** in the English-Japanese section), change **na** to **ni**:

shizka na heya	**Keiko-san wa shizka ni hanashimas**
['quiet room']	['Keiko' + polite form + sub. part. + 'quietly speaks']
a quiet room	Keiko speaks quietly

Word Order

The normal word order in Japanese sentences is:

subject – object – verb

ane wa sushi o suki des ga, watashi wa suki dewa arimasen
['sister' + sub. part. + 'sushi' + ob. part. + 'like but I' + sub. part. + 'like not']
my sister likes sushi but I don't

Adjectives usually precede the noun they modify while particles and conjunctions follow the noun they refer to.

'Yes' and 'No'

The words for 'yes' and 'no' are **hai** (or sometimes **ē**) and **īe** (or **ie**):

hai, onegai shimas	**īe kek·kō des**
yes, please	no thanks
yomimashta ka?	**hai, yomimashta**
have you read the paper?	yes, I have

In general, however, it is possible to omit **hai** and **īe** and answer simply by using the verb.

When the question is a negative one, however, **hai** and **īe** are used in quite a different way to English. This is because **hai** is used to confirm the statement, whether the answer is affirmative or negative:

anata wa Amerika-jin dewa arimasen ka?
['you' + sub. part. + 'American' + negative + question part.]
aren't you American?

hai, Igirisu-jin desu
['yes (I am not) English']
no, I'm English

This kind of negative question (as in English) implies the speaker may be slightly surprised or incredulous or wants to confirm something that they are almost sure of. If a positive question were asked, with no prior assumptions, the answer would be **īe**.

In the same way, when the question is a negative one, **īe** is used to deny the sentence whether the answer is affirmative or negative:

soba o tabemasen deshíta ka?
['noodles' + ob. part. + 'eat did not' + question part.]
didn't you eat the noodles? (implying you should have)

īe, tabemashíta
['no, did eat']
yes, I did eat them

'And'

There are different words for 'and' in Japanese. **To** is used with nouns and pronouns:

shio to koshō	**Tōkyō to Rondon**
salt and pepper	Tokyo and London

kōhī to satō o kaimashíta
['coffee and sugar' + ob. part. + 'bought']
I bought coffee and sugar

Soshite also means 'and'; it is used with verbs, adjectives and adverbs:

watashitachi wa onsen ni hairi soshite shokji o shimashta
['we' + sub. part. + 'hot spring in go and meal did']
we had a bath in the hot spring and had a meal

kare wa hayak, soshite utskushik, ji o kakimas
['he' + sub. part. + 'fast and neatly characters' + ob. part. + 'writes']
he writes both fast and neatly

Sorekara means 'and then':

terebi o mite, sorekara benkyō shimas

['television' + ob. part. + 'watched and then study']

I'll watch television and then I'll study

Masculine and Feminine Forms of Speech

In the past, there were many different levels of courtesy in Japanese speech and special words and phrases were used, for example, to praise one's superiors, and to deprecate oneself. As well as this, women's speech was traditionally more polite than men's. Although the differences between male and female speech patterns are now less pronounced than they used to be, there are still many ways of speaking that are exclusively used by either men or women. Men speak with a more even tone of voice, whereas women speak in a more lilting manner. Men and women use different pronouns and interjections. Also, in informal speech, men tend to use **yo** or **zo** at the end of sentences for emphasis, whereas women will use **wa**, for example:

bok wa Eigo ga hanaseru yo/zo! (said by a man)

['I' + sub. part. + 'English' + ob. part. + 'speak can emphasis']

I can speak English!

watashi wa okoto ga hikeru wa! (said by a woman)

['I' + sub. part. + polite prefix + 'Japanese harp' + ob. part. + 'play can' + emphasis]

I can play the Japanese harp!

Women make more use of the polite prefix **o-** or **go-**, as in:

denwa/odenwa

(said by a man/woman)

(your) telephone

gokazoku wa ogenki desu ka?

[polite prefix + 'family' + sub. part. + polite prefix + 'well' + question part.]

are your family all well?

Women also tend to use emotional interjections more than men, such as '**kawaī**' (cute!) or '**suteki!**' (marvellous!). To express surprise when meeting somebody unexpectedly, women tend to say '**mā!**' or '**ara!**', which are never used by men, who tend to say '**yā!**' or '**ō!**'.

Counting

Japanese has two sets of numbers from one to ten:

	set 1	set 2
1	ichi	hitotsu
2	ni	futatsu
3	san	mit·tsu
4	yon/shi*	yot·tsu
5	go	itsutsu
6	roku	mut·tsu
7	nana/shichi*	nanatsu
8	hachi	yat·tsu
9	kyū/ku*	kokonotsu
10	jū	tō

The first set is used when referring to expressions of time, quantities and measurements. They are used with the classifiers on the opposite page or with count words such as 'minute', 'yen' etc:

go-fun
five minutes

ichijikan mae
an hour ago

gozen shichiji ni
at 7am

jū-en
10 yen

★ The alternative numerals in the first set above must be used in the following time expressions:

yoji
four o'clock

shichiji
seven o'clock

kuji
nine o'clock

The second set of numbers is used for counting any other things not mentioned above. The number is placed after the object and is used without a count word (like 'minute') or a classifier:

bīru futats, onegai shimas
two beers, please

If you use the two sets of numbers in the way described above, this will be acceptable, but a further method of counting, using a counting word known as a classifier, is more commonly used. Classifiers equate roughly to English words like 'glassful', 'cupful', 'bottle of', 'sheets of' etc. Nouns or groups of nouns in Japanese have specific classifiers which are used when they are counted or quantified.

The most common classifiers are:

-dai	machines, cars, bikes, stereos
-hai	glassfuls, cupfuls
-hiki	animals
-hon	pens, cigarettes, other cylindrical objects
-ko	fruit, cakes, eggs and small chunky objects
-mai	pieces of paper, tickets, other things that are thin and flat
-nin	people
-sats	books
-tsū	letters

kuruma ni-dai
['car two' + classifier]
two cars

kip·p o sam-mai, kudasai
['ticket' + ob. part. + 'three' + classifier + 'please']
three tickets, please

Nihon·go no hon o go-sats*u* kaimash*i*ta
['Japanese of book' + ob. part. + 'five' + classifier + 'bought']
I bought five Japanese books

mājan wa yo-nin de shimas*u*
['mahjong' + sub. part. + 'four' + classifier + 'by do']
mahjong is played by four people

There is only one set of numbers above ten. See pages 292–293.

Dates

The word order for dates is:

year – month – day

There are two common ways of counting years in Japanese. The Western system is used thus:

sen-kyū-hyaku-kyū-jū-hachi-nen
〔thousand-nine-hundreds-nine-tens-eight-year〕
1998

ni-sen-ichi-nen
〔two-thousand-one-year〕
2001

There is also a traditional system of counting from the first year of the current emperor's reign. The Heisei period (of Emperor Akihito) began in 1989:

Heisei ni-nen
〔Heisei two year〕
second year of Heisei (1990)

Heisei jū-nen
〔Heisei ten year〕
tenth year of Heisei (1998)

Kugatsu tsuitachi
〔nine-month (September) first〕
the first of September

Jūnigatsu futsuka
〔twelve-month (December) second〕
the second of December

ni-sen-ichi-nen Gogatsu san-jū-nichi
〔two-thousand-one-year five-month (May) thirtieth〕
the thirtieth of May 2001

Heisei jū-nen Rokgats ni-jū san-ichi
〔Heise-ten-year six-month (June) twenty-third〕
the twenty-third of June 1998

Dates are formed using the versions of the ordinal numbers below:

1st	tsuitachi	一日
2nd	futska	二日
3rd	mik·ka	三日
4th	yok·ka	四日

288

5th	itska	五日
6th	muika	六日
7th	nanoka	七日
8th	yōka	八日
9th	kokonoka	九日
10th	tōka	十日
11th	jū-ichi-nichi	十一日
12th	jū-ni-nichi	十二日
13th	jū-san-nichi	十三日
14th	jū-yok·ka	十四日
15th	jū-go-nichi	十五日
16th	jū-rok-nichi	十六日
17th	jū-shichi-nichi	十七日
18th	jū-hachi-nichi	十八日
19th	jū-ku-nichi	十九日
20th	hatska	二十日
21st	ni-jū-ichi nichi	二十一日
22nd	ni-jū-ni-nichi	二十二日
23rd	ni-jū-san-nichi	二十三日
24th	ni-jū-yok·ka	二十四日
25th	ni-jū-go-nichi	二十五日
26th	ni-jū-rok-nichi	二十六日
27th	ni-jū-shichi-nichi	二十七日
28th	ni-jū-hachi-nichi	二十八日
29th	ni-jū-ku-nichi	二十九日
30th	san-jū-nichi	三十日
31st	san-jū-ichi-nichi	三十一日

Japanese ordinals are written using the Chinese characters (kanji) above if writing vertically; otherwise, when writing left to right, Arabic numbers can be used instead.

Days

Monday	Getsuyōbi	月曜日
Tuesday	Kayōbi	火曜日
Wednesday	Suiyōbi	水曜日
Thursday	Moku·yōbi	木曜日
Friday	Kin·yōbi	金曜日
Saturday	Doyōbi	土曜日
Sunday	Nichiyōbi	日曜日

Months

January	Ichigatsu	一月
February	Nigatsu	二月
March	San·gatsu	三月
April	Shigatsu	四月
May	Gogatsu	五月
June	Rokgatsu	六月
July	Shichigatsu	七月
August	Hachigatsu	八月
September	Kugatsu	九月
October	Jūgatsu	十月
November	Jūichigatsu	十一月
December	Jūnigatsu	十二月

Time

what time is it? ima nanji desu ka? 今何時ですか？
it's one o'clock ichiji desu 一時です
it's two o'clock niji desu 二時です
at one o'clock ichiji ni 一時に
at two o'clock niji ni 二時に
five past one ichiji go-fun 一時五分

ten past one ichiji jup·pun　一時十分

quarter past one ichiji jū-go-fun　一時十五分

quarter past two niji jū-go-fun　二時十五分

half past one ichiji-han　一時半

half past two niji-han　二時半

quarter to one ichiji jū-go-fun mae　一時十五分前

quarter to two niji jū-go-fun mae　二時十五分前

twenty to one ichiji nijup·pun mae　一時二十分前

ten to two niji jup·pun mae　二時十分前

am gozen　午前

pm gogo　午後

at 1am gozen ichiji ni　午前一時に

at 1pm gogo ichiji ni　午後一時に

13.00 jū-sanji　十三時

14.00 jū-yoji　十四時

18.30 jū-hachiji sanjup·pun　十八時三十分

noon shōgo　正午

midnight mayonaka　真夜中

hour jikan　時間

minute fun　分

one minute ip·pun　一分

two minutes ni-fun　二分

second byō　秒

quarter of an hour jū-go-fun　十五分

half an hour san-jup·pun　三十分

three quarters of an hour yon-jū-go-fun　四十五分

Minutes are expressed by adding **-fun** (minute) to the numbers below. This sometimes changes to **-pun** depending on the preceding sound:

ni-fun	**go-fun**	**jup-pun**
two minutes	five minutes	ten minutes

Numbers

See Counting pages 286.

0 zero	ゼロ	
1 ichi	一	
2 ni	二	
3 san	三	
4 shi	四	
5 go	五	
6 rok	六	
7 shichi	七	
8 hachi	八	
9 kyū	九	
10 jū	十	
11 jū-ichi	十一	
12 jū-ni	十二	
13 jū-san	十三	
14 jū-shi	十四	
15 jū-go	十五	
16 jū-rok	十六	
17 jū-shichi	十七	
18 jū-hachi	十八	
19 jū-kyū	十九	
20 ni-jū	二十	
21 ni-jū-ichi	二十一	
22 ni-jū-ni	二十二	
30 san-jū	三十	
31 san-jū-ichi	三十一	
32 san-jū-ni	三十二	
40 yon-jū	四十	
50 go-jū	五十	
60 rok-jū	六十	

70 shichi-jū	七十	
80 hachi-jū	八十	
90 kyū-jū	九十	
100 hyak	百	
101 hyak-ichi	百一	
102 hyak-ni	百二	
200 ni-hyak	二百	
1,000 sen	千	
2,000 ni-sen	二千	
3,000 san-zen	三千	
4,000 yon-sen	四千	
5,000 go-sen	五千	
10,000* ichi-man	一万	
20,000 ni-man	二万	
1,000,000 hyak*u*-man	百万	
10,000,000 is-sem·man	一千万	
100,000,000 ichi-ok*u*	一億	

*For 10,000 and above, use **man** instead of **sen**.

Japanese numbers are written using the Chinese characters (kanji) above if writing vertically; otherwise, when writing left to right, Arabic numbers can be used instead.

Ordinals

In Japanese, the words used for the dates (1st of March etc) and the ordinals in English sense (for example, 'third chair from the window') are different. The English ordinals can usually be translated by adding **-bam·me** to numbers.

1st ichi-bam·me	時十五
2nd ni-bam·me	分二時
3rd san-bam·me	十五分
4th yon-bam·me	一時半
5th go-bam·me	二時半
6th rok-bam·me	一時十
7th nana-bam·me	五分前
8th hachi-bam·me	二時十
9th kyū-bam·me	五分前
10th jyū-bam·me	一時二

See pages 288-289 for the set of ordinals used to form dates.

Conversion Tables

1 centimetre = 0.39 inches   1 inch = 2.54 cm

1 metre = 39.37 inches = 1.09 yards   1 foot = 30.48 cm

1 kilometre = 0.62 miles = 5/8 mile   1 yard = 0.91 m

                                      1 mile = 1.61 km

km	1	2	3	4	5	10	20	30	40	50	100
miles	0.6	1.2	1.9	2.5	3.1	6.2	12.4	18.6	24.8	31.0	62.1

miles	1	2	3	4	5	10	20	30	40	50	100
km	1.6	3.2	4.8	6.4	8.0	16.1	32.2	48.3	64.4	80.5	161

1 gram = 0.035 ounces   1 kilo = 1000 g = 2.2 pounds

g	100	250	500
oz	3.5	8.75	17.5

1 oz = 28.35 g

1 lb = 0.45 kg

kg	0.5	1	2	3	4	5	6	7	8	9	10
lb	1.1	2.2	4.4	6.6	8.8	11.0	13.2	15.4	17.6	19.8	22.0

kg	20	30	40	50	60	70	80	90	100
lb	44	66	88	110	132	154	176	198	220

lb	0.5	1	2	3	4	5	6	7	8	9	10	20
kg	0.2	0.5	0.9	1.4	1.8	2.3	2.7	3.2	3.6	4.1	4.5	9.0

1 litre = 1.75 UK pints / 2.13 US pints

1 UK pint = 0.57 l   1 UK gallon = 4.55 l
1 US pint = 0.47 l   1 US gallon = 3.79 l

centigrade / Celsius $°C = (°F - 32) \times 5/9$

°C	-5	0	5	10	15	18	20	25	30	36.8	38
°F	23	32	41	50	59	64	68	77	86	98.4	100.4

Fahrenheit $°F = (°C \times 9/5) + 32$

°F	23	32	40	50	60	65	70	80	85	98.4	101
°C	-5	0	4	10	16	18	21	27	29	36.8	38.3